B.R. Ambedkar

The Quest for Justice

B.R. Ambedkar

The Quest for Justice

VOLUME III

Legal and Economic Justice

Edited by
Aakash Singh Rathore

OXFORD
UNIVERSITY PRESS

OXFORD
UNIVERSITY PRESS

Oxford University Press is a department of the University of Oxford.
It furthers the University's objective of excellence in research, scholarship,
and education by publishing worldwide. Oxford is a registered trademark of
Oxford University Press in the UK and in certain other countries.

Published in India by
Oxford University Press
22 Workspace, 2nd Floor, 1/22 Asaf Ali Road, New Delhi 110002, India

First Edition published in 2021

ISBN-13 (print edition): 978-0-19-012684-1
ISBN-10 (print edition): 0-19-012684-1

ISBN-13 (eBook): 978-0-19-099338-2
ISBN-10 (eBook): 0-19-099338-3

Typeset in Trump Mediaeval LT Std 10/13
by Tranistics Data Technologies, Kolkata 700 091
Printed in India by Rakmo Press, New Delhi 110 020

Contents

PART TWO: ECONOMIC JUSTICE

Figures, Tables, and Chart

Figures

Tables

Chart

Foreword

By intellect, industry, and perseverance, Dr Bhimrao Ramji Ambedkar (1891–1956) became a great scholar, statesman, chief architect of India's Constitution, and leader of the oppressed. He combined in himself the distinction of being a great scholar, social revolutionary, and statesman. An intellectual giant and prolific writer, his knowledge was encyclopaedic. His erudition and experience covered such diverse fields as law and economics, which the present volume covers, but also politics (as was covered in Volume I), sociology (Volume II), comparative study of culture, history, and, of course, religion (the themes of later volumes in this collection). The range of his topics, the breadth of his vision, the depth of his analysis, the rationality of his outlook, and the essential humanity of his argument—all these marked Dr Ambedkar out as a man of destiny.

Dr Ambedkar was driven by a desire to understand the troubling issues of his times and to find their solutions. Thus motivated, he decisively shaped economic and legal developments of India during a crucial period of history. There was no issue of salience between the 1920s and 1950s to which Ambedkar did not apply his illuminating intelligence; for example, the problems surrounding the minorities, the reorganization of states, Partition, and, of course, the legal and economic framework for the Indian Republic. Not content with confining himself to scholarly expositions, he attended to all the related issues that came within his discretionary authority. Indeed, even where these were not directly within his authority, he aided those in authority so that solutions could be found and implemented. Most remembered among Dr Ambedkar's innumerable contributions are his indefatigable efforts toward the making of the Indian Constitution, his social and political efforts to uplift the socially downtrodden, and his remarkable revival of Buddhism.

Questions of legal justice stretch out farther than constitutionalism, but the Constitution, as the basic law of the land, remains the soil from whence various roots and trunks emerge, branching out in myriad directions. Ambedkar was involved in all the deliberations surrounding the drafting of the Constitution, even preceding the Montagu–Chelmsford Reforms of 1919. Prior to these reforms, a franchise committee was appointed under the chairmanship of Lord Southborough. Giving extensive evidence before this committee, Ambedkar argued forcefully for political representation for the Depressed Classes on the basis of population. Dr Ambedkar also presented a memorandum to the Indian Statutory Commission under the chairmanship of Sir John Simon in 1928, which revised the Government of India Act of 1919. He played a crucial role at the Round Table Conferences in London in the early 1930s, and later as well during the earliest stages of the Constituent Assembly.

Dr Ambedkar was appointed a member of the Constitution Drafting Committee by the Constituent Assembly and soon after, unanimously, its chairman. Working with incredible energy, he almost single-handedly produced the revised draft within two years of the initial meeting of the Constituent Assembly, and just over a year later, the final Constitution. Recalling his contribution, T.T. Krishnamachari, himself a member of the Drafting Committee, said on 5 November 1948:

> The House is perhaps aware that of the seven members nominated by you one resigned from the house and was replaced. One died and was not replaced. One was away in America and his place was not filled up and another person was engaged in state affairs and there was void to the extent. One or two people were far away from Delhi and perhaps reason of health did not permit them to attend. So it happened ultimately that the burden of drafting the Constitution fell on Dr Ambedkar and I have no hesitation in saying that we are grateful to him for having achieved this task in a manner which is undoubtedly commendable.[1]

[1] Dananjay Keer, *Dr. Ambedkar: Life and Mission* (Bombay: Popular Prakashan, 1954).

In his concluding speech to the Constituent Assembly, Dr Rajendra Prasad, its president, remarked about Dr Ambedkar:

> Sitting in the chair and watching the proceedings from day to day, I have realised as nobody else could have, with what zeal and devotion the members of the Drafting Committee and especially its Chairman Dr Ambedkar, in spite of his indifferent health, have worked. We would have never made a decision which was or could be ever so right as when we put him on the Drafting Committee and made him its Chairman. He has not only justified his selection but has added lustre to the work which he has done.

With respect to economic justice, a great deal of the scholarship that I myself have produced over the past decades has been dedicated to exploring Dr Ambedkar's work and the implications that can and ought to be drawn from it. These go as far back as the 1990s with publications such as *Ambedkar's Role in Economic Planning, Water and Power Policy* (1998) up to more recent works such as *Blocked by Caste: Economic Discrimination in Modern* India (2010; co-authoured with K. Newman). The present volume is dedicated more to the pursuits of economic justice inspired by Ambedkarite interests and methods rather than to Ambedkar's own positions and actions with respect to economic justice. Hence, I have mentioned the preceding material as potential resources for those readers eager to understand the latter.

Back to the present volume, it is the third of a five-volume set of chapters exploring major themes of research surrounding the prolific writings of Dr Ambedkar, primarily in terms of political, social, legal, economic, gender, racial, religious, and cultural justice. This volume, in particular, focuses specifically on the two themes of legal justice and economic justice. The first part explores the Constitution and its institutions, the idea of constitutional morality, rights and the rule of law, and the idea of an Ambedkarite jurisprudence.

The second part turns to a variety of issues in economic justice anchored in Ambedkar's economic methodology and philosophy. This collection on legal and economic justice adds an essential component to the overall project captured in the five volumes, and

I am pleased to invite readers to explore the lively and sophisticated research that follows. They form a crucial contribution to the international and multidisciplinary studies of and inspired by Dr B.R. Ambedkar.

Sukhadeo Thorat
Professor Emeritus,
Jawaharlal Nehru University, New Delhi;
Distinguished Professor in Social Science,
Savitribai Phule University, Pune, Maharashtra; and
K.R. Narayanan Chair for Human Rights and Social Justice,
Mahatma Gandhi University, Kottayam, Kerala

Preface

This book forms part of a five-volume publication entitled *B.R. Ambedkar: The Quest for Justice*, an ambitious project that originated during the B.R. Ambedkar International Conference, 'Quest for Equity', held at Bengaluru, India, in July 2017, with some 350 speakers and thousands of participants. That conference took place keeping in view that the values of social, political, and economic justice that were so vigorously championed by Dr Ambedkar are now under attack at several levels: constitutional norms and public institutions created to fight against dominance and subservience have proved inadequate or have been subverted; norms and policy often merely pay lip service to egalitarian considerations; and the rise of social intolerance and exclusion tends to effectively whittle down and even sabotage an inclusive conception of polity and citizenship. The complexity of the social, political, and economic environment in which the value of social justice has to be envisaged too has undergone significant changes: we understand social inequality and diversity to be layered and multidimensional; and the State has to reckon with several competing centres of religious, communal, and cultural allegiances. Despite these serious challenges, new sites for social and political assertions have re-emerged, renewing the call for justice. These five volumes are very much part of that engagement.

Social activism in India today is inspired by Dr B.R. Ambedkar's insightful lifework analysing complex social and political challenges and proposing daring and radical policy measures in response. His approach to critical intellectual and policy challenges may inspire similar interventions elsewhere in the world, particularly throughout the Global South. Thus, in the light of the conference, this five-volume collection emerged as an invitation to scholars and policymakers to substantially rethink current political, social, legal, economic, gender, racial, religious, and cultural paradigms motivated by Dr B.R. Ambedkar's imaginative and creative work.

The project has succeeded in encouraging a wide interdisciplinary engagement among academics, scholars, activists, and policymakers on each of these themes, which are treated across the five volumes. This is apparent from a review of their tables of contents:

B.R. Ambedkar: The Quest for Justice

(in five volumes)

Volume I: *Political Justice*

1. Bhikhu Parekh *The Intellectual and Political Legacy of B.R. Ambedkar*
2. Cosimo Zene *B.R. Ambedkar and Antonio Gramsci: Justice for the Excluded, Education for Democracy*
3. Anand Teltumbde *Ambedkar and Democracy: Critical Reflections*
4. Neera Chandhoke *Repairing Complex Historical Injustice*
5. Pradeep Gokhale *Dr Ambedkar and the Trio of Principles: Liberty, Equality, and Fraternity*
6. Vidhu Verma *Discrimination, Colonial Injustice, and the Good Society*
7. Scott Stroud *Communication, Justice, and Reconstruction: Ambedkar as an Indian Pragmatist*
8. J. Daniel Elam *Of Castes and Crowds: B.R. Ambedkar's Anticolonial Endosmosis*
9. Pushparaj Deshpande *A Constellation of Ideas: Revisiting Ambedkar and Gandhi*
10. Shaunna Rodrigues *Self-Respect as a Primary Political Ideal: Ambedkar's Challenge to Political Theory*

Volume II: *Social Justice*

1. Martin Fuchs *Ambedkar's Theory of the Social: The Universal Condition of Recognition*
2. James Manor *B.R. Ambedkar: Visionary and Realist*
3. G.C. Pal *Caste and Delivery of Social Justice: Revisiting Ambedkar*
4. Meena Dhanda *'Made to Think and Forced to Feel': The Power of Counter-Ritual*
5. David N. Gellner, Krishna P. Adhikari, Arjun Bahadur B.K. *Dalits in Search of Inclusion: Comparing Nepal with India*
6. Navyug Gill *Ambedkar, Labour, and the Political Economy of Dalit Conversion in Colonial Panjab*
7. Shailaja Menon *The Fractured Society of the Republic*
8. Karen Gabriel and Prem Kumar Vijayan *Whose State Is It Anyway? Reservation, Representation, Caste, and Power*
9. Jagannatham Begari *Reclaiming Social Justice and Deepening Democracy*
10. Suraj Yengde *Ambedkar's Internationalization of Social Justice*
11. Karthik Raja Karuppusamy *Foregrounding Social Justice in Indian Historiography: Interrogating the Poona Pact*
12. Ajay Verma *Ambedkar and the Metaphysics of Social Justice*

Volume III: *Legal and Economic Justice*

Part One: Legal Justice

1. Upendra Baxi *Lawless Law, Living Death, and the Insurgent Moral Reason of Babasaheb Ambedkar*
2. R. Sudarshan *B.R. Ambedkar's Exemplary Adherence to Constitutional Morality*
3. Arvind Narrain *Radical Constitutionalism: Towards an Ambedkarite Jurisprudence*
4. Antje Linkenbach *B.R. Ambedkar's Imaginations of Justice*
5. Umakant *The Significance of Rights and Rule of Law under the Indian Constitutional Framework*
6. Anupama Rao *B.R. Ambedkar and Indian Democracy*

Part Two: Economic Justice

7. Vijay Gudavarthy *Development through Informalization and Circulation of Labour: The Emerging Anatomy of an Uncivil Society*
8. Joseph Tharamangalam *India's Paradox of 'Hunger Amidst Plenty' Has a Name: Caste-Based Discrimination and Exclusion*
9. Aseem Prakash *Dalits Enter the Indian Markets as Owners of Capital: Adverse Inclusion, Social Networks, and Civil Society*
10. Pritam Singh *Ambedkar's Economic Methodology for Social Justice: The Centrality of Dalits*
11. Jawed Alam Khan *Economic Justice: Policy and Public Investment for Pasmanda Muslims*

Volume IV: *Gender and Racial Justice*

Part One: Gender Justice

1. Sanghmitra S. Acharya *Double Disadvantage of Sanitation Workers and Government Responses*
2. Mushtaq Ahmad Malla *The Shame of India: Stigma and Shame among Dalit Women in Rural Agricultural Relations*
3. Rajesh Raushan *Gender Equality and Women's Empowerment: Ambedkar in Contemporary Context*
4. Sunaina Arya *Ambedkar as a Feminist Philosopher*
5. Mala Mukherjee *Ambedkar on Women's Empowerment and the Status of Dalit Women in Karnataka*
6. Komal Rajak and N. Sukumar *Constructing a New Female Subjectivity: Ambedkar's Perspective*

Part Two: Racial Justice

7. Moses Seenarine *Organic Resistance: The Relevance of Ambedkar, Du Bois, and Garvey to Diaspora, Caste, Race, and Women's Liberation*
8. Goolam Vahed and Ashwin Desai *Racelessness and Ambedkar's Idea of Annihilation: Post-apartheid South Africa*

9. Kevin Brown and Lalit Khandare *Common Struggles? Why There Has Not Been More Cooperation between African-Americans and Dalits*
10. Goolam Vahed *Can Ambedkar Speak to Africa? Colour, Caste, and Class Struggles in Contemporary South Africa*

Volume V: *Religious and Cultural Justice*

Part One: Religious Justice

1. Laurence R. Simon *Searching for a Theology of Liberation in India*
2. Kanchana Mahadevan *Ambedkar's Critical Hermeneutics of Religion*
3. Debora Spini *Civil Religion, Uncivil Society: A Reflection on Baba Sahib Dr B.R. Ambedkar's Conception of a 'Religion for Civil Society'*
4. Priyanka Jha *The Gaze on Justice: A Genealogy from Anagarika Dharmapala to B.R. Ambedkar*
5. Bansidhar Deep *B.R. Ambedkar's Philosophy of Religion*
6. Matthew H. Baxter *Two Concepts of Conversion at Meenakshipuram: Seeing through Ambedkar's Buddhism and Being Seen in EVR's Islam*

Part Two: Cultural Justice

7. Pramod K. Nayar *Marginality, Suffering, Justice: Questions of Dalit Dignity in Cultural Texts*
8. Y. Srinivasa Rao *Asura: Myth into Cultural Reality*
9. John Clammer *Cultural Rights in the Context of Ambedkarite Social Justice*
10. Raju Sakthivel *Education in a Hierarchical Culture*
11. Jadumani Mahanand *Ambedkar in/and Academic Space*

Despite the wide range of themes spread across these five volumes, the collection as a whole is oriented towards articulable specific aims and objectives. These aims and objectives are inspired by and fully consistent with the life and legacy of Dr Ambedkar, a man who was, on the one hand, a scholar of indubitable genius, and on the other hand, a dynamic agent of social and political action.

1. *B.R. Ambedkar: The Quest for Justice* seeks to explore the multifaceted idea of justice in dialogue with Ambedkar's *opus* for a society that encompasses manifold social inequalities, deep diversities, exclusion, and marginality.
2. In dialogue with Ambedkar's writings, the contributions to the collection aim in an overall way to suggest constitutional, institutional, and policy responses to the concerns of justice, and to reformulate the conceptual and policy linkages between social justice and other related norms and concerns.
3. Through high-level scholarship, this collection aims to help identify modes of thought and agency and social and political practices inimical to the pursuit of justice, and to delineate social and political agency and modes of action conducive to the furtherance of justice in line with Dr Ambedkar's own writings and mission.

Thus, in sum, Dr Ambedkar's conception of justice and his life's work shaping the idea of India offer this collection the vantage points for sustained reflection on concerns of justice and its relation to other human values. This is particularly relevant, indeed urgent, in our day, not only in India but also throughout the world.

As convener of the organizing committee of the Dr B.R. Ambedkar International Conference, 'Quest for Equity', held at Bengaluru, India, in July 2017, where many of the chapters included in this volume were originally presented, I would like to gratefully acknowledge the people and institutions that made the conference a success and helped to make these volumes possible.

First and foremost, I must acknowledge the Government of Karnataka with Chief Minister Siddaramaiah at the helm, which hosted and funded the conference. Many put in extraordinary time and effort: Dr H.C. Mahadevappa, convenor and hon'ble minister for Public Works Department (PWD); H. Anjaneya, hon'ble minister for Social Welfare Department; Dr G. Parameshwara, hon'ble minister for home affairs; Shri T.B. Jayachandra, hon'ble minister for law and minor irrigation; Shri R. Roshan Baig, hon'ble minister for infrastructure development and information; Shri Basavaraj Rayareddy, hon'ble minister for higher education; Shrimati Umashree, hon'ble minister for women and child welfare development; Priyank M. Kharge, publicity convener and hon'ble minister for information technology and biotechnology; Krishna Byre Gowda, logistics convener and hon'ble minister for agriculture;

and Captain Manivannan, secretary, Social Welfare Department. Thanks also to Dr M.C. Srinivasa, joint director, Social Welfare Department, and Dr H. Nataraj, secretary, State Safai Karmachari Commission, both nodal officers attached to Captain Manivannan, for taking care of the logistics of the conference organization. I would also like to thank Dr Nagalakshmi and Mehroz Khan, who were coordinators for the conference; Shri Srinivasulu, managing director, Ambedkar Development Corporation, attached to Krishna Byrc Gowda; and Dr Nandan Kumar, officer on special duty to Priyank Kharge. I must also thank Luthfulla Atheeq, principal secretary to the chief minister; Shri Venkataiah, special advisor to Social Welfare Department; M.V. Savithri, commissioner, Social Welfare Department; and numerous other officials and staff of the Social Welfare Department who worked so diligently.

Special thanks are due to the Scheduled Castes Department team of the All India Congress Committee: Shri K. Raju, head of the Congress President's Office, for his ideation and immense political support, and Pushparaj Deshpande, in-charge of the Quest for Equity website and other logistical support. I cannot fail to mention Oum, Navil, Deepika, and the rest of the Phase I team, who worked tirelessly.

I would like to express my profound thanks to the members of the various committees, specially members of the academic committee, Professors Sukhadeo Thorat, Valerian Rodrigues, G. Haragopal, Aakash Singh Rathore, Rochana Bajpai, Sudhir Krishnaswamy, S.G. Siddaramaiah, K. Marulasiddappa, Siddalingaiah, L. Hanumanthaiah, Mallika Ganti, and K.B. Siddaiah. Special thanks are also due to the editorial advisory board for their invaluable advice and assistance throughout, including those members from the academic committee mentioned earlier, as well as Dr Suraj Yengde and Professors Anand Teltumbde, Kalpana Kannabiran, Lawrence R. Simon, and Meena Dhanda. My heartful thanks to Professor Aakash Singh Rathore for taking the responsibility of editing these volumes.

Of course, I cannot fail to mention the support of Shabin John and Chandrashekar for their office and logistics support and Dr Ramkhok Raikhan for research assistance to the editor.

S. Japhet
Professor and Vice Chancellor,
Bengaluru Central University, India

Abbreviations

ACRs	additional class rooms
AISCF	All-India Schedule Caste Federation
AWC	Anganwadi centres
BJP	Bharatiya Janata Party
BPL	below poverty line
BSP	Bahujan Samaj Party
BSUP	Basic Service to the Urban Poor
CASI	Centre for the Advanced Study of India
CASM	Critical Ambedkar Studies Movement
CBGA	Centre for Budget and Governance Accountability
CSO	Central Statistics Office
CSS	centrally sponsored schemes
DAY-NRLM	Deendayal Antayodaya Yojana – National Rural Livelihoods Mission
DPR	detailed project report
DTDC	desk-to-desk courier
EOC	Equal Opportunity Commission
ESI	employee's social insurance
FIR	first information report
FSA	Food Security Act
FYP	five-year programme
GBD	global burden of disease
GDP	gross domestic product
GHI	global hunger index
GLP	gross legislative product
GoI	Government of India
HDI	human development index

HDR	human development report
IAY	Indira Awas Yojna
ICDS	integrated child development services
IDMI	infrastructure development for minority institutions
IHSDP	Integrated Housing and Slum Development Programme
IMR	infant mortality rate
IPC	Indian Penal Code
ITI	Industrial Training Institute
JNNURM	Jawaharlal Nehru National Urban Renewal Mission
KGBV	Kasturba Gandhi Balika Vidyalaya
LE	life expectancy
LGBT	lesbian, gay, bisexual, transgender
MAEF	Maulana Azad Education Foundation
MCB	minority concentrated blocks
MCD	minority concentrated districts
MCT	minority concentrated towns
MGNREGA	Mahatma Gandhi National Rural Employment Guarantee Act
MPI	multidimensional poverty index
MSDP	Multi-sectoral Development Programme
NCDHR	National Campaign on Dalit Human Rights
NCR	National Capital Region
NCRB	National Crime Records Bureau
NDB	National Data Bank
NITI	National Institution for Transforming India
NMDFC	National Minorities Development Finance Corporation
NRDWP	National Rural Drinking Water Programme
NULM	National Urban Livelihoods Mission
OBC	Other Backward Classes
PDS	public distribution system
PF	Provident Fund
PIL	public interest litigation
PMAY	Pradhan Mantri Awas Yojana
PRI	Panchayati Raj Institution
PSL	public sector lending
PUCL	People's Union for Civil Liberties
PWD	Public Works Department
QEHWP	Queen Elizabeth House, Working Papers

RBI	Reserve Bank of India
RSS	Rashtriya Swayamsevak Sangh
SCC	Supreme Court cases
SCR	Supreme Court reports
SCs	Scheduled Castes
SCSP	Scheduled Caste Sub-Plan
SGSY	Swarnajayanti Gram Swarozgar Yojana
SJRSY	Swarna Jayanti Shahari Rozgar Yojana
SPQEM	Scheme to Provide Quality Education in Madrasas
SSA	Sarva Shiksha Abhiyan
SSC	Staff Selection Commission
STs	Scheduled Tribes
TMT	thermo-mechanical treatment
TSP	Tribal Sub-Plan
U5MR	under-five mortality rate
UIDSSMT	Urban Infrastructure Development Scheme for Small & Medium Towns
UIG	urban infrastructure and governance
ULBs	urban local bodies
UNDP	United Nations Development Programme
UP	Uttar Pradesh
UPSC	Union Public Service Commission
WB	World Bank

Introduction

AAKASH SINGH RATHORE

Legal Justice and Economic Justice

Unlike the previous two volumes in this collection that were each devoted to a single theme (first, political justice, and second, social justice), this volume includes two themes, as will all of the subsequent volumes in the collection. These two themes, legal justice and economic justice, are treated in two different parts of the book. Thus, this volume and the remaining volumes in the collection are like double issues. By this, we do not mean to suggest an inherent link between the two different themes covered in these volumes. It is simply a matter of organizational convenience.

However, in the present case it must be said that the two subjects covered in this volume, legal justice and economic justice, were actually the two pre-eminent academic disciplines of B.R. Ambedkar. Although Ambedkar was a polymath and made pioneering innovative contributions in fields as diverse as political science, sociology, historiography, religious studies, and so on, law and economics were the two disciplines in which he was formally trained and officially credentialled. Among other degrees, Ambedkar earned an MSc and DSc in economics, as well as the Bar-at-Law (Barrister) degree.

It is worth touching on a sample of a few ways by which Dr Ambedkar operationalized his academic training in law and economics, as well as some ways by which his concerns and efforts continue to be our own right up to this day, as his legacy continues to inspire us.

After the completion of his formal education abroad in economics and law, Ambedkar returned once again to Bombay, where he started his legal practice in 1923. He took on some noteworthy cases, often hopeless ones where he championed the underdog.

In 1927, Ambedkar was appointed as a member of the Legislative Assembly of Bombay Province for a term of five years (it was renewed in 1932 for another five years). In this capacity, he submitted a statement before the Simon Commission on 29 May 1928, which was noteworthy because it departed radically from all other submissions by pontificating on the nature of constitutional democracy and, within that framework, raising attention to the plight of Untouchables. Thus was launched the era of his large-scale political prominence.

In August of 1936, Ambedkar founded the Independent Labour Party, a party based not on caste but on class. He joined hands with the Left and attempted to apprise Marxists about their shared interests. Ambedkar was a champion of labour rights at a time when the concept of workers' rights did not exist. In India, much before other nations even started thinking about instituting just and fair conditions for workers, Ambedkar successfully led the struggle for reducing working hours from 12 to 8 in 1942. He also vehemently (and successfully) protested against the 'Black Bill' which the colonial government was using to suppress workers' strikes. His commitment to labour rights was also visible in Article 19(c) of the Indian Constitution, which guarantees the fundamental right to form associations or unions.

Dr Ambedkar was also inextricably connected with the Reserve Bank of India (RBI). The RBI was created on the basis of guidelines that Ambedkar had presented to the 'Royal Commission on Indian Currency and Finance' in 1925 and in his definitive book *The Problem of the Rupee—Its Problems and Its Solution.*

In August 1947, Ambedkar joined Prime Minister Jawaharlal Nehru's cabinet as law minister. He had hoped to be given the portfolio for development so he could pursue massive projects in electricity, transportation, health, and so on, to improve the quality of life for the millions of destitute. Nevertheless, he accepted the law ministry portfolio, thereby launching his uneasy tenure in the Union Cabinet, from which he resigned in protest after four years of service.

Two weeks after being inducted into Nehru's cabinet, Ambedkar was made the chairman of the Drafting Committee of the Indian Constitution. There is a great deal of controversy about a moment when Ambedkar seems to have denounced the Constitution and referred to himself as a 'hack' for Congress; however, he remains revered for the decisive role that he played in creating that abiding instrument.

As law minister, Ambedkar spearheaded the introduction of the Hindu Code Bill, giving rights of inheritance and property ownership to women. Both he and Nehru believed it was a 'vital step in the introduction of true democracy in India, and would remove the practices and the logic that underpinned the caste system' (Rathore 2020, 65). Yet, all dispersed factions from the right united to defeat the bill as well as to vilify and attack Ambedkar personally. When Nehru himself withdrew support from the bill due to political expediency, Ambedkar resigned from the cabinet.

Over the course of his life and vocation, Ambedkar's understanding of the nature of legal justice and economic justice evolved, but his commitment to them never faltered. Ambedkar envisaged a proactive role for the State and public policy to intervene in favour of the disadvantaged and marginalized. While he supported State intervention in the economy, he also stressed the need to adopt strong policies for affirmative action that reshaped the State and made it representative, responsive, and accountable. Ambedkar developed a pragmatic view on the relative ability of the State and the market to achieve social, political, and economic justice. The turn to market-oriented economic reforms in India and elsewhere poses new challenges for the social vision that Ambedkar bequeathed. With these sorts of challenges in view, numerous scholars, policymakers, and activists came together in Bengaluru in 2017, both to celebrate the life of B.R. Ambedkar and to carry his legacy forward. Concerns of legal justice and economic justice were central to the engagement. These were given formal recognition through numerous recommendations within the Bengaluru Declaration (see Volume 2 of this set, 'Introduction'). Consider, for example, the following excerpts:

Safeguarding the People

Upholding the Rule of Law: The State must be unequivocal in its protection of fundamental rights and constitutional values. To do this:

- Irrespective of religious identities or institutional affiliations, the State needs to strictly reassert political and legal accountability for any violence. This is the only way to prevent lynchings and uphold the rule of law.
- The police services must be freed from political control, and reformed by fully implementing police reforms, so that they become a service provider to citizens rather than a force to impose control.
- Just like the Prevention of Sexual Harassment at Workplace Act, a special Act for the prevention of caste, religious and gender discrimination in educational institutions must be passed. This will prevent discrimination in admission, enhance access to quality education, and ensure equality as an integral part of the education process.
- The State must uphold the Constitution in letter and spirit. Any attempt at reviewing the Constitution shall be opposed forthwith.

Protecting Individual Rights and Freedoms: All provisions that place constraints on freedom of speech, expression and individual rights should be reformed or removed. These include those on defamation, sedition, art/film censorship and social media.

Strengthening Democratic Institutions

Judicial reforms: To ensure that the judiciary is robust and reflective of the social diversity of India, reservations for SCs/STs/OBCs in the higher judiciaries must be institutionalised. Furthermore, as per the recommendation of the National Judicial Commission, an All India Judicial Services should be created with provisions of reservation for SCs/STs/OBCs.

Deepening Social Justice

Economic Empowerment of SCs/STs/OBCs and Minorities: The State shall ensure adequate special funds to boost entrepreneurship among the SCs/STs, OBCs and Minorities, to ensure they attain economic liberty. The State shall also reserve at least 10 per cent of Stakes/Shares in PSUs/Corporations/Companies, for SCs/STs/OBCs to enhance their participation in the economic activities of the State. For this, the State shall create a special corpus fund for SCs/STs/OBCs to buy these stakes/shares. Similar other mechanisms to increase representations of SCs/STs/OBCs in Government's financial institutions should also be ensured.

Comprehensive reform of caste based occupational vocations: All caste based occupational vocations must be comprehensively reformed so that they are modernised, formalised and it is ensured that those entering the particular occupation are not representative of a particular caste or community. At the same time, through the above mentioned educational and employment recommendations, the State should liberate people from caste based occupational oppression.

Immediate publishing of Socio-Economic Caste Census: The State shall immediately publicise the results of the socio-economic and caste census undertaken in the urban and rural areas.

Promoting Social Security

Universal social security for unorganised sector: All labourers working in the unorganised sector should be covered with a comprehensive social security scheme providing for life, disability and health insurance. In addition, monthly pensions should be provided to those who have crossed 60 years.

Living wage for unorganised sector: Workers in the unorganised sector must be secured with a 'Living Wage' which ensures a decent standard of life, full enjoyment of leisure and social and cultural activities.

Ensuring Dignity in Retirement through enhanced pensions: To ensure that the old, disabled and widows are able to lead a dignified life, pensions will be enhanced to Rs. 1500 p.m., with an increase every year in tune with the Consumer Price Index.

Enhanced safety net: To uplift and empower the most vulnerable, the State's safety net should be expanded by universalising access to all poverty elimination programmes for every family where no members of the family pays income tax.

Fund for landless labourers: All loan waivers should have an additional 20 per cent kept aside as a fund for rehabilitating and uplifting landless labourers.

Low cost housing for the urban poor in all private housing layouts: To ensure affordable housing for the urban poor, all private housing layouts must allocate 20 per cent of land for low cost housing.

Contextualizing these specific recommendations for policies and practices, and giving teeth to many of Dr Ambedkar's preoccupations within his pursuit of legal justice and economic justice for all, the Bengaluru Declaration closes with these words:

> We need to address these concerns urgently. ... India needs to return to its noblest ideals, the spirit of its Constitution. It is time for the Indian people to recognise the constitutional path we chose 70 years ago and dedicate ourselves to protect and enhance this legacy. In this quest, the Bengaluru Declaration hopes that all progressive forces, collectively and across party lines, will adopt and implement these recommendations to fulfil Babasaheb Ambedkar's dream of an equitable, just and egalitarian society.

It is very much within this spirit that this volume on legal justice and economic justice functions as a platform to think along with Ambedkar and to offer imaginative strategies to achieve legal justice and economic justice in contemporary India.

Turning now to its specific contents, in the first chapter, foremost legal scholar **Upendra Baxi** ('Lawless Law, Living Death, and the Insurgent Reason of Babasaheb Ambedkar') explores how Ambedkar's lifelong struggles contributed to the making of a Constitution that accentuated the values of liberty, equality, fraternity, and dignity, but at the same time ushered in massive lived and basic contradictions between the established caste order and the promised normative change. Dwelling on the multifaceted and violent social exclusion, Ambedkar showed how the caste system is based on the notions of 'living death' and 'lawless law'. The contradictory unity of State and law which he indefatigably explored ultimately led him away from law and towards religion as a means of social change. According to Baxi, in tracing this great itinerary, one also chases the various shades of meaning of emancipation as justice.

In the next chapter, **R. Sudarshan** ('B.R. Ambedkar's Exemplary Adherence to Constitutional Morality') inaugurates a theme that is common within several of the following chapters: an exploration of the significance of Ambedkar's idea of 'constitutional morality'. Sudarshan asks why one of the main architects of a Constitution that anticipated the abolition of zamindari, and who crafted its first amendment in order to protect land reform laws from being struck down by courts for violating the right to property, would resign from his office as law minister and argue cases on behalf of zamindars? Was this a principled stand or was it motivated by mere expediency? The answer is to be found in unravelling the notion of constitutional morality.

Arvind Narrain ('Radical Constitutionalism: Towards an Ambedkarite Jurisprudence') elaborates further upon constitutional morality, and also explores other legal concepts put forward by Ambedkar that he believes are of great relevance today. Narrain argues that a key Ambedkarite idea is that legal activism cannot stop at norm articulation but must struggle with the difficult task of actualizing the norm in a deeply flawed society. In these days of a rising tide of Hindutva, it is integral that we also go back to the Ambedkarite corpus and retrieve key notions such as fraternity and constitutional morality as guides to a more constitutional future.

In the fourth chapter, **Antje Linkenbach** ('B.R. Ambedkar's Imaginations of Justice') explores the complex relationship between Ambedkar's sociopolitical vision of a just society, based on concepts deriving from various scholarly and religious contexts his idea of constitutional morality, the possibilities of constitutional law, and the realities of oppression in the everyday life of marginalized groups in India. Linkenbach also reflects upon the basic challenge in Ambedkar's imagination of justice: A just society requires a fundamental change of the 'philosophy of life' or 'outlook' of the ruling classes. Law and legislation can enforce procedures of justice, but altering attitudes deeply rooted in unjust cultural traditions and mindsets needs long-term peaceful forms of persuasion and struggle.

Umakant ('The Significance of Rights and the Rule of Law under the Indian Constitutional Framework'), in a tacit sense in dialogue with the concerns of the previous chapter, examines Ambedkar's view on the relationship between the underlying concepts of an inclusive constitution (wherein liberty, equality, and fraternity are foundational) and the objectives of the Constitution for a newly liberated country such as India, where inequality, social divisions, lack of harmony, and fraternal relations had been the defining characteristics for a long time in its history. As Umakant points out, with arduous deliberations, Ambedkar played a key role in formulating a constitution which professes the country's unity and diversity, its egalitarian society, ensuring rights to all through the rule of law.

Anupama Rao ('B.R. Ambedkar and Indian Democracy') offers further social and historical context for the claims that Umakant makes in the previous chapter. Rao argues that we ought to think about B.R. Ambedkar as an insurgent thinker, just as Upendra Baxi had proposed. This means that Ambedkar challenged established modalities of thought and activism by drawing on political and ethical possibilities that were globally conceived, though deeply engaged with forms of subaltern difference. The author focuses on Ambedkar as a figure whose thought and activism transcends the divide of colonial/postcolonial history, which is typically framed around the dual axes of the political Partition and Britain's transfer of power. She attends to his powerful efforts to challenge a restricted conception of the caste question and the foreclosure of more radical conceptions of social equality in the aftermath of political Independence.

With this, the first part of the volume—on legal justice—is brought to a close.

Part two, on economic justice, begins with a chapter by **Vijay Gudavarthy** ('Development through Informalization and Circulation of Labour: The Emerging Anatomy of an Uncivil Society'). Gudavarthy attempts to address the question of whether modes of social coordination through social networks and social capital resolve the challenge of extra economic force to develop a competitive labour market across the economy. The author accomplishes this by studying the problem of segmentation of employment and whether the processes underlying the intra– and inter–social network relations as modes of organization and coordination are resolving it. This is done by focusing on two streams of inter-state labour circulation; namely informal workers employed in the unorganized brick kilns on the one hand and organized manufacturing on the other. Both of the streams consist of temporary migrants from Odisha to Telangana characterized by illiteracy, low levels of education, and/or low level of skills. Gudavarthy's title gives a clear hint at what he finds the data to reveal.

Joseph Tharamangalam ('India's Paradox of "Hunger amidst Plenty" Has a Name: Caste-Based Discrimination and Exclusion') continues to analyse conundrums in the Indian economy. The records of the Human Development Index (130 of 188) and Multidimensional Poverty Index (55 per cent) have presented a paradox for India, a country touted as one of the fastest growing economies in the world and a rising economic powerhouse. Tharamangalam attempts to show that this Indian puzzle begins to unravel when we disaggregate the data and see the nature of a large pool of chronic and endemic poverty/hunger that disproportionately consists of historically excluded castes, especially Dalits (also Adivasis) who continue to be the victims of an entrenched system of exclusion and deprivation from livelihood resources, including knowledge. The author reveals thereby the structural and cultural violence that sustains the paradox.

In the third chapter on economic justice, **Aseem Prakash** ('Dalits Enter the Indian Market as Owner of Capital: Adverse Inclusion, Social Networks, and Civil Society') analyses how Dalits continue to find themselves included in India's markets on adverse terms. The root cause is their lack of social networks based on caste locations. Prakash thus argues for considering caste as a specific Indian form of civil society—as a site of accumulation. In doing so, the author sheds light on some of the problems inherent in the recent celebration of Dalit entrepreneurs and explores a host of related challenges from the perspective of economic sociology.

Pritam Singh ('Ambedkar's Economic Methodology for Social Justice: The Centrality of Dalits') returns the focus to the nature of Ambedkar's own economic thought. According to Singh, Ambedkar did not view economics as 'neutral' between conflicting economic interests in society, but looked upon economic concepts as analytical tools for multiple and conflicting uses. The unifying theme behind his eclectic use of economic concepts was the defence of Dalit economic interests for social and economic justice. This method was particularly used in analysing various economic phenomena and policies during British rule in India. Singh elaborates this interpretation of Ambedkar's economic thought by examining his writings on issues in the domain of money and banking, agriculture, and federalism.

The final chapter on economic justice as well as the final chapter of the volume as a whole is by **Jawed Alam Khan** ('Economic Justice: Policy and Public Investment for *Pasmanda* Muslims'). Unlike the previous chapter that explores Ambedkar's own economic methodology, Khan's chapter is an example—as several earlier ones—of practising the discipline in line with central concerns shared between the author and Dr Ambedkar. In this case, Khan assesses the policy initiatives and scheme designs, availability of financial resources, fund utilization, physical performance, and status of implementation of development programmes meant for *Pasmanda* (socially and educationally backward) Muslims. The author highlights that they have largely not been targeted directly and properly through ongoing schemes and programmes meant for minorities, mainly initiated since the Eleventh Five-Year Plan. The Pasmanda Muslims face exclusion in planning, budgeting, and implementation processes of development programmes at various levels of governance. Along with uncovering these profound defects, the chapter also offers important corrective measures that we can adopt in order to overcome the current failures.

Each one of these eleven, often interrelated, contributions précised here lays a single foundation stone toward erecting the pillars of legal and of economic justice. This volume on legal and economic justice, in turn, serves as a unit of support for the broader edifice formed by the five volumes taken together. This broader edifice of research and scholarship may seem imposing from the academic point of view. However, when viewed from the more panoramic perspective of Dr Ambedkar's lifelong quest for justice, it may rightly be seen as itself only a single foundation stone set toward the achievement of colossal goals. These are goals that will only be achieved by accumulating the momentum of critical masses enlightened and thundering forward. Speaking on behalf of the 70 or so participants in this particular project, I think we can take some satisfaction in the small part that we are playing through what we have achieved. The intersection and synergy between Dr Ambedkar's own profound and prolific writings and the most current scholarship and intellectual insights on offer here is a crucial step in the right direction. The Bengaluru Declaration stands as testament to the fact. But, of course, a mere declaration is not enough.

In a touching anecdote, the head of the Western Buddhist Order, Sangharakshita, described his final encounter with Dr Ambedkar shortly before the latter's death. He described Ambedkar as very ill and unable to speak clearly—a shocking change from his usual booming voice. Ambedkar was repeating something in an impassioned manner but inaudibly to Sangharakshita. Sangharakshita placed his ear to Ambedkar's lips to be able to hear what he was saying. Ambedkar's last words to the monk to whom he had entrusted the Buddhist education of hundreds of thousands of new converts were: 'There is still so much to be done. ... So much to be done' (Sangharakshita 1986, 20).

Indeed, in our own efforts to carry forward the torch of B.R. Ambedkar's quest for justice, there is still so much to be done.

References

Rathore, Aakash Singh. 2020. *Ambedkar's Preamble: A Secret History of the Constitution of India*. Delhi: Penguin.

Sangharakshita. 1986. *Ambedkar and Buddhism*. London: Windhorse Publications.

Part One

Legal Justice

1

Lawless Law, Living Death, and the Insurgent Moral Reason of Babasaheb Ambedkar

UPENDRA BAXI

It is impossible to narrate precisely Babasaheb Ambedkar's political and juridical thought because he did not primarily pursue abstract theory; in fact, much of his writing aimed to clarify the history and workings of the system of untouchability as a means of reflexive political solidarity against suffering, repression, and humiliation. More than Jacques Derrida, who pursued a theory of relationship between writing and violence (Derrida 1978; see also Landau 2010), Babasaheb showed the linkages between inscription, violence, and counter-power.

His life was a constant struggle in organizing the negation of systemic realities that sought to legitimate social repression and violence. No doubt, there are threads of unity in his oceanic writings, but equally, if not more, there are also tides of difference. The corpus is diverse, heterogeneous, even if not fragmentary, and constantly evocative of difference and otherness.

As a small versifier, I wrote: 'Kaetlii Ankho Radi Hase/Samandar Ansuaau no Bhandarchhe' (lit. how may eyes must have cried/to create the ocean which is the treasure of tears). The ocean as a collection of suffering people's tears, constantly replenished, is a powerful imagery and I am of the opinion that Babasaheb's oceanic writings express the power of hope as well as of despair—civic lamentation at the continuing acts of injustice. Civic lamentation has been a powerful voice of subaltern protest.

I engage primarily with the theme of contradictory unity of State and law and try to understand the theory of contradictions, latent and patent, in Ambedkar. I also explore the relation between law and religion in Ambedkar. I am aware that I remain, in doing so, only at the outskirts of his thought but that also provides valuable starting points. I write this in furtherance of my programme of the critical Ambedkar studies movement (CASM), which is critical in two senses: it is non-hagiographical[1] (as opposed to hero-worship[2]) and it is a critical resource for the Indian renaissance of a constitutional republic, in its seventieth year. However, the term 'critical' should itself be viewed critically: obviously, quilt quotations from the *Collected Works* (the journalistic fashion today) is not the way ahead, because the entire spirit of Ambedkar may not be grasped by isolated passages. Rather, a very close study of the man and his thought is necessary. To be critical is to understand gestures at thought and the overall thought itself, not just to offer

[1] I sounded this theme in my Ambedkar University Ambedkar Memorial Lecture 2013, 'Restoring "Title Deeds to Humanity": Lawless Law, Living Death, and the Insurgent Reason of Babasaheb Ambedkar'. Some of the themes here owe to that meditation. I pointed out how thinkers such as Gopal Guru, Valerian Rodrigues, and Sharmilla Rege recognized CASM (without naming it so). (See Guru 1970; 1998, 156–7; Rege 2006; 2008, 17–20; 2013; Rodrigues 2002. See also, Teltumbde 2013, 10–11.)

[2] So fierce is the recent appropriation by competitive politics that it is worth quoting what Ambedkar famously said:

> There is nothing wrong in being grateful to great men who have rendered life-long services to the country. But there are limits to gratefulness. As has been well said by the Irish Patriot Daniel O'Connell, no man can be grateful at the cost of his honor, no woman can be grateful at the cost of her chastity and no nation can be grateful at the cost of its liberty. This caution is far more necessary in the case of India than in the case of any other country. For in India, Bhakti or what may be called the path of devotion or hero-worship, plays a part in its politics unequalled in magnitude by the part it plays in the politics of any other country in the world. Bhakti in religion may be a road to the salvation of the soul. But in politics, Bhakti or hero-worship is sure road to degradation and to eventual dictatorship. (Ambedkar 1994: 13, 125–6)

miscellaneous and fragmentary criticisms based on contextual quotations. One must always have in view (as Kumar [2015] puts it) the figure of Ambedkar not only as a 'thinker of sacrifice' but also as a 'sacrificial thinker'.[3]

While we will analyse Ambedkar's understanding of the contradictory unity of State and law in some detail later, it needs to be said at the outset that he himself lived a life of contradictions. He was the chief architect of the Constitution,[4] yet as Eleanor Zelliot (1996, 69) wryly notes, the Constitution was adopted with a chant: 'Mahatma Gandhi ki jai! [Let Mahatma Gandhi be victorious!]' The naming of Ambedkar as a modern Manu is deeply antinomic, especially when we recall that he burnt a copy of *Manusmriti*.[5] We may note that his desire was to extend similar treatment to the Constitution too.[6] It shows how Babasaheb was deeply ambivalent

[3] The invocation of 'sacrifice' is summoning. So is the implicit linkage between repression of the dominant and the counter-power of resistance, where the subaltern despite constant struggle yields and defers emancipation. (In many ways, Ambedkar himself felt repressed, even when he mobilized variously the struggles for emancipation.) Sacrificial thought and action does not mean trading off the present for a better future, but the courage to combat the miserable present on its own terms, with or without any promise of future redemption or deliverance.

[4] The expression is probably emanating from Brecher (1959). But Dr Ambedkar, with becoming modesty, attributed credit to Sir B.N. Rau as well as others. The Constitution was indeed (as Granville Austin notes) framed by an 'oligarchy' (see Austin 1967).

[5] He burnt a copy of *Manusmriti* on 25 December 1927; the day is called *Manusmriti Dhahan Din* ever since. His action was based on the ground of equality of all humans. Whether the burning of books gains anything and whether book-burning should ever be considered an act of symbolic protest are important issues; so is the question whether such protest is an aspect of freedom of speech and expression. These questions, which I will not pursue here, deserve analysis and reflection.

[6] The Constitution had many illiberal provisions which he detested. For example, the notion of the undemocratic nature of discretionary powers with the governor: 'We have inherited the idea that the Governor must have no power at all, that he must be a rubber-stamp'; Babasaheb stated that if 'a minister, however scoundrelly he may be', puts 'up a proposal before the Governor, he has to ditto it. That is the kind of conception about democracy which we have developed in this country' (quoted in Shourie 2008).

about the writing of the Constitution. Not wholly in a self-deprecatory way he described himself not as chief 'maker of the Constitution' but as its 'hack'; he added, 'What I was asked to do, I did much against my will.' He went on to say, '[M]y friends tell me that I have made the Constitution. But I am quite prepared to say that I shall be the first person to burn it out. I do not want it. It does not suit anybody.'[7]

How does one understand this disenchantment with the law, rights, and constitutionalism? As an act of constitutional nihilistic observations—a complete loss of belief in constitutionalism or constitutional justice? Or does it signify 'passive nihilism' (evacuation of all existing values)? Or active nihilism (installation of new desired values) (see Heidegger 1991, 55–6, 66)? 'Burning it' because it 'does not suit anybody' remarkably suggests passive nihilism. On the other hand, the Constitution that he partly drafted is directed both against casteism and coloniality. Perhaps, as many of his contemporary critics maintained, he was a tragic figure not able to do much either without the Constitution and rights or also with them, and organizing negation was indignation entrepreneurship of an ultimately impotent rage. I think the better view is that he was an active nihilist.

However, Babasaheb also says that he was a 'hack' writer; not the chief architect of the Constitution. His rejection of the qualifier the 'author' or the 'chief architect' was, of course, based on being surrounded by co-equal giants of the national struggle. Was this an act of exasperation, this simultaneous ownership and dispossession of the constitutional text? Or was he expressing a guarded expression of the liberal elements of the law and the Constitution? Or was it even more? It is true that there were many aspects that he did not like but equally true that many other aspects walked into the text because of his historic presence and insistence.

More than any other thinker of his time, Ambedkar grasped the character of caste governance. He characteristically said (Ambedkar 1990: 9, 217): '[C]an anyone who realizes the outlook, tradition, and social philosophy of the governing class in India' ever believe that 'under the Congress regime, a sovereign and independent India will be different from the India we have today?' He was referring

[7] See https://www.thequint.com/news/india/father-of-the-indian, last accessed on 8 April 2018.

both to the nationalist and the casteist profile of the freedom movement but also addressing the liberal competitive politics ensured by the Constitution.

Perhaps, then, the great contradiction was the return to religion after a sojourn in Constitution-making. We all know the notion, still very strong, that law is an instrument of social control and social change, and Ambedkar did rely upon that instrumentality of control and change in the Indian society. But like the nineteenth-century Western founders of social theory, Ambedkar also believed that religion and education were such major instrumentalities too. He placed a major emphasis on all the three as pillars of emancipation in the struggle against the mass illegalities imposed on Untouchables by the dominant Brahmanism.[8] His thesis of 'Broken Men', the violated Buddhists Atisudras,[9] indicated early on his preference for Buddhism as a religion of equality, and displayed a remarkable degree of non-revolutionary 'pragmatism' (Stroud 2016, 5–27)[10] in ultimately reforming the established Buddhist religion and leading a mass conversion on 14 October 1956. Nearly half a million Untouchables embraced the Buddhist fold. He scandalized many by declaring: 'By discarding my ancient religion which stood for inequality and oppression today I am reborn' (Keer 1990). The metaphor of being reborn articulates a stage in resistance and insurrection. That social rebirth (in a finite life) beckons the transcendent only in struggles within the terrestrial—in a sense Ambedkar does engage the courage to be an act of love for the oppressed and repressed, and further develops

[8] See 'Annihilation of Caste' (Ambedkar 1989: 1, 23–95); Ambedkar (2011); see also 'Buddha or Karl Marx' (Ambedkar 1987: 3, 441–64).

[9] See, generally, Ambedkar (1990: 7), but particularly the description of 'Broken Men' and specific references and perspectives (370–9).

[10] Stroud (2016, 35–6) rightly concludes that 'Ambedkar's temporally drawn-out rhetoric of religious reorientation is a project in changing the social through a free and self-directed mental revolution in the commitments one takes as most central to the conception of self and other, and it behooves us to explore the fundamentally rhetorical nature of his actions, in the execution of this endeavor' (also see Skaria 2015, 450–65). One may also read into Aishwary Kumar's notions of 'fearless civility' and *maitri* as a constant struggle for justice: not merely the act of conversion but also the founding of a new religion (see Kumar 2015, especially Chapter 1 and Epilogue).

'a moral ontology of action ... from the dialectic of nation and empire, a commitment to virtue and sovereignty that placed itself in the interstices between the just and unjust (rather than in the difference between colonizer and colonized) as its primary site of intervention' (Kumar 2015, 339).

The contrast between the constitutional and religious Ambedkar must, however, be noted. Just to take one example of the many interventions made by Dr Ambedkar as a member of Governor General's Executive Council during 1942–6, he reminded his colleagues that as Hindus the Untouchables were not entitled to any special benefits and 'if fraternity is to involve this cost then I say I am their cousin and not their brother'. He further said:

> I shall not live on their *charity*. I am *entitled* to claim from the Government Treasury whatever right and benefit every other community is claiming for itself. I do not want charity: charity, the object of which is to *enslave and demoralize my community. The Scheduled Caste*[s] *want to stand on their rights ... if their claims are met with opposition, they will not hesitate to shed their blood to get their rights.* (Ambedkar 1991: 10, 363; emphasis added)[11]

Note the fundamental contrast Ambedkar makes between *charity* and *rights*. Not all acts of charity are pious or benevolent (in the sense they fulfil the duty of beneficence); in fact, there is a form of charity that colonizes (to evoke the phrase of Jürgen Habermas) the 'lifeworld' (see Fairtlough 1991 and White 1988, 90–127), a form of colonizing that enslaves rather than liberates. In contrast, claiming and having rights sets humans free from domination by the other. The rights are collective by their nature; and they are a promise of liberation as well as *threats* (of resistance, opposition,

[11] The context of discussion was the project for a college for the scheduled caste which Pandit Govind Malaviya found as 'nothing but the introduction of a sectarian spirit in the educational field'. He decried this attitude as nothing short of 'imprudence' and 'misnomer'. Ambedkar also said that though it was only recently that he became a member, he had read every word of the Council debates and that 'it is very seldom that any member of the Opposition has asked any question of any member of the Government ... with regard to the many atrocities, tyrannies, and oppression that have been practiced upon the Scheduled Castes in every village from day to day' (Ambedkar 1991: 10, 356, 361–2, respectively).

and bloodshed) to a form of domination that 'enslaves' and 'demoralizes' entire communities. These communities have a right to be, and to remain, human. They have also (in Hannah Arendt's terms) the 'right to have rights' (Arendt 2004, Chapter 9; see also Kesby 2012 and Birmingham 1996).

Ambedkar seems to limit 'entitlement' (and resistance) to 'whatever right and benefit very other community is claiming for itself': that is, entitlement to *justice as reciprocity*. Freedom, equality, and dignity are presented as universal moral goods to which each member of the species is entitled, and just social order is based on (and pursues) this. Ambedkar is not very explicit here but it is clear from his corpus that collective violence for rights is also justified when claims of justice as reciprocity are wholly ignored.

Ambedkar makes a very telling point when he says (as late as 1946) that the Hindu 'friends' only notice him when he makes '*a political question of* [his] *existence*' (Ambedkar 1991: 10, 361; emphasis added).[12] This is a profound biopolitical observation in the sense that the idea of having a body is itself constituted by the specific forms of biopower in State and society (see Foucault 2003, 2009, 2010; see also Deleuze 1988 and Cisney and Morar 2015). An untouchable is only noticed when she makes a 'political question of … existence' (see Norris 2005, 1–30). One may well ask: Was the act of mass conversion such a question?

Socially, the Untouchables were not merely untouchables but also *invisible*. Making them visible was a question of *rights*. But there was also the question of what is the *right thing to do*. The constitutional Ambedkar followed the logic of human rights, of equal dignity, which can only be done by making the Untouchables politically *visible*. The religious Ambedkar emphasized ahimsa as a moral and political virtue: the rivers of blood will not earn *nibbana*. Not the *rights* (being human and having rights) but *the right* (the highest good) was the principal question for the Buddhist Ambedkar. If the event of mass conversion is reformation of the self, no issue of political and social visibility survives. It, however, does when one fully embraces constitutionalism as a path of social progress in a finite world.

[12] He instanced issues such as separate electorates, reservations in services, and education grants.

'Living Death' and Untouchability

Taking recourse to Giorgio Agamben to understand Bhim Rao Ambedkar may appear anachronistic, and at first sight they seem to almost belong to different planets! Ambedkar was an eminent political leader of the Indian Depressed Classes and had the singular honour of being a principal draftsperson of the Constitution of India, while Professor Giorgio Agamben is far removed from the worlds of colonial/postcolonial politics. He is an Italian philosopher whose work has in some ways revolutionized political philosophy. Ambedkar, who died in 1956, had no occasion to read Agamben, and Agamben (despite being a progressive Eurocentric thinker) is probably entirely unaware of the existence of Ambedkar's voluminous, and yet still incomplete, collected works.

Agamben suggests, in the context of Auschwitz, that the space between 'literary and philosophic texts' is constituted by the problem or the affair of 'testimony' of 'obscure' and 'ordinary' people (who in the Camp) combine a 'great majority of people'—'both executioners and victims'. This is the space where the 'banality of evil' indwells (Agamben 1999, 13). Ambedkar's *Collected Works*, in my reading, fully archive this. Ambedkar is among the handful of modern Indian political thinkers to have taken sufferings of the Untouchables seriously.[13]

Understating Agamben requires accomplished grasp of classics and hermeneutic traditions in European theology, philosophy, and

[13] For Professor Agamben the task of 'completing Foucault' remains decisive; for Ambedkar remains imperative the task of critiquing Mohandas Gandhi. Agamben pursues abstract and often abstruse areas of philological, genealogical, aesthetic, and philosophical enquiry and does so remarkably giftedly. Ambedkar remains engaged with the tasks and challenges of applied political reason and ethics. Ambedkar spoke to the plights and rights of the masses of Untouchable peoples in India during the freedom struggle and the first decade of a free India and he continues to inspire their struggles even today, whereas Agamben speaks luminously to the global epistemic (theory-producing) classes. Ambedkar remains gifted in polemical prose (indeed reading him almost reminds one of Lenin!); Agamben has uses for rhetoric but not for polemics (a distinction which I may not for reasons of space here develop). Ambedkar always remains an easy read.

aesthetics (Agamben 1998, 180).[14] But not all the seven Ambedkars (Baxi 1994, 122–49) remained engaged with the production of knowledges; rather, many of them pursued critical social action, thus always haunted by formative life-experience.

Dr Ambedkar pointed out the brutal repression and destruction of Untouchable lives in ways reminiscent of Agamben's description of the conditions of 'living death' in concentration camps. He even described the camp as the 'Nomos of modern law' (Agamben 1998, 181). Ambedkar would have certainly held the law of Manu (and all forms of the most ancient law that practised discrimination and exclusion) as the nomos of the ancient law.

As we know, for Agamben, 'the state of exception is neither internal nor external to the juridical order', and the problem of defining it concerns precisely a threshold, or a zone of indifference (or a realm of indistinction), where 'inside and outside do not exclude each other but rather blur one another'; his basic question is: 'How can an anomie be inscribed within the juridical order?' (2005, 207). For him, 'the state of exception is "a *fictioiuris* par excellence which claims to maintain the law in its very suspension", but creates a space "without law", a zone of anomie' (2005, 59).[15]

Perhaps, it may be useful to distinguish between dharmic and constitutional conceptions of equality. A social order based on dharma—where social stands determined by birth in a caste, where discrimination and violence are considered as the only available legal fate possible, and where rigid exclusion prevails—offers a conception of graded inequality which legalizes a 'space without law' for those who live a living death. It is *fictio*(*iuris*) (legal fiction) which is at the same moment terribly real.

Although at first sight Dr Ambedkar did not have this language of biopower/biopolitics, he said pretty much the same about the law of Manu and its folk survivals till today. However, a deep comparison between Ambedkar and Agamben would show that the conditions of living death were not a state of exception but remain

[14] The nearest Agamben comes to Ambedkar is when he says (1998, 180) that 'in a different and analogous way, today's democratic capitalist project of eliminating poor classes through development not only reproduces within itself the people that is excluded, but also transforms the entire population of the Third World into bare life'.

[15] See also Humphreys (2006, 677–87).

integral to the very idea of law and justice. The discrimination against fellow humans appears as anomic from the outside but is the very *grundnorm* (fundamental norm) for the denial of dignity in a system of 'graded inequality'.[16]

Untouchability is partly a religious system, but Dr Ambedkar also identified it as economic. As an economic system, 'the Hindu takes no responsibility for the maintenance of the Untouchable' (a difference from American slavery)—a sort of an adieu to them, a moral ontology of non-presence, or an existence which is apolitical and, therefore, belonging to the bare and non-political life. The economic system can, therefore, organize both '*unmitigated* economic exploitation' and '*uncontrolled* economic exploitation' (Ambedkar 1990: 7, 197; emphasis added).[17] Ambedkar believed that it was this system which would be given a long lease of renewal by the Independence of India: the 'hard facts of the present and their certainty to continue in the indefinite future' require recognition that 'Swaraj, instead of putting an end to Untouchability, may extend its life' (Ambedkar 1990: 7, 198).[18]

In the absence of fully efficient constitutional safeguards freedoms of other citizens would mean 'tyranny' over others, and that other freedom will continue to be the '*Freedom to Enslave*' (Ambedkar 1990: 7, 199; emphasis added). Multiple caste-based tyrannies which occur daily cannot be eliminated only by religious reformation; nor can they be resisted by a 'scattered' people who are themselves weak and disarmed, by threat and use of force. What is needed is a new economic system which will put an end to these forms of exploitation.

[16] See Ambedkar (1990: 7, 215) where graded inequality is listed as a cluster conception.

[17] I do not think that Ambedkar meant by equality a state of affairs beyond all gradations of hierarchy. Indeed, secular 'hierarchical inequality' is built into constitutional structure (as hierarchy within administration of justice, bureaucracy, armed forces, learned professions, and so forth). Ambedkar's lifelong struggles can best be explained not so much through the notion of *graded inequality* but by *degrading inequality* (the justification of the manifestly unjust).

[18] Agamben was referring specially to developments since World War I, described as 'a laboratory for testing and honing the functional mechanisms and apparatuses of the state of exception as a paradigm of government' (Agamben 2005, 7).

Ambedkar would have agreed with Agamben that a 'state of exception' which 'becomes the rule' permits then the conversion of 'the juridicopolitical system itself into a *killing machine*' (Agamben 2005, 86; emphasis added). How is then the economic system to be changed entirely?[19] That 'how' is important if violence and force have to be abjured as methods of social change and control, and redistribution is to be achieved through a non-hegemonic but revolutionary consensus for social change. At the time of the making of the Constitution, Dr Ambedkar tried valiantly to accomplish this task through the Constitution by the alchemy of post-liberal rights, before he turned to the invention of religious tradition which would be further renovated toward the requirement firmly anchoring the equality of all human beings, animal life, and even the non-human worlds of some non-animate matter. Incidentally, relating Ambedkar's thought and corpus to the contemporary tasks of developing an Anthropocene justice theory will be extremely rewarding: for example, his implicit approaches to future persons, notions of intra-generational and intergenerational justice, and approaches to sustainable development and environmental justice.[20]

Post-liberal Fundamental Rights Paradigm

Constitutions are usually concerned with governance institutions, even when they enunciate the minima of justice and rights. Ambedkar helped make the world's first truly postcolonial Constitution. The latter form explicitly enshrines a contradiction between four key ideas: governance, development, rights, and justice. These values, or goals/ends, are deeply antinomic. The values

[19] There is much wisdom too in studying the transnational theory and practice. See Berg (2018, 843–64): The author insists that 'Ambedkar identifies a contingency in the constitution of caste based domination, namely the distinction between touchable and untouchable castes' and names it an 'embedded contingency', as 'it is rooted in religious beliefs, hegemony, social organization, and labor relations'. Insightful as this analysis is, it does not take fully into account Babasaheb's observations concerning caste as an economic system, unless the last expression ('labour relations') is meant to include this.

[20] Some beginnings have been made: see, for example, Sharma (2017) and https://kafila.online/2016/10/01/ambedkar-and-the-environmental-tradition/.

themselves contain and carry a deep, perhaps even abiding, conflict. And Dr Ambedkar made no pretence of concealing that conflict. He was simultaneously a proponent of horizontal equality of all citizens and of constitutional vertical group-based rights,[21] and further a stern critic of Indian constitutionalism at work and for the future of fraternity. However, it may not be gainsaid that it was 'Ambedkar's struggle [that] resulted in placing the Dalit problem at the heart of India's Constitution' (Berg 2011, 2).[22]

Sailing against the scholarly wind, I name the Indian Constitution as post-liberal rather than merely liberal in the classical sense, because of three reasons. First, Ambedkar constructed constitutional provisions which departed from a liberal model of basic rights by including some social rights as basic human rights;[23] second, he accomplished the creation of enforceable basic rights;[24] and third, the Constitution declared the suspension of the principle and details of federalism, imposing a power coupled with duty to make laws regarding those practices declared as offences by Part 111 (as fundamental rights).[25] The constitutionally desired social order[26] is

[21] For an analysis of Will Kymlika's notion of what he called 'polyethnic rights', see Baxi (2013, 221–3).

[22] I have often called Article 17 as the 'bleeding heart of the Indian Constitution'.

[23] Article 17 abolishes 'untouchability' in any form, forbids discrimination, and declares it as an offence. Here is a constitutional provision that, together with Articles 23/24, defines elements of a crime and prescribes a constitutional duty on Parliament to expeditiously and effectively prevent and punish the proscribed behaviour and conduct.

[24] Articles 23 and 24 deal respectively with (*a*) traffic in human beings, beggar, forced labour, and related forms of agrestic serfdom, and (*b*) prohibition of children in employment by any factory, or mine, or hazardous employment; significantly, the marginal notes describe these several rights as 'rights against exploitation'—the only place where that term appears in the Constitution. The mention of the term 'exploitation' is extremely significant, and Article 17 is also an integral aspect of it. I have developed some types of exploration as carceral, status, authority, economic, and other forms of exploitation (see Baxi 1993: Chapter 4, 60–8).

[25] Article 35 provides that 'not withstanding anything in the Constitution, Parliament shall have the power, and state legislatures will not have power to make law … for prescribing punishment for those acts which are declared to be offences under this Part' and Parliament shall do this 'as soon as it may'.

[26] For an elaboration of this notion, see Baxi (1967, 323–430).

at war with the social justifications for status quo (radical inequality). In a sense, it is a paradigmatic instance of what Andre Beteille (1971) once called a 'disharmonic' social system.

To be sure, Ambedkar shared certain features of liberalism but his conceptions of basic rights were already post-liberal, at least in the sense that he directed the logics and paralogics of human rights not just at the level of the State but also civil society (religious institutions, associations, and networks).

Constitutionalism thus means a revolutionary normative social change which provokes dissidence (discriminatory and illegal behaviour) into a new conformity. Reminiscent of Lon Fuller, we have here the idea of law as *enterprise*: Fuller defined law as an enterprise of subjecting behaviour to norms (Fuller 1969; Lovett 2015; Rundle 2012). The entire Constitution was drafted as an exercise and enterprise towards a democratic future, although Ambedkar was aware of its characteristic trait of ingrained inequality. Ambedkar believed in the Constitution and the laws favouring Atisudras (the economic and social propertiat) but he was aware of the glacial pace of legal change. He believed that law should remain a programme of social action directed towards the promotion of social change, and not a programme of social revenge.

Dr Ambedkar's ambivalence towards the law was shaped by the discrimination he himself suffered in his life, and also by knowing the pain, suffering, ostracism, and denial of dignity suffered by the Untouchables. Reputedly, he narrates how law is dumb, lame, and visually challenged when it approaches the Untouchables. In Agamben's terms it can be characterized as 'lawless law', to which we now briefly turn.

Lawless Law

Any legal positivist for whom positive law is the will of the sovereign or the State is bound to remain anxious at the expression 'lawless law'. But even postmodern criticisms of law do not recognize how Hinduism (its civilization and culture) protects and promotes lawless law. Chapter 23 in Volume 5 of the *Collected Works* of Ambedkar (1989) entitled 'Their Wishes Are Law for Us' offers an interesting thought. Law as the articulation of sovereign will is an idea that we are accustomed to, but what is meant by 'sovereign' here is an amalgam of religious and this-worldly (secular) authority. The king and the emperor are each bound by dharma, and so is the civil society, but what is dharma? Is it that which is only to be enunciated by certain kinds of uppermost castes? Can its maxims, standards, precepts, and doctrines be read as providing standards of critical morality which legitimize customs and practices of violent discrimination, exclusion, and violence against the Untouchables? May even critical morality justify the Brahmanic will to discriminate against the Untouchables with exclusionary force? May domination go so far as to eliminate visages and residues of justice? If the response is in the affirmative, then by its very nature, as it were, law in a caste society is irredeemably lawless.

The lawlessness of the law will also affect the administration of law and justice. Talking about the late colonial times, Ambedkar shows us how 'injustice and persecution can be perpetrated within the limits of the law':

> A Hindu may well say that he will not employ an Untouchable, that he will not sell him anything, that he will evict him from his land, that he will not allow him to take his cattle across his field without offending the law in the slightest degree. The law does not see with what motive he does it. *The law does not see what injury it causes to the Untouchable.* (Ambedkar 1989: 5, 106; emphasis added)

Second, the 'police may misuse its powers and authority' in various ways. Among these ways are: deliberate falsification of records, disclosure of evidence to the interested side, coercive manipulation of witnesses, and refusal to arrest. 'He may do a hundred other things to spoil the case. All this he can do without the slightest fear of being brought to book. The loopholes of law are many, and he knows how to use them well' (Ambedkar 1989: 5, 106).

Third is the problem of judicial arbitrariness in deploying judicial power; characteristically, this discretion has been 'exercised ... to the prejudice of Untouchables'.[27] Further, 'the forces ... are arrayed against the struggling Untouchables. There is simply no way to

[27] Ambedkar (1989, 107n39): The Magistrates have taken a common line by saying: 'I disbelieve the witnesses. And nobody has questioned this discretion. What sentence to inflict is also a matter of discretion with the magistrate.' An appeal is a way of 'getting redress but this may be blocked by a magistrate by refusing to give an appealable sentence'.

overcome because there is no way of punishing *a whole society which is organized to set against the law*' (Ambedkar 1989, 270–1; emphasis added).[28] What does Ambedkar mean by 'whole society'? Obviously, he signifies the law and the constitutional elites who discriminate yet profess a contradictory belief, or even faith, in equality and the rule of law, and also form and organize dominance as a means to perpetrate gross injustice. What Ambedkar means by 'whole society' here is the whole dominant society, including the State–law institutions. The notion in the italicized phrase sets two entities at war: law and 'society', or the Constitution and 'established order', but this Hobbesian state of nature—war of all against all—not just constitutes the denial of legal equality to the Untouchables but also repudiates at the very threshold the idea of law as a constraint against the threat or use of organized force. Set against the law, 'whole society' signifies the impossibility of the idea of law itself.

At a different level, Ambedkar emerges as the foremost critic of governance discretion that is despotic, that is, where it is used systematically to perpetuate violent social exclusion. While he knew that discretion is unavoidable and that abuse of power is never a ground against its conferral, for him casteist misuse of discretion was unjustified and unjustifiable. Instead, what remains sufficient for him is the validation of a general institutional bias of the police and magistracy against Untouchables and to question it. Only such questioning, it is said, enables the power to practice a reversal of perspectives so essential to doing and achieving justice. But does it? As Ambedkar himself said, the law as administered has a certain quality of 'impregnability': 'If the Hindu society plays its part in maintaining the Established Order, so does the Hindu officials [*sic*] of the State. The two have made the Established Order impregnable' (see Ambedkar 1989, 107). Sure, the 'impregnability' is addressed by the normative law (the law in books) but is restored daily on the ground (existential administration of justice or law in action). No amount of constitutional law writing affects the administration of discretionary (in)justice. The 'Established Order' triumphs over the normative law's commandments and

[28] See also Ambedkar (1989: 5, 62–74); this chapter, entitled 'Why Is Lawlessness Lawful?', is a poignant account of prohibitions and lynching still widely prevalent, especially in the countryside.

aspirations. Impunity makes law impregnable. In such a situation, as Hannah Arendt writes, certain humans act as a force of nature and history:

> Guilt and innocence become senseless notions; 'guilty' is he who stands in the way of the natural or historical process which has passed judgment over 'inferior races', over individuals 'unfit to live', over 'dying classes and decadent peoples'. Terror executes these judgments, and before its court, all concerned are subjectively innocent: the murdered because they did nothing against the system, and the murderers because they do not really murder but execute a death sentence pronounced by some higher tribunal. The rulers themselves do not claim to be just or wise, but only to execute historical or natural laws; they do not apply laws, but execute a movement in accordance with its inherent law. Terror is lawfulness, if law is the law of the movement of some supra-human force, Nature or History. (Arendt 2004, 456)

Leaving aside here Ambedkar's critique of Gandhi's adroit uses of fasting unto death as an act of biopower militating against the emancipation of India's Untouchables (Ambedkar 2017, notes 14, 24, 25, 42; Baxi 1994),[29] his historic summons of 'Educate, Organize, Agitate' for India's postcolonial Untouchable subjects evokes some biophilic imageries of Indian constitutional futures. He believed somehow that forms of postcolonial Indian constitutionalism may still mitigate 'minute by minute' what Hannah Arendt named as the 'lesson' of the 'terrifying, unswayable and unimaginable banality of evil' (Arendt 2004, 456–7) or—as with stateless persons, 'in a Kafkaesque legal vacuum' of 'non-persons'—'legal ghosts'.[30] But 'legal ghosts' remain crucial to any narrative of law, if only because this spectral non-presence that is always a presence haunts the very naming of the idea of law.[31]

In a way, one is talking about the totalitarian uses of law as extended to societies which call themselves both liberal and

[29] See also the incisive critique of 'reconciliation between Gandhi and Ambedkar' in Rathore (2017, 168–91). See also Vajpeyi (2012).

[30] See http://www.unhcr.org/basics/BASICS/4523b0bb2.pdf, last accessed on 5 May 2018.

[31] As is, in many ways, shown acutely by Derrida (2006). Derrida famously coined the term 'hauntology' without which he said the (Western) science of 'ontology' is radically incomplete.

modern today. The essence of the 'totalitarian attempt is to *make men superfluous*' and this is replicated today in the 'experience of modern masses of their superfluity on an overcrowded earth' (Arendt 2004, 589n47; emphasis added). The superfluous already belong to the '*world of the dying, in which men are taught they are superfluous through a way of life* in which punishment is meted out without connection with crime, in which *exploitation is practiced without profit, and where work is performed without product, is a place where senselessness is daily produced anew*' (Arendt 2004, 589n47; emphasis added). It is this everyday production of senselessness and of superfluity that Ambedkar depicted in describing the system as 'evil', though as an encomist he would have differed a great deal from the notion that this evil system was one where 'exploitation [was] without profit' and work was 'without product'.

Contradiction, Order, and Change

Despite all this, Ambedkar also emphasized his view that it is 'only a Government of the people, for the people, and by the people' that will make possible 'undivided allegiance to the best interest of the country' (Ambedkar 1982: 2, 504). Such a government—knowing full well '*where obedience will end and resistance will begin*'—will not be afraid to deploy its constitutional and legal power to '*amend the social and economic code of life which the dictates of justice and expediency so urgently call for*' (Ambedkar 1982: 2, 504; emphasis in original). In this sense, Ambedkar perceived the tasks of the constitutional State and political action and association as amending the established social order; at the same time, he was also apperceptive of constitutions and laws as obstacles as well as opportunities for social action and change.

It is probably true that amongst the Constitution-makers Dr Ambedkar had a lively grasp of contradictions, but it remains doubtful if he had something deep to say about the nature of contradictions or entertained a theory of contradictions. His famous speech on the subject, on the eve of the adoption of the Constitution, is worth reiteration. He said:

> On the 26th January, 1950, we are going to enter into a life of contradictions. In politics, we shall be recognizing the principle of one man one vote one value. In our social and economic life, we shall,

> by reason of economic structure continue to deny [this principle]. How long shall we continue to live this *life of contradiction*? If we continue to deny it for long, we will do so by putting our democracy in peril. (Lok Sabha Secretariat 1949, Volume 19, 979, emphasis added)

Clearly, constitutionalism was transforative in a deep normative sense, but sociologically and existentially it embodied a 'life of contradictions'. The nature of these contradictions, however, remains on the agenda of theoretical debate. Prescinding here logical contradictions, any theory of contradictions will have to take account of broadly six related but distinct types—material, civilizational, cultural, normative, institutional, and juristic/legal contradictions. As already discussed earlier, no biography of Ambedkar may fail to note that he himself lived a life of contradictions. But how did he thematize these in his pedagogic and polemical work?

As a jurist, he stressed the normative contradiction between the constituent power (the power to make and unmake the Constitution) and the constituted power (power within the Constitution). In a way, Ambedkar's articulation comes closest to the notion of constitutional insurgency enunciated by Antonio Negri. Negri carries the understanding of transformative constitutionalism farthest as entailing normative, institutional, and material labours requiring us all actually living an 'ethics of transformation' (Negri 1999). However, Negri more clearly perceived the state of play and war between the two; constituent power thus diminished the range of the political as the 'the origin of the political' and invited continual 'struggles ... in order to emerge as strength' (Negri 1999).[32] Ambedkar, the chief architect of the Constitution, was for non-violent order and change; he was not in favour of judicial review powers that may even invalidate an amendment of the Constitution in the name of the people. In other words, he did not wish the normative to transform itself into an institutional contradiction (between legislative and judicial powers).[33] Presumably, he wished institutional

[32] Ambedkar's thinking on insurgent reason of the constituent power of the demos is certainly not as radical as that of Negri (1999). Yet, we cannot accept that so militant a thinker as Ambedkar would have acquiesced into a version of absolute `constituent' power in the Parliament to amend Articles 17, 23, 24, 25, 30, and 35, or the democratic, secular, and socialist Constitution of India.

[33] Ambedkar made the distinction this way: 'It is the right and privilege of the highest Court of the land to interpret the Constitutional law,

accommodation rather than conflict and to take as self-evident or axiomatic the objectives and the framework of the Constitution as providing interpretation beyond all interpretation.

Ambedkar certainly saw contradictions between political and economic inequality. Were all contradictions material, as entailing the relations of production between the capital and labour, or between the forces of production and relations of production? Did Ambedkar distinguish between antagonistic and non-antagonistic contradictions, as Mao Zedong was to do in his famous August 1937 essay 'On Contradiction'?[34] This question must be left open for future study, especially when considerable theoretical work remains yet to be done on Ambedkar's labour movement participation and socialist philosophy.[35]

---

however, at the same time; it is also the duty of the Parliament to see that objects aimed at in the Constitution are fulfilled or not by the judgement based on such interpretation' (Lok Sabha Secretariat 1951, 9616–17). The 'privilege' of interpretation is contrasted here with the duty of the Parliament to fulfil the objectives. But is it not the judicial duty to further these constitutional objectives through interpretation?

[34] Mao carefully distinguished between contradictions in a semi-colony and the antagonistic/non-antagonistic contradictions. He held that in a 'semi-colonial' country,

> the contradiction between imperialism and the country concerned becomes the principal contradiction, while all the contradictions among various classes within the Country (including what was the principal contradiction, between the feudal system and the great masses of the people) are temporarily relegated to secondary and subordinate position. … [Hence] if in any process there are a number of contradictions, one of them must be the principal contradiction playing the leading and decisive role, while the rest occupy a secondary and subordinate position. Therefore, in studying any complex process … he must devote every effort to funding [*sic*] its principal contradiction.

As to the other category, quoting Lenin, Mao said that 'Antagonism and contradiction are not at all one and the same'. In socialism, 'the first will disappear' but 'the second will remain'. See, www.maoism.org (excerpted by Professor William A. Joseph), last accessed on 8 May 2018; see also Hong (1957: 2, 128–32).

[35] See www.india-seminar.com/2012/633/633_anupama_rao.htm, last accessed on 7 May 2018. See also Rao (2009) and Omvedt (1973).

Ambedkar was most explicit and at his scathing best when he exposed the systematic and endemic exposition of contradiction in Hinduism. It stemmed from the cultural and civilizational traditions of the pious Hindus who justified it, and some still continue to do so. The styles of constitutional secularism contradict the lived religion of the Hindus. The 'lawlessness' of their 'law' is in contradiction with the civic religion of a secular constitution; both its spirit and provisions stand wholly desecrated by the justifications offered for 'radical inequality'.

The greatness of Ambedkar lies in demonstrating that all the three agencies of social control and social change are critical for achieving transformation, and taking these singly is neither good in principle nor as a strategy. However, is their collective use a sword to social, political, and spiritual emancipation and a shield against exploitation? The answer that we must seek through the contradictory unity of the State and the law even as we struggle is also a standing invitation to rethink our constitutional and democratic futures.

References

Agamben, Giorgio. 1998. *Homo Sacer: Sovereign Power and Bare Life*, translated by Daniel Heller-Roazen. Stanford: Stanford University Press.

———. 1999. *Remnants of Auschwitz: The Witness and the Archive*, translated by Daniel Heller-Rosen. New York: Zone Books.

———. 2005. *The State of Exception*, translated by Kevin Attlee. Chicago: Chicago University Press.

Ambedkar, B.R. (1989–2003). *Collected Works*. 17 volumes. Bombay: Education Department, Government of Maharashtra.

———. 2017. *What Congress and Gandhi Have Done to Untouchables*. Delhi: Kalpaz Publishers.

Arendt, Hannah. 2004. *The Origins of Totalitarianism*. New York: Schocken Books.

Austin, Granville. 1967. *The Indian Constitution: Cornerstone of a Nation*. Delhi: Oxford University Press, 1967.

Baxi, Upendra. 1967. 'The Little Done, The Vast Undone: Some Reflections on Reading Granville Austin's *The Indian Constitution*'. *Journal of Indian Law Institute* 9, no. 3: 323–430.

———. 1993. *Marx, Law and Justice*. Bombay: N. M. Tripathi; Delhi: Lexis Nexis.

———. 1994. 'Justice as Emancipation: The Legacy of Babasaheb Ambedkar'. In *Crisis and Change in Contemporary India*, edited by Upendra Baxi and Bhikhu Parekh, 122–49. New Delhi: Sage.

———. 2013. *The Future of Human Rights*. Delhi: Oxford University Press.

Berg, Dag-Eric. 2011. 'Dalits, and the Constitutional State: Untouchability, Dalit Movements and Legal Approaches to Equality and Social Justice for India's Scheduled Castes'. PhD dissertation, University of Bergen, Norway.

———. 2018. 'Foregrounding Contingency in Caste-Based Dominance: Ambedkar, Hegemony, and the Pariah Concept'. *Philosophy and Social Criticism* 44, no. 8: 843–64.

Beteille, Andre. 1971. *Harmonic and Disharmonic Social Systems*. Sydney: Sydney University Press.

Birmingham, Peg. 1996. *Hannah Arendt and Human Rights: The Predicament of Common Responsibility*. Bloomington, Indiana: Indiana University Press.

Brecher, Micheal. 1959. *Nehru: A Political Biography*. Oxford: Oxford University Press.

Cisney, Vernon W., and Morar Nicolae, eds. 2015. *Biopower: Foucault and Beyond*. Chicago: Chicago University Press.

Deleuze, Gilles. 1988. *Foucault*, translated by Seán Hand. London: Athlone.

Derrida, Jacques. 1978. *Writing and Difference*, translated by A. Bass. Chicago: University of Chicago Press.

———. 2006. *Specters of Marx: The State of the Debt, the Work of Mourning and the New International*. London: Routledge.

Fairtlough, Gerard H. 1991. 'Habermas' Concept of "Lifeworld"'. *Systems Practice* 4: 547–63.

Foucault, Michel. 2003. *Society Must Be Defended*. New York: Picador.

———. 2009. *Security, Territory, Population*. New York: Picador.

———. 2010. *The Birth of Biopolitics*. New York: Picador.

Fuller, Lon. 1969. *The Morality of Law*. Connecticut, NH: Yale University Press.

Guru, Gopal. 1970. *Dalit Cultural Movement and Dialectics of Dalit Politics in Maharashtra*. Mumbai: VAK Publication.

———. 1998. 'Understanding Ambedkar's Construction of National Movement.' *Economic and Political Weekly* 4, no. 33 (24 January): 156–7.

Heidegger, Martin. 1991. *Nietzsche*, translated by David Farrell Krell. San Francisco: Harper Collins.

Hong, Shan. 1957. 'An Attempt to Discuss "Antagonism" and "Antagonistic Contradictions"'. *Philosophical Research* [哲学研究]: 128–32.

Humphreys, Stephen. 2006. 'Legalizing Lawlessness: On Giorgio Agamben's State of Exception', *The European Journal of International Law* 17, no. 3: 677–87.

Keer, Dhananjay. 1990. *Dr. Ambedkar: Life and Mission*. Bombay: Popular Prakashan.

Kesby, Allison. 2012. *The Right to Have Rights: Citizenship, Humanity, and International Law*. Oxford: Oxford University Press.

Kumar, Aishwary. 2015. *Radical Equality: Ambedkar, Gandhi, and the Risk of Democracy*. Stanford: Stanford University Press.

Landau, Iddo. 2010. 'Violence and Postmodernism: A Conceptual Analysis.' *Reason Papers* 32–67: 73.

Lok Sabha Secretariat. 1949. *Constituent Assembly Debates: Official Reports*, vols 11 and 19.

———. 1951. *Parliamentary Debates*, vols 12–13, part 2.

Lovett, Frank. 2015. 'Lon Fuller, The Morality of Law'. *The Oxford Handbook of Classics in Contemporary Political Theory*, edited by Jacob T. Levy. Oxford: Oxford University Press.

Negri, Antonio. 1999. *Insurgencies: Constituent Power and the Modern State*, translated by Maurizia Boscagli. Minnesota: Minnesota University Press.

Norris, Andrew. 2005. 'Introduction' to 'Giorgio Agamben and the Politics of the Living Dead'. In *Politics, Metaphysics, Death: Essays on Giorgio Agamben's Homo Sacer*, 1–30. Durham: Duke University Press.

Omvedt, Gail. 1973. 'Non-Brahmans and Communists in Bombay'. *Economic and Political Weekly* 8, no. 16 (21 April): 749–59.

Rao, Anupama. 2009. *The Caste Question: Dalits and the Politics of Modern India*. Berkeley, CA: University of California Press.

Rathore, Aakash Singh. 2017. *Indian Political Theory: Laying the Groundwork for Svaraj*. London: Routledge.

Rathore, Aakash Singh, and Ajay Verma 2011. *The Buddha and His Dhamma*. New York: Oxford University Press.

Rege, Sharmilla. 2006. *Writing Caste/Writing Gender: Reading Dalit Women's Testimonies*. Delhi: Zubaan Publications.

———. 2008. 'Interrogating the Thesis of "Irrational Deification"'. *Economic and Political Weekly* 43, no. 7 (16–22 February): 17–20.

———. 2013. *Against the Madness of Manu: B.R. Ambedkar's Writings on Brahmanical Patriarchy*. Delhi: Navyana publications.

Rodrigues, Valerian. 2002. *The Essential Writings of B. R. Ambedkar*. New Delhi: Oxford University Press.

Rundle, Kristen. 2012. *Forms Liberate: Reclaiming the Jurisprudence of Lon L Fuller*. Oxford: Hart.

Sharma, Mukul. 2017. *Caste and Nature: Dalit and Environmental Politics*. Delhi: Oxford university Press.

Shourie, Arun. 2008. 'The Manu of Our Times?' Available at https://arunshouri.blogspot.com>2008>05>manu-of-our-times.html. Last accessed on 2 July 2020.

Skaria, Ajay. 2015. 'Ambedkar, Marx, and the Buddhist Question'. *South Asia: Journal of South Asian Studies* 38, no. 3: 450–65.

Stroud, R. Scott. 2016. 'Pragmatism and the Pursuit of Social Justice in India: Ambedkar and the Rhetoric of Religious Reorientation'. *Rhetoric Society Quarterly* 46, no. 1: 5–27.

Teltumbde, Anand. 2013. 'Ambedkerite against Ambedkar.' *Economic & Political Weekly* 48, no. 19 (11 May): 10–11.

Vajpeyi, Ananya. 2012. *The Righteous Republic: The Political Foundations of Modern India*. Massachusetts: Harvard University Press.

White, Stephen K. 1988. *The Recent Work of Jurgen Habermas: Reason, Justice, Modernity*. Cambridge: Cambridge University Press.

Zelliot, Eleanor. 1996. 'Gandhi and Ambedkar: A Study in Leadership'. In *From Untouchable to Dalit: Essays on Ambedkar Movement*. New Delhi: Manohar.

2

B.R. Ambedkar's Exemplary Adherence to Constitutional Morality

R. SUDARSHAN

This essay explores the significance which Dr Ambedkar attached to 'constitutional morality' and his own conduct demonstrating his adherence to it. This exploration was prompted for me by the surprising discovery that Dr Ambedkar appeared as an advocate for a zamindar of Uttar Pradesh and the Maharaja of Kapurthala, who owned estates in the erstwhile province of Oudh.

Why would one of the main architects of India's Constitution—which anticipated the abolition of zamindari and distribution of land to hitherto exploited tenants—and also the first law minister of independent India, who crafted the first amendment to that Constitution in order to protect land reform laws from being struck down by courts for violating the right to property, resign from his office and argue cases on behalf of zamindars? Was this a principled stand or was it motivated by mere expediency? Answers to these questions demand a careful scrutiny of Dr Ambedkar's actions after he had brilliantly emphasized the importance of constitutional morality in the Constituent Assembly.

Constitutional Morality

On 4 November 1948, Dr Ambedkar, as chairman of the Drafting Committee in the Constituent Assembly, provided a lengthy justification for the draft proposed for adoption by the Assembly (Lok Sabha Secretariat 1948, 38). He noted the criticism that the draft Constitution contained a good deal of the provisions of the Government of India Act, 1935. He said that it was not plagiarism because no one had any patent rights over the fundamental ideas of a Constitution; however, he regretted that many of the borrowed provisions related to administrative details.

However, he went on to justify why the Drafting Committee had borrowed these provisions. He invoked the idea of 'constitutional morality', and quoted George Grote, a historian of democracy who wrote on the city state of Athens (1888, 1846–56):

> The diffusion of constitutional morality, not merely among the majority of any community but throughout the whole, is the indispensable condition of government at once free and peaceable; since even any powerful and obstinate minority may render the working of a free institution impracticable, without being strong enough to conquer ascendency for themselves.

Elucidating, Ambedkar said:

> By constitutional morality Grote meant 'a paramount reverence for the forms of the Constitution, enforcing obedience to authority acting under and within these forms yet combined with the habit of open speech, of action subject only to definite legal control, and unrestrained censure of those very authorities as to all their public acts combined too with a perfect confidence in the bosom of every citizen amidst the bitterness of party contest that the forms of the Constitution will not be less sacred in the eyes of his opponents than in his own.' (Lok Sabha Secretariat 1948, 38)

This observation was greeted with applause.

Grote, it must be noted, has the distinction of rehabilitating Athenian democracy which had to bear the guilt of prosecuting and executing Socrates. Before Grote rewrote Greek history, Athenians had a bad name. Aristophanes ridiculed their dishonesty and selfishness. Plato denounced their incompetence and perversions of justice. Thucydides and Xenophon emphasized their capriciousness.

The extent of people's participation (estimated to be about 30,000 adult males) in Athens's governance was amazing. Athenians convened 40 *ekklesiai* (a regularly convoked assembly; Athenians' general assembly) which were attended by about 6,000 citizens. Most Athenians served at least one year in the council of 500, and every year at least 700 other magistrates were elected or selected by the drawing of lots. It is rare in the history of democracies to find such strong commitment to participation in public affairs. Athenian democracy's first principle is *isonomia*—the equal right of all citizens to exercise their political rights. Through *sortition*, all citizens who wished to serve in public office had an equal chance and high likelihood of doing so. This is very different from the extremely unequal chance that poor people have of being elected to political office through election. The second principle is *isegoria*—the right of every citizen to speak in the people's assembly and make proposals. This right remained even if only a few wished to exercise it or make the most of it, as did Cleon—the demagogue master of rhetoric of persuasion, and a hero for Grote.

As a radical member of the Westminster Parliament in the UK, Grote played an important part in the 1832 Parliamentary Reform Act. This brought the vote to many ordinary men in the country. Dispelling the notion that Athens stood for the dangers of mob rule, Grote saw Athenian democracy as an inspiration for the extension of franchise and electoral change.

Constitutional morality is the safeguard against authoritative claims to popular sovereignty. It entails self-restraint, respect for plurality, and deference to processes. It emphasizes that there is a proper way of doing things; no ends can justify forsaking constitutional means that have been stipulated to achieve them. Ambedkar's reference to Grote underlines his concern about the rarity of genuinely democratic decision-making in world history.

Ambedkar's comments on the importance and rarity of constitutional morality and his reference to the *spirit of the Constitution* deserve repeated emphasis. He said:

> While everybody recognizes the necessity of the diffusion of the Constitutional morality for the peaceful working of a democratic Constitution, there are two things interconnected with it which are not, unfortunately, generally recognized. One is that the form of administration has a close connection with the form of the Constitution. The form of the administration must be appropriate to and in the same sense as the form of the Constitution. The other is that it is perfectly possible to prevent the Constitution, without changing its form by merely changing the form of the administration and to make it inconsistent and opposed to the spirit of the Constitution.

> It follows that it is only where people are saturated with Constitutional morality such as the one described by Grote, the historian, that one can take the risk of omitting from the Constitution details of administration and leaving it for the Legislature to prescribe them. The question is, can we presume such a diffusion of Constitutional morality? Constitutional morality is not a natural sentiment. It has to be cultivated. We must realize that our people have yet to learn it. Democracy in India is only a top-dressing on an Indian soil, which is essentially undemocratic. In these circumstances it is wiser not to trust the Legislature to prescribe forms of administration. This is the justification for incorporating them in the Constitution. (Lok Sabha Secretariat 1948, 38)

Dr Ambedkar did not profess great faith that democratic politics in India would produce rational outcomes. In the chapter on fundamental rights he wanted to introduce principles of 'state socialism' and 'economic democracy'. He did not wish to 'leave the fulfillment of so fundamental a purpose to the exigencies of ordinary law which simple majorities (whose political fortunes are never determined by rational causes) have a right to make and unmake'.[1] In his 1947 proposals on safeguards for the Scheduled Castes, submitted to the Constituent Assembly on behalf of the All India Scheduled Castes Federation, Ambedkar included a section on remedies against 'economic exploitation'. The remedies included nationalization of key industries and State ownership of agricultural land. Ambedkar believed that a modified form of state socialism in industry was required for rapid industrialization. He believed that for landless labourers, especially those belonging to the 'Untouchable' castes, collective farming was the only means of salvation.

The Constituent Assembly regarded his proposals as too radical to insert in the chapter on fundamental rights, as they would then become justiciable in courts. Instead, social, economic, and cultural rights were moved to Part IV of the Constitution, the non-justiciable 'Directive Principles of State Policy'. Mahboob Ali Baig, a Muslim League member from Madras, pointed out the depoliticizing implications of granting constitutional status to a particular set of ideological norms that the Congress party

[1] Note to the Fundamental Rights Sub-committee (Rao 1965–71, 101–2). See also Ambedkar (1947).

favoured. He argued that a set of principles 'to bind and tie down political parties was contrary to the principles of parliamentary democracy' (Lok Sabha Secretariat 1948, 488–9). B.N. Rau, advisor to the Constituent Assembly (described as one of the more 'Europeanized intellectuals' by Granville Austin, who chronicled the framing of the Constitution [Austin 1966, 20]), overruled his objections.

The reference to Grote and constitutional morality by Ambedkar was meant to underline that he was painfully aware of how incorrigibly segmented Indian society remained and how his kinsfolk, the untouchable Dalit, were cast out beyond the pale. Ambedkar realized that when people in India cast their votes, they are most likely to vote in their respective castes. Communal majority undermines *isonomia* and *isegoria*. He made a crucial distinction between communal majority and political majority:

> A political majority is changeable in its class composition. A political majority grows. A communal majority is born. The admission to a political majority is open. The door to a communal majority is closed. The politics of a political majority are free to all to make and unmake. The politics of a communal majority are made by its own members born in it. (Ambedkar 1979, 169)

Ambedkar clearly set out the effects of India's segmented society on its voting behaviour in elections:

> (1) Voting is always communal. The voter votes for the candidate of his community and not for the best candidate.
> (2) The majority community carries the seat by sheer communal majority.
> (3) The minority community is forced to vote for the candidate of the majority community.
> (4) The votes of the minority community are not enough to enable the candidate to win the seat against the candidate put up by the majority community.
> (5) As consequence of social system of graded inequality the voter of the higher (major) communities can never condescend to give his vote to a candidate of a minority community. On the other hand, the voter of the minority community who is socially on a lower level takes pride in giving his vote to the candidate of the majority community. That is another reason why a candidate of a minority community loses in election. (Ambedkar 1979, 168)

In his last major speech in the Constituent Assembly on 25 November 1949, Ambedkar again elaborated on what adherence to constitutional morality entails:

> If we wish to maintain democracy not merely in form, but also in fact, what must we do? The first thing in my judgment we must do is to hold fast to constitutional methods of achieving our social and economic objectives. It means we must abandon the bloody methods of revolution. It means that we must abandon the method of civil disobedience, non-cooperation and satyagraha. When there was no way left for constitutional methods for achieving economic and social objectives, there was a great deal of justification for unconstitutional methods. But where constitutional methods are open, there can be no justification for these unconstitutional methods. These methods are nothing but the Grammar of Anarchy and the sooner they are abandoned, the better for us. (Ambedkar 1994, 1295)

The way in which Ambedkar functioned as the chair of the Drafting Committee in the Constituent Assembly is an object lesson in adherence to proper form and respect for the opinion of others. Even though he had very strong views on what provisions should be included and not included in the Constitution, Ambedkar never misused his office or attempted to browbeat others in the process of drafting the Constitution. He did not press for his impassioned belief in separate electorates for Dalits; he had proposals, other than the first-past-the-post electoral system in single-member constituencies, to solve the communal deadlock through multi-member constituencies and cumulative voting within the framework of parliamentary democracy; he restrained his zeal for a uniform civil code among Hindus; he gracefully accepted the defeat of his programme for social and economic equality, besides the one for political equality in terms of universal adult franchise that got accepted; and he went along with the Congress Party's preference for the abolition of zamindari, instead of pushing harder for the nationalization of land and its redistribution as cooperative, collective farms.

Ambedkar, as an outstanding professional learned in the law, took great pains to give reasons for accepting or rejecting amendments proposed to the draft Constitution. The final Constitution that was adopted was not the one that he wanted, but that did not stop him from discharging his responsibilities and deferring with grace to the collective will of the members of the assembly.

Land in the Constituent Assembly

Ambedkar was particularly knowledgeable about inequities in the ownership of land in India, which were part and parcel of the inequities in a society segmented by caste. In 1918, he published a paper entitled 'Small Holdings in India and Their Remedies' (Ambedkar 1918), where he argued that land consolidation and increasing the size of land holdings would not result in optimal productivity unless there was a commensurate increase in other factors of production, especially capital. As the people who depended on land had low savings, their capacity for investing in agriculture would be seriously limited. The remedy for this state of affairs, according to Ambedkar, did not lie in ill-conceived programmes of land consolidation. He pointed out:

> In short, strange though it may seem, industrialization of India is the soundest remedy for the agricultural problems of India. The cumulative effects of industrialization, namely, a lessening pressure and an increasing amount of capital and capital goods will forcibly create the economic necessity of enlarging the holding. Not only this, but industrialization by destroying the premium on land will give rise to few occasions for its sub-division and fragmentation. (Ambedkar 1918, 492; 1979: 1, 470–96)

Ambedkar regarded the programme to take over the estates of zamindars and to distribute the land among the tenants who cultivated it and paid rents to zamindars as unimportant, particularly from the point of view of the Scheduled Castes who were landless and would not get any land. He acquiesced with Prime Minister Nehru and other leaders of the Congress Party in their extraordinary efforts in the Constituent Assembly to ensure that state legislation abolishing zamindari did not fall foul of the judiciary.

The draft article on the right to property (Article 31) was introduced by Nehru himself and it was the only one among the provisions of the fundamental rights that he introduced in the assembly.

By that time, in late 1949, the legislation of Bihar and the United Provinces did not provide for full compensation at market value for taking over the estates of zamindars. Nehru, after noting that the State should normally pay a compensation if it acquired any property, made an exception to the rule in the case of zamindars. He said:

> The law should provide for the compensation for the property and should either fix the amount or specify the principles under which or

the manner in which the compensation is to be determined. The law should do it. Parliament should do it. There is no reference to any judiciary coming into the picture. ... Naturally the judiciary comes in to see if there has been a fraud on the Constitution or not. But normally speaking one presumes that any Parliament representing the entire community of the nation will certainly not commit a fraud on its own Constitution and will be very much concerned with doing justice to the individual as well as the community. (Lok Sabha Secretariat 1949, 1193)

Land in the Courts and the First Amendment to the Right to Property

As passed by the Constituent Assembly, Article 31 excluded judicial review *only for* zamindari and similar large holdings, described as 'estates'. Soon after the Constitution of India came into force on 26 January 1950, the Patna High Court delivered its judgement in a case brought against the Bihar Land Reforms Act by the Maharaja of Darbhanga, Kameshwar Singh. The court held that Article 31(4), as it was then in the Constitution, merely saved the law from judicial challenge on the ground of the right to property but not on the ground of contravening any of the other fundamental rights.

The Patna High Court struck down the law for violating the right to equality in Article 14 because it discriminated between rich and poor zamindars by providing different rates of compensation for estates of different sizes.[2] Meanwhile though, the high courts at Allahabad and Nagpur upheld the validity of similar zamindari abolition laws passed by the Uttar Pradesh and Madhya Pradesh legislatures. Without waiting for the Supreme Court to hear the appeal of the state of Bihar against the ruling of the Patna High Court, the government of India introduced in the Parliament a bill to amend the Constitution.

Even though Ambedkar was then the law minister, and had proposed provisions that could protect the takeover of zamindari estates from possible judicial obstruction, it was Prime Minister Nehru who introduced in the Parliament the Constitution (First Amendment) Bill.

[2] *Kameshwar Singh* v *State of Bihar* [1951], All India Reporter (AIR) Patna, 91.

The First Amendment, with respect to the right to property, inserted the new Article 31 (A) with the provision that

> notwithstanding anything in the foregoing provisions of this Part, no law providing for the acquisition by the State of any estate or of any of the rights therein or for the extinguishment or modification of any of such rights shall be deemed to be void on the ground that it is inconsistent with, or take away or abridges any of the rights conferred by, any provisions of that Part.

This protection against judicial review for violation of any of the fundamental rights was accorded retrospective effect by providing that this Article 'shall be deemed always to have been inserted'.

Going beyond this, the First Amendment inserted another new article—31 (B). Thirteen state land-reform laws were listed in the Ninth Schedule of the Constitution. This article provided that none of them 'shall be deemed to be void, or ever to have become void ... notwithstanding any judgement, decree or order of any court or tribunal to the contrary'.

The idea of creating a Schedule in the Constitution, which will list laws that are deemed to be valid even if they violated any of the fundamental rights, was proposed to the then law secretary, K.V.K. Sundaram, by the then advocate general of Madras, V.K.T. Chari (Austin 1999, 85).

He suggested this to then law secretary, K.V.K. Sundaram. The precedent for inserting into the Constitution itself laws inconsistent with other provisions comes from Ireland. In that country, the law providing for preventive detention was not consistent with its Constitution and could have been struck down by the judiciary. To prevent that possibility, the entire text of the preventive detention law was inserted by a constitutional amendment into Ireland's Constitution. As there were multiple land reform laws that Parliament in India wanted to protect from judicial review, the more elegant option of listing those laws in the Ninth Schedule was adopted.[3]

In the time to come, the 39th Amendment to the Constitution of India—passed when a state of internal emergency was in force—placed the Maintenance of Internal Security Act, 1971, in the Ninth

[3] Letter from V.K.T. Chari to K.V.K. Sundaram, 14 March 1951, Law Ministry File F34/51-C. Cited also in Austin (1999, 85n45).

Schedule to the Constitution, thereby making it totally immune from any judicial review; even on the grounds that it contravened the fundamental rights guaranteed by the Constitution or violated its basic structure.[4]

Issues of constitutional morality loomed large in the context of what seemed to many members of the Provisional Parliament an 'indecent haste' to amend the Constitution's provisions on property rights even before the Supreme Court could dispose Bihar's appeal against the judgement of the Patna High Court. Shyama Prasad Mookerjee of the Hindu Mahasabha said that the Constitution was being treated as a 'scrap of paper' (Lok Sabha Secretariat 1951, col. 9626).

In the Select Committee which considered the First Amendment Bill, S.P. Mookerjee reiterated his arguments against the bill, adding that the president should scrutinize the state laws before placing them in the Ninth Schedule.[5] K.T. Shah objected to the Ninth Schedule as 'a dangerous precedent which should not be allowed'. The bill was passed on 2 June 1951 and a reluctant President Rajendra Prasad assented to the bill on 18 June 1951.

The charges brought against its validity included the fact that as there was only one house of Parliament and no Rajya Sabha, the procedure for amending the Constitution had not been followed, and that Article 13 prohibited its enactment because it prohibited any law that curtailed the fundamental rights in Part III (this was the argument that was accepted by the majority led by Justice K. Subba Rao in *Golak Nath* v *Union of India* in 1967). On 5 October 1951, in *Shankari Prasad Singh Deo* v *The Union of India and the State of Bihar*,[6] Chief Justice Patanjali Shastri, for the majority, held that the amendment had been enacted validly and that the Parliament had unlimited power to amend the Constitution.

Ambedkar, while serving as law minister till he demitted office at the end of the life of the Provisional Parliament, did not make any pronouncements that could have embarrassed the government.

[4] As laid down by *Kesavananda Bharati* v *State of Kerala* [1973] (4) Supreme Court Cases (SCC) 225ff.

[5] *The Constitution (First Amendment) Bill, 1951: Report of the Select Committee*, p. 8.

[6] 1952 (3) Supreme Court Reports (SCR) 89ff.

The question that troubled him was how could the Provisional Parliament take liberties with the Constitution that had been adopted by the Constituent Assembly without having to seek a mandate from the electorate for amending the Constitution. He held his peace till after he resigned from the council of ministers. What must have rankled him all the more was the fact that Prime Minister Nehru did not heed the objections of the president of India to the enactment of the First Amendment Bill, because zamindari abolition was a personal crusade for him.

However, the prime minister decided not to proceed with the enactment of the Hindu Code Bill, an ordinary statute and not an amendment to the Constitution, because President Prasad objected on 15 September 1951 to that legislation, maintaining that the Parliament should seek a mandate from the electorate before changing the personal law of Hindus. The president believed that the Hindu Code Bill was discriminatory in that it altered only Hindu law and not Muslim law. The president warned that when it came to him for his assent he could act consistently with the dictates of his own conscience. Prime Minister Nehru capitulated to the president's threats on the Hindu Code Bill, while maintaining that if the president acted against the advice of his council of ministers, the council, having the confidence of the Parliament, must resign.

The prime minister's abandonment of the Hindu Code Bill, on which Ambedkar and the Ministry of Law and Justice had worked very hard, was the last straw heaped upon many other previous humiliations that Ambedkar had borne with equanimity in the interest of discharging his constitutional obligations, adhering to his conception of constitutional morality.

After resigning from the cabinet on 27 September 1951, Ambedkar published as a press note a statement on 15 October 1951 on the reasons for his resignation. He was not permitted to make a statement in the House by the deputy speaker who insisted upon an advance copy, and was given a later time. Ambedkar left the House and did not return at the appointed time. It was left to Prime Minister Nehru to read out to the House, on 11 October 1951, extracts from Ambedkar's resignation statement. In that statement Ambedkar said that he had acceded to the Prime Minister's request to discharge the duties of law minister ('a request to which I was, in obedience to constitutional convention, bound to assent') till the session of the Parliament ended and the first general elections began from 25 October 1951 till 21 February 1952.

Ambedkar said:

> I have never been a party to the game of power politics inside the cabinet or the game of snatching portfolios which goes on when there is a vacancy. I believe in service, service in the post which the Prime Minister, who as the head of the Cabinet, thought fit to assign to me. It would have, however, been quite unhuman for me not to have felt that a wrong was being done to me. (Ambedkar 1995, 1317–27)

Ambedkar stoically bore the prime minister's neglect of his competence and capacity to contribute to policymaking in the Cabinet. He pointed out that he was not included in any of the main committees of the Cabinet, such as the Foreign Affairs Committee or the Defence Committee. He said, 'When the Economics Affairs Committee was formed, I expected, in view of the fact that I was primarily a student of Economics and Finance, to be appointed to this Committee. But I was left out' (Ambedkar 1995, 1319).

Another reason for being dissatisfied with the government that he served so diligently was its neglect of the cause that was dearest to him: justice for backward classes and the Scheduled Castes. He explained that he was

> very sorry that the Constitution did not embody any safeguards for the Backward Classes. It was left to be done by the Executive Government on the basis of the recommendations of a Commission to be appointed by the President. More than a year has elapsed since we passed the Constitution. But the Government has not even thought of appointing the Commission. (Ambedkar 1995, 1320)

Ambedkar also recorded his dissatisfaction with the government over its conduct of foreign policy and its failure to resolve the dispute with Pakistan over Kashmir by partitioning the province: 'The real issue to my mind is not who is in the right but what is right. Taking that to be the main question, my view has always been that the right solution is to partition Kashmir. Give the Hindu and Buddhist part to India and the Muslim part to Pakistan as we did in the case of India' (Ambedkar 1995, 1322).

Ambedkar's main reason to resign at the time he did must be cited in full:

> It may be said that my resignation is out of time and that if I was dissatisfied with the Foreign Policy of the Government and the treatment accorded to Backward Classes and the Scheduled Castes I should have gone earlier. The charge may sound as true. But I had reasons which held me back. In the first place, most of the time I have been a member of the Cabinet, I have been busy with the framing of the Constitution. It absorbed all my attention till 26th January 1950 and thereafter I was concerned with the Peoples' Representation Bill and the Delimitation Orders. I had hardly any time to attend to our Foreign Affairs. I did not think it right to go away leaving this work unfinished. In the second place, I thought it necessary to stay on, for the sake of the Hindu Code. In the opinion of some it may be wrong for me to have held on for the sake of the Hindu Code. I took a different view. The Hindu Code was the greatest social reform measure ever undertaken by the Legislature in this country. No law passed by the Indian Legislature in the past or likely to be passed in the future can be compared to it in point of its significance. To leave inequality between class and class, between sex and sex which is the soul of Hindu Society untouched and to go on passing legislation relating to economic problems is to make a farce of our Constitution and to build a palace on a dung heap. This is the significance I attached to the Hindu Code. It is for its sake that I stayed on notwithstanding my differences. (Ambedkar 1995, 1325–6)

Ambedkar in the Supreme Court

Ambedkar qualified for law practice on 28 June 1922 when he got his barrister-at-law degree from Gray's Inn. He was admitted to the Bombay Bar Council in 1923 and began his practice. He worked in the Bombay High Court and in the district courts of Thane, Nagpur, and Aurangabad. He had some notable successes in his early days as a lawyer but could not devote time to practice as he became increasingly involved in the pursuit of justice for the Scheduled and backward Castes (Sumit 2017).

Ambedkar did not think that the abolition of zamindari would bring about any improvement in the lot of the population groups that he cared about the most. But Ambedkar was also committed to socio-economic equality and opposed to exploitation. He could not be expected to hold any brief for zamindars who had exploited their tenants for decades since the introduction of the Permanent Settlement Act in 1783 and the Mahalwari system for the collection of land revenue in 1833. The government decided to amend the Constitution, barely months after it had been brought into force, to safeguard its policy over zamindari estates and distribute that land to their tenants. Ambedkar, as a member of the Cabinet and committed to the principle of collective responsibility, worked hard on the draft of the First Amendment (which modified the right to property in Article 31 and enabled restrictions to be placed on the right to free speech in Article 19).

It is undoubtedly surprising that soon after he resigned from the council of ministers he opted to appear as an advocate for some of the zamindars opposing the land reform law of Uttar Pradesh, in appeals to the Supreme Court of India against judgements delivered by the high courts in Patna and Allahabad. Ambedkar appeared as the advocate for some of the zamindars from Uttar Pradesh and also for the Maharaja of Kapurthala who owned some property in Oudh and was aggrieved by the Uttar Pradesh land reform law.

On 12 March 1951 the Supreme Court began hearing these appeals. On 2 May 1951 the verdicts were delivered.[7] Three judges of the five-judge bench (Justices M.C. Mahajan, B.K. Mukherjea, and N. Chandrasekhara Aiyar) declared the Bihar land reform law to be invalid, even though the First Amendment had placed this law in the Ninth Schedule to give it immunity from judicial review. The three-judge majority reached beyond the right to property, as amended by the First Amendment, and based their ruling on an entry in the Concurrent List which provided that real principles of compensation had to be fixed and this had not been done properly. The majority ruled that some provisions of the Bihar law amounted to a 'colourable exercise [of] legislative power' and a 'fraud on the Constitution'.[8] These phrases echoed Prime Minister Nehru's remarks in the Constituent Assembly when he said that these factors were the only grounds on which a court might strike down land reform laws, which it could not on the ground of inadequate compensation. However, Chief Justice Patanjali Sastri and S.R. Das

[7] *State of Bihar* v *Maharajadhiraja Sir Kameshwar Singh of Darbhanga and Others* [1952] (3) SCR 889ff.

[8] *State of Bihar* v *Maharajadhiraja Sir Kameshwar Singh of Darbhanga and Others* [1952] (3) SCR 889ff.

dissented and held that the First Amendment fully protected the Act from judicial scrutiny.

On the same day, however, the same bench was unanimous in upholding the Uttar Pradesh and Madhya Pradesh zamindari abolition acts.[9] The arguments advanced in the Supreme Court by former Law Minister Ambedkar against the validity of the legislation that the government had gone to extraordinary lengths to safeguard are interesting.

According to Chief Justice Patanjali Shastri, Ambedkar argued for:

> a constitutional prohibition against compulsory acquisition of property without public necessity and payment of compensation was deducible from what he called the 'spirit of the Constitution', which, according to him, was a valid test for judging the constitutionality of a statute. The Constitution, being avowedly one for establishing liberty, justice and equality and a government of a free people with only limited powers, must be held to contain an implied prohibition against taking private property without just compensation and in the absence of a public purpose. He relied on certain American decisions and text books as supporting the view that a constitutional prohibition can be derived by implication from the spirit of the Constitution where no express prohibition has been enacted in that behalf. Article 31-A and 31-B barred only objections based on alleged infringements of the fundamental rights conferred by Part III, but if, from the other provisions thereof, it could be inferred that there must be a public purpose and payment of compensation before private property could be compulsorily acquired by the State, there was nothing in the two articles aforesaid to preclude objection on the ground that the impugned Acts do not satisfy these requirements and are, therefore, unconstitutional.[10]

According to Justice Mahajan, Ambedkar told the court that he

> would have been content had the State nationalised the zamindaries because then the acquisition would be for a public purpose, but as under the impugned Act the State had merely constituted itself a trustee for distribution of the intermediaries' interests

[9] *Raja Suryapal Singh* v *State of Uttar Pradesh* [1952] SCR 1056; *Viseshwar Rao* v *State of Madhya Pradesh* [1952] SCR 1020ff.

[10] *State of Bihar* v *Maharajadhiraja Sir Kameshwar Singh of Darbhanga and Others* [1952] SCR 252.

amongst the 'haves' and not amongst the 'have nots': i.e., amongst the bhumidars, sirdars, asamis and adhivasis and not amongst the landless, the Act was not for a public purpose at all but was an unfortunate piece of legislation as property was being acquired for the private benefit of persons and not for public use and that giving of property to gaonsamaj also could not be held to be for public benefit or public use.[11]

Pressing his point about the lack of public purpose in the zamindari abolition laws, Ambedkar argued:

> 'public purpose' was not a new concept when the Constitution of India was framed; on the other hand, it had a settled meaning in the past legislative history of this country and it must be presumed that the Constitution used the expression in the same sense in which it had been used in the earlier Acts and in the Government of India Act, 1935, and that it should not be construed in the light of the Directive Principles laid down in Part IV of the Constitution. He contended that had the constitution makers intended to give this concept a different meaning than it had acquired in the past, they would have clearly given expression to that intention by saying that the expression 'public purpose' includes purposes which aim at implementing the Directive Principles of State Policy and that Part IV of the Constitution merely contained glittering generalities which had no justification behind them and should not be taken into consideration in construing the phrase 'public purpose'.[12]

Ambedkar's arguments did not persuade the court. With respect to the Uttar Pradesh law, the unanimous verdict was that the jurisdiction of the court to question its validity on the ground that it did not provide for payment of compensation was barred by Articles 31(4), 31-A, and 31-B of the Constitution. The court also declared that the Act was not a fraud on the Constitution; it did not delegate essential legislative power to the executive and was not liable to be impugned on the ground of absence of a public purpose. Justice Mahajan said that recourse could not be had to the spirit of the Constitution when its provisions were explicit; and when the fundamental law had not limited either in terms or by necessary implication the general powers conferred on the legislature, it was

[11] *Raja Suryapal Singh* v *State of Uttar Pradesh* [1952] SCR 1056.
[12] *Raja Suryapal Singh* v *State of Uttar Pradesh* [1952] SCR 1056.

not proper to deduce a limitation from something supposed to be inherent in the spirit of the Constitution.

Ambedkar held strong views on the irrelevance of the State takeover of zamindari estates for the plight of marginalized and landless people, and his anger at the fact that the government had ignored 'constitutional morality' in its attempt to circumvent judicial decisions must have motivated his opposition to what was a matter of the highest priority for the government of Prime Minister Nehru.

Ambedkar voiced his objections to the amendments designed to overrule judicial decisions in his statement on the Constitution's Fourth Amendment Bill. On 11 December 1953, the Supreme Court held that taking of land for the rehabilitation of refugees required payment of 'compensation', which meant 'a just equivalent of what the owner has been deprived of'.[13] The Supreme Court's decisions in some other cases involving takeover by the government of a bus transport company and a textile mill affirmed the judiciary's authority to examine the adequacy of compensation. The Fourth Amendment was crafted to overcome judicial decisions on the right to property other than those regarding the land reform cases which concerned the takeover of zamindari estates. It received the president's assent in April 1955.

It should be noted that Ambedkar lost the election to the Lok Sabha in 1952 to the Congress Party nominee. He was subsequently elected to the Rajya Sabha where he remained in opposition to Prime Minister Nehru's government, which had an overwhelming majority in the Parliament. In an exemplary exposition of what he had described in the Constituent Assembly as 'constitutional morality', Ambedkar, objecting to the Fourth Amendment Bill in 1955, said in the Rajya Sabha:

> In our country the dogma on which we proceed is that the Prime Minister can do no wrong and that he will do no wrong. Therefore, anything that the Prime Minister proposes to do must be accepted as correct and without question. This devotion in politics to a personality may be excusable in some cases, but it does not seem to me excusable where the fundamental rights are being invaded. The fundamental rights are the very basis of the preamble to the

[13] *State of West Bengal* v *Mrs. Bela Banerjee and Others* [1954] AIR SC 170.

> Constitution. The Preamble says that this Constitution will have as its basis liberty, equality and fraternity. These objectives of the Constitution are carried out by the fundamental rights. And it is, therefore, the duty, I should have thought, of every Member of Parliament, apart from personal loyalty, to be critical when any invasion is made of the fundamental rights. Unfortunately, one does not find this kind of critical attitude. (Ambedkar 1997: 15, 944)

Ambedkar advised the government not to tamper with the Constitution and said:

> In other countries wherever a clause of the Constitution has been interpreted by the judiciary in a way which the Government does not like, Government concurs, it does not like to upset the decision of the court. Here, in our country, we have cultivated a different mentality. Our mentality is that if the judges of the Supreme Court do not give a judgement which is to our liking, then we can throw it out. That is what it is. I am rather glad with regard to the behaviour of our Supreme Court. ... I do not find that the Supreme Court has given any judgement which, any independent man can say, is not in consonance with the terms of the Constitution. (Ambedkar 1997: 15, 955)

He criticized the Fourth Amendment Bill for adding seven laws in the Ninth Schedule, which had been declared void either because the compensation was judged to be inadequate or because they provided for taking over the management of private property without making provisions for the payment of compensation. Ambedkar said:

> We are asked to give constitutional validity to laws passed by State Legislatures. We have not seen those laws; they have not been circulated; they have not been debated here. And yet we are asked here to exercise the constituent powers of Parliament not only to validate them but to give them constitutional immunity from the other clauses of the Act. Sir, I think it is very derogatory to the dignity of the House that it should be called upon to validate laws passed by some other State which laws it has not seen, it has not considered. The proper thing for the Government to do is to put these subjects in the concurrent field so that Parliament may at least give them validity by the powers vested in it. But it is a very wrong thing. Because we did it in the case of the first amendment where we added the Ninth Schedule to the Constitution, that is no reason why we should widen this anomaly and this ugliness in the Constitution. (Ambedkar 1997: 15, 961)

***

Unlike those who have criticized the judiciary for its class bias, Ambedkar appreciated in the very early years itself that the Supreme Court was attempting to establish the authority of the Constitution in order to ensure a proper form of political rule, which is the hallmark of the modern state. The *Privy Purses* case is a good example of this. The court struck down a 'midnight executive order' that 'derecognized' the former rulers of princely states after a constitutional amendment to terminate their privileges fell short of the required majority by one vote. The judges struck down the order not because their class bias inclined them to think that the maharajas should continue to have anachronistic privileges but because the commitments made in the Constitution to the rulers, whose territories were merged into the Union of India, could not be reneged by executive fiat. Proper form of political rule required that the abolition of the privileges of former rulers had to be done properly, through a proper amendment of the Constitution.[14]

A more recent reference to constitutional morality, which Ambedkar would have appreciated, is in the judgement of the Delhi High Court that invalidated Section 377 of the Indian Penal Code, which criminalizes 'unnatural sex'.[15] Justice A.B. Shah in his judgement (concurred by Justice Muralidhar) wrote:

> Popular morality, as distinct from a constitutional morality derived from constitutional values, is based on shifting and subjecting notions of right and wrong. If there is any type of 'morality' that can pass the test of compelling state interest, it must be 'constitutional' morality and not public morality. This aspect of constitutional morality was strongly insisted upon by Dr. Ambedkar in the Constituent Assembly.

Andre Beteille, elaborating on Ambedkar's emphasis on constitutional morality, noted:

> The strength or weakness of constitutional morality in contemporary India has to be understood in the light of a cycle of escalating

[14] *H. H. Maharajadhiraja Madhav Rao Scindia Bahadur* v *Union of India* [1971] SCR (3) 9.

[15] *Naz Foundation* v *NCR Delhi* [2009], available at https://indiankanoon.org/doc/100472805/, last accessed on 16 July 2018.

> demands from the people and the callous response of successive governments to those demands. In a parliamentary democracy, the obligations of constitutional morality are expected to be equally binding on the government and the opposition. In India, the same political party treats these obligations very differently when it is in office and when it is out of it. This has contributed greatly to the popular perception of our political system as being amoral. ... [P]oliticians may devise ingenious ways of getting round the Constitution and violating its rules from time to time, but they do not like to see the open defiance of it by others. In that sense the Constitution has come to acquire a significant symbolic value among Indians. But the currents of populism run deep in the country's political life, and they too have their own moral compulsions. It would appear therefore that the people of India are destined to oscillate endlessly between the two poles of constitutionalism and populism without ever discarding the one or the other. (Béteille 2008, 35–42)

There can be no doubt that Ambedkar was passionately committed to the cause of justice for the downtrodden people. He greatly lamented the failure of the ideal of fraternity in India. Yet, in the course of his professional conduct he upheld the highest standards of integrity. For the sake of upholding the sanctity of the Constitution as it was adopted on 26 November 1949 and brought into force on 26 January 1950, he risked being charged with opprobrium of being a defender of zamindars. There can be no more exemplary adherence to the ideal of constitutional morality than this.

References

Ambedkar, B.R. 1918. 'Small Holdings in India and Their Remedies'. *Journal of the Indian Economic Society* 1. Available at http://www.ambedkar.org/ambcd/11.%20Small%20Holdings%20in%20India%20and%20their%20Remedies.htm. Last accessed on 10 July 2018.

———. 1947. *States and Minorities* (Memorandum on the Safeguards for the Scheduled Castes Submitted to the Constituent Assembly on Behalf of the All India Scheduled Castes Federation). Available at http://www.ambedkar.org/ambcd/10A.%20Statesand%20Minorities%20Preface.html. Last accessed on 10 July 2018.

———. 1979. 'Thoughts on Linguistic States'. In *Dr. Babasaheb Ambedkar: Writings and Speeches*, vol. 1. Bombay: Education Department, Government of Maharashtra.

———. 1994. 'Draft Constitution'. In *Dr. Babasaheb Ambedkar: Writings and Speeches*, vol. 13, 134–345. Bombay: Education Department, Government of Maharashtra. Available at https://www.mea.gov.in/Images/attach/amb/Volume_13.pdf. Last accessed on 10 July 2018.

———. 1995. *Dr. Babasaheb Ambedkar: Speeches and Writings*, vol. 14, part 2. Bombay: Education Department, Government of Maharashtra.

———. 1997. *Dr. Babasaheb Ambedkar: Writings and Speeches*, vol. 15. Bombay: Education Department, Government of Maharashtra.

Austin, Granville. 1966. *The Indian Constitution: Cornerstone of a Nation*. Delhi: Clarendon Press.

———. 1999. *Working a Democratic Constitution: The Indian Experience*. Delhi: Oxford University Press.

Béteille, Andre. 2008. 'Constitutional Morality'. *Economic and Political Weekly* 43, no. 40 (4–10 October): 35–42.

Lok Sabha Secretariat. 1948. *Constituent Assembly Debates: Official Reports*, vol. 7, 4 November.

———. 1949. *Constituent Assembly Debates: Official Reports*, vol. 9, 10 September.

———. 1951. *Parliamentary Debates*, vol. 2, part 2, 29 May.

Grote, George. 1888. *A History of Greece: From the Earliest Period to the Close of the Generation Contemporary with Alexander the Great*, 10 vols. London: J. Murray.

Rao, Shiva, ed. 1965–71. *The Framing of India's Constitution*, vol. II. New Delhi: Indian Institute of Public Administration.

Sumit. 2017. 'Ambedkar: A Jurist without Equals'. *The Forward Press*, 13 July. Available at https://www.forwardpress.in/2017/07/ambedkar-a-jurist-with-no-equals/. Last accessed on 10 July 2018.

3

Radical Constitutionalism

Towards an Ambedkarite Jurisprudence

ARVIND NARRAIN

In India, caste was the law for centuries.

—Balagopal (n.d.)

The right which is grounded by law but is opposed by society is of no use at all.

—Ambedkar (quoted in Jadhav 2013: I, 186)

This tyranny of the majority must be put down with a firm hand if we are to guarantee to the untouchable the freedom of speech and action necessary for their uplift.

—Ambedkar (quoted in Jadhav 2013: I, 232)

[The Constitution only] *contains legal provisions, only a skeleton. The flesh of the skeleton is to be found in what we call constitutional morality.* [The framework of constitutional morality would mean that] *there must be no tyranny of the majority over the minority. ... The minority must always feel safe that although the majority is carrying on the Government, the minority is not being hurt, or the minority is not being hit below the belt.*

—Ambedkar (quoted in Jadhav 2013: I, 292)

Without equality, liberty would produce the supremacy of the few over the many. Equality without liberty would kill individual initiative. Without fraternity, liberty and equality could not become a natural course of things. It would require a constable to enforce them.

—Ambedkar (Lok Sabha Secretariat 1949, 979)

Ambedkar's presence in the politics, culture, and society of contemporary India is ubiquitous.[1] Innumerable statues of Ambedkar holding the Constitution in his hand and looking into the distance dot villages, towns, and cities around the country. For the Dalit community, these statues symbolize pride in the achievements of Ambedkar as well as a continuing resistance to caste-based oppression.

Though the Constitution was central to the Ambedkar which India has chosen to remember (Baxi 1995, 122–49),[2] there has been only scattered research into understanding what Ambedkar's contribution was to thinking about the law, apart from the epithet that Ambedkar was the 'father of the Indian Constitution'. At least until recently, Ambedkar was 'ritually celebrated' even as he was 'intellectually marginalized'. Professor Baxi tellingly notes that 'the Indian social science landscape has disarticulated Babasaheb Ambedkar by studious theoretical silence' (1995, 122–49).[3]

In this climate of silence, Professor Baxi asserts that Babasaheb Ambedkar was the originator of the idea of the 'lawless laws of Hinduism', which not only denied 'equality before the law as a principle to the untouchables, thus erecting a permanent edifice of subalternity over them down the ages' but also 'inscribed the extra territorialisation of whole communities of human beings and their castigation as being outside the pale of humanity' (1995, 141).

However, while the 'lawless laws of Hinduism' were what enabled the expulsion of Dalits from the political community, it

[1] Perhaps indicative of Ambedkar's posthumous popularity was an *Outlook* poll on the most popular Indian after Gandhi; the winner by far was Ambedkar. See http://www.outlookindia.com/magazine/story/the-greatest-indian-after-gandhi/281103, last accessed on 13 June 2018.

[2] In this germinal article, Professor Baxi talks about seven Ambedkars, including Ambedkar the authentic Dalit, the exemplary scholar, the activist journalist, the pre-Gandhian activist, the constitutionalist, and the renouncer.

[3] However, this silence is beginning to be broken. See the recent works of Aishwary Kumar (2015) and Soumyabrata Choudhury (2018).

was law to which Ambedkar turned in order to right the millennial wrongs of history.

Ambedkar's vision of the law was deeply rooted in his own experience of discrimination under the rigid laws of caste. It was arguably this experience of suffering due to the caste laws authored by society which turned him to the unceasing quest to combat caste discrimination through various forms of law and love. He experimented with norm creation through the prohibition of untouchability and ceaselessly sought to operationalize the norm through a close attention to procedure. He introduced the term 'constitutional morality' to public and constitutional discourse to make the point that Indian democracy must not be founded on majoritarianism but rather on a constitutional ethic of respect for dispersed and powerless minorities. While working closely with law he was intensely aware of its limitations, as seen by his advocacy of the concept of fraternity. Fraternity, in his understanding, pushed positive law to its limits, as its operationalization had to be premised on a form of love of a citizen for her fellow citizens.

Caste as Law

When Balagopal asserts that in India 'caste was the law for centuries', what does it mean? Is caste law a command of the sovereign in the Austinian sense or do we rather understand caste law, following Hart, as a system of rules that impose obligations which members of a society accept and are in the habit of obeying (Hart 2012)?

Clearly, if we have to think of caste as law, we have to go beyond the idea that it is a command of the sovereign and should be able to account for the fact that the rules of caste have a deep-rooted acceptance within the Hindu society, corresponding to what Hart would call 'an internal point of view'.[4] Caste-based norms govern every aspect of human behaviour in the society, and a large majority of persons accept and are in the habit of obeying norms which they see as just. In some cases where these norms are violated, members

[4] Law, Hart points out, depends not only on the external social pressures which are brought to bear on human beings, but also on the inner point of view that such beings take towards rules conceived as imposing obligations (Lloyd and Freeman 1985, 406).

of the society take vigilante action to punish the violators. Other cases of violation of these norms are adjudicated upon by caste-based Panchayats, which then prescribe punishment.

Some of the norms prescribed by the caste Hindu order might be of merely ritualistic or religious significance. Other norms prescribed by the caste Hindu order violate the basic postulates of citizenship, including the rights to equality, dignity, freedom of movement, expression, and other fundamental rights, especially of the Dalit community.

It is Ambedkar's deep insight that unless one came to terms with the system of caste law it would not be possible to even speak of the rights of the Dalit community. Ambedkar comes to the question of rights and law from his personal experience of being at the receiving end of caste-based discrimination. The young Ambedkar notes:

> I knew that in the school I could not sit in the midst of my class students according to my rank but that I was to sit in a corner by myself. I knew that in the school I was to have a separate piece of gunny cloth for me to squat on in the class room and the servant employed to clean the school would not touch the gunny cloth used by me. I was required to carry the gunny cloth home in the evening and bring it back the next day. (Ambedkar 1990)

This lifelong experience of discrimination in all aspects of social life arguably became the basis of Dr Ambedkar's viewpoint that to understand law in India one had to go beyond State law.

> Custom is no small thing as compared to law. It is true that law is enforced by the state through its police power and custom unless it is valid is not. But in practice this difference is of no consequence. Custom is enforced by people far more effectively than law is by the state. This is because the compelling force of an organized people is far greater than the compelling force of the state. (Moon 2014: V, 283)

The fact that the rules of caste enjoy the status of law in Indian society has the inverse implication that laws prohibiting caste-based behaviour suffer from a lack of social legitimacy. In this context, Dr Ambedkar doubts whether the rights which guarantee the Untouchables freedom from discrimination have the character of rights at all.

As he puts it:

> Law guarantees the untouchables the right to fetch water in metal pots. ... Hindu society does not allow them to exercise these rights. ... In short, that which is permitted by society to be exercised can alone be called a right. The right which is grounded by law but is opposed by society is of no use at all. (Jadhav 2013: I, 186)

From Ambedkar's writings one can identify three factors which make caste law such a powerful system of subjugation.

At the first level, in Ambedkar's understanding, caste law has behind it the authority of society, and these norms, in turn, derive from religion. He says, '[S]ocial force has an imperative authority before which the individual is often powerless. In the matter of a religious belief the imperative authority of the social force is tempered as steel is by the feeling that it is a breach of a graver kind and gives religious sanction a far greater force than a purely social sanction' (Moon 2014: V, 180).

At the second level, it is the divine authority of caste law (which Ambedkar traces to the *Manusmriti*) which emboldens the ordinary Hindu to feel that vigilante action (even if unlawful) to punish the supposed infractions of caste law is justified. Ambedkar painstakingly documents myriad incidents of brutal violence against the Dalits who violated the caste law and the impunity of those who perpetrated such violence, and traces such impunity to the sanction of religious codes. These systematic acts of violence spread the fear that any infraction of the caste law would result in severe consequences (Moon 2014: V, 35–61).

At the third level, violations of caste law are adjudicated upon by a caste Panchayat which arrogates to itself the authority to punish the supposed infractions. Ambedkar cites instances when the 'chavadi' (public assembly) courts have inflicted their 'lynch law' against Dalits. The lynch law consists of arbitrary punishments meant to strip the Dalit of both humanity and dignity. The apposite analogy to the arbitrary punishments meted out by the chavadi courts is the punishments meted out by the British post the Jallianwala Bagh massacre when Indians were made to crawl on the road, flogged on the street, made to salaam all British persons, and so forth. Both aimed to rob the human being of what Ambedkar was to call the 'title deeds of his humanity'. The only difference being that in one case the British authorities were inflicting the punishment, while in the other it was the Indians themselves (Moon 2014: V, 120).

Thus, caste law in the Ambedkarite rendering emerges as a totalitarian system meant to keep the Dalit in a continued state of servility. How did caste law interact with the modern legal system? Mark Galanter observes that colonial India was rife with instances of courts interpreting state law to reinforce the caste-based order. Thus, for example,

> [c]ourts granted injunctions to restrain members of particular castes from entering temples—even ones that were publicly supported and dedicated to the entire Hindu community. Damages were awarded for purificatory ceremonies necessitated by the pollution of lower castes; such pollution was actionable as a trespass on the person of the higher caste worshippers. It was a criminal offence for a member of the excluded caste knowingly to pollute a temple by his presence. (Galanter 1969)

The limitations of state law are apparent to Ambedkar as he notes:

> The worst of it is that all this injustice and persecution can be perpetrated within the limits of the law. A Hindu may well say that he will not employ an Untouchable, that he will not sell him anything, that he will evict him from his land, that he will not allow him to take his cattle across his field without offending the law in the slightest degree. In doing so, he is only expressing his right. The law does not care with what motive he does it. The law does not see what injury it causes the untouchable. (Moon 2014: V, 270)

Combating Caste Discrimination through State Law

Even as Ambedkar was conscious of the limitations of state law, he saw in it a potential to begin attacking caste law. One principle of modern law which Ambedkar found of value was that law should be no respecter of persons. He referred approvingly to the provisions of the draft Penal Code and the commitment of the law commissioners to the principle that '[it] is an evil that any man should be above the law' and their reasoning that the promulgation of the code was an opportunity to ensure that 'the Code was binding alike on persons of different races and religions' (Moon 2014: V, 103). It is clear that Ambedkar, very early on, saw the emancipatory possibilities of a universal law which applied to all persons as a welcome movement away from a law which differentiated between people based on race and religion. That was the strength of the Draft Penal Code.

Ambedkar also sought to draw on the principles of common law to assert the civil rights of the Dalits. After the famous Mahad satyagraha, in which the Untouchables drew water from Chawdar tank against caste Hindu prohibitions, the caste Hindus of Mahad filed a civil suit, making Ambedkar a party and seeking to assert their customary right to the use of the water in Chawdar tank as well as their right to exclude the Untouchables from the use of the tank from then on. For the caste Hindus to succeed in their claim they had to prove that the exclusion of Untouchables was a custom which was certain, existed from time immemorial, and was not against public policy.

Justice Broomfield[5] of the Bombay High Court, in his judgment in the case, held that there was no such immemorial custom and hence the caste Hindus could not exclude the Untouchables from the use of the tank.[6] He did not adjudicate the question as to whether untouchability was a custom which was against public policy.

Ambedkar expressed his disappointment at this judgment and its failure to address the question as to whether the custom of excluding Untouchables from the use of the tank was contrary to public policy. During the pendency of the litigation the court granted a temporary injunction against the Untouchables using Chawdar tank, and the Untouchables under the leadership of Ambedkar did not violate the order of the court and go and drink water from the tank for a second time. According to Ambedkar, the strategic reason for suspending their civil disobedience was because

> they wanted to have a judicial pronouncement on the issue whether the custom of untouchability can be recognized by the Court of law as valid. The rule of law is that a custom to be valid must be

[5] Interestingly, Justice Broomfield was the same judge before whom Gandhi was tried for sedition.

[6] *Narhari Damodar* Vaidya v *Bhimrao Ramji Ambedkar* [1937] 39 BOMLR 1295. Justice Broomfield held, 'We therefore, agree with the learned Assistant Judge that the appellants have not established the immemorial custom which they allege. Had they succeeded on this point, it might have been necessary to consider whether the custom was unreasonable or contrary to public policy (though strictly speaking that was not pleaded in the lower Courts).'

> immemorial, must be certain and must not be opposed to morality or public policy. The Untouchables' view is that it is a custom which is opposed to morality and public policy. But it is no use unless it is declared to be so by a judicial tribunal. Such a decision declaring the invalidity of the custom of untouchability would be of great value to the Untouchables in their fight for civil rights because it would seem illegal to import untouchability in civic matters. (Moon 2014: V, 252)

What is apparent in both examples is that Ambedkar was thinking about the possibilities and the potential of state law. It is true that state law, when it comes to combatting the millennial injustices of Indian society, lacks social legitimacy. As such it is a deeply weakened instrument when it comes to dealing with caste-based discrimination. However, in an otherwise totalitarian environment where all aspects of life are controlled by the rigid laws of caste, state law provides an entry point to begin questioning caste domination.

Dr Ambedkar asks whether, in a society with a deep-rooted majoritarian bias, the law can be mobilized to protect the interests of a geographically scattered minority? He argues that the coercive power of the law is a force which should be mobilized against the culturally and socially sanctioned prejudice of the majority community.

> Sin and immorality cannot become tolerable because a majority is addicted to them or because the majority chooses to practise them. If untouchability is sinful and an immoral custom, then in the view of the depressed classes, it must be destroyed without any hesitation even if it was acceptable to the majority. (Ambedkar 2017, 109)

In the context of this majoritarian bias, the coercive force of the law must be mobilized on the side of right and morality. Speaking of the most insidious form of violence faced by the Untouchables, namely the social boycott, he cites the State Committee which concluded: '[T]his tyranny of the majority must be put down with a firm hand if we are to guarantee to the untouchable the freedom of speech and action necessary for their uplift' (Jadhav 2013: I, 232).

The coming of Independence saw Ambedkar drawing upon this legacy of struggle to mobilize the counter-majoritarian power of the law to first articulate the norm that untouchability was a constitutional offence, then to legislate the norm through the enactment of the Civil Rights Act, 1955. This Ambedkarite legacy was taken forward through the subsequent enactment of the SC/ST Atrocities Act, 1989, and succeeding amendments.

Articulating the Norm of Untouchability as a Constitutional Crime

In a speech in 1930 at the First Round Table Conference, Dr Ambedkar first articulated the idea that untouchability should be considered a criminal offence.

> First of all, we want a Fundamental Right enacted in the Constitution which will declare 'Untouchability' to be illegal for all public purposes. We must be emancipated from this social curse before we can at all consent to the Constitution; and secondly, this Fundamental Right must also invalidate and nullify all such disabilities and all such discriminations as may have been made hitherto. Next, we want legislation against the social persecution to which I have drawn your attention just now, and for this we have provided certain clauses which are based upon an Act which now prevails in Burma in the document which we have submitted. (Jadhav 2013: III, 126)

Sixteen years after the idea was first articulated by Dr Ambedkar, the practice of 'untouchability' was criminalized, with the Constituent Assembly passing what was to become Article 17 of the Indian Constitution.

Article 17 reads:

> Abolition of 'Untouchability'
>
> 'Untouchability' is abolished and its practice in any form is forbidden. The enforcement of any disability arising out of 'Untouchability' shall be an offence punishable in accordance with law.

The debate in the Constituent Assembly was overwhelmingly in support of the said article (draft Article 11), with member after member seeing it as a new dawn. One such member, Shri Muniswamy Pillai, opined that 'the very clause about untouchability and its abolition goes a long way to show the world that the unfortunate communities that are called "untouchables" will find solace when this Constitution comes into effect' (Lok Sabha Secretariat 1948, 665).

Another, Dr Manomohon Das, said that 'for the sake of fairness and justice to the millions of untouchables of this land, for the sake of sustaining our goodwill and reputation beyond the boundaries of India, this clause which makes the practice of untouchability a punishable crime must find a place in the Constitution of free and independent India' (Lok Sabha Secretariat 1948, 666). In addition to this support, there was a note of caution. Shri Santanu Kumar Das stated:

> [T]he fact is that we merely want to enact laws about it and expect the rural people to observe these laws. We must ourselves first observe the law for otherwise there would be no sense in asking others to act upon it. If we fail to observe it, it would be impossible to root out this evil. ... [O]ur members act as fifth columnists in the rural areas, for they tell the people there that these laws are not in force and thus themselves act against the law. (Lok Sabha Secretariat 1948, 667)

A predominant sentiment in the speeches of both Shri Muniswami Pillai and Dr Manomohon Das is that the enactment of what was to become Article 17 meant that a practice which had defined Hindu society would no more be tolerated once the Constitution came into force. The amendment made untouchability a 'punishable crime', which meant that a law had to be enacted to effectively outlaw and punish a practice which was otherwise sanctioned by the society. However, the note of caution by Shri Santanu Kumar Das indicated that the key challenge would remain the enforcement of such a law which was avowedly counter-majoritarian.

The contribution of Dr Ambedkar was to the articulation of the norm on which all subsequent work with respect to ensuring the dignity of the Dalit community is based, namely that the practice of 'untouchability' should be considered a constitutional crime.

At the heart of Article 17 is a recognition of what Gautam Bhatia describes as 'Ambedkar's revolutionary insight: that the denial of human dignity, both material and symbolic, is caused not only by public power, but by *private* power as well—and the task of constitutionalism is not limited to satisfactorily regulating public power in service of liberty, but extends to positively guaranteeing human freedom even against the excesses of private power'.[7]

[7] Gautam Bhatia (2016) argues that Article 17, Article 15(2), and Article 23 should be seen as a golden triangle: 'Each of these articles protects the individual not against the State, but against other individuals, and against *communities*.'

Articulating the Necessary Elements of a Counter-Majoritarian Law

While it was important for the Constitution to recognize the practice of untouchability as a crime, for this constitutional prohibition to have any impact it needed to find statutory expression. The bill which was moved in the Parliament to actualize this constitutional vision was the Untouchability Offences Bill in 1954. Dr Ambedkar's responses to the bill in a speech that he delivered in the Rajya Sabha addressed the key question of how to legislate when the law is against the sentiments of the majority.

Dr Ambedkar began by making clear that he was uncomfortable with calling the statute the Untouchability Offences Bill and preferred the title Civil Rights (Untouchables) Protection Act. The reason for this was because the original title of the bill

> gives the appearance that it is a Bill of a very minor character, just a dhobi not washing the cloth, just a barber not shaving or just a mithaiwala not selling laddus and things of that sort. People will think that these are trifles and piffles and why has parliament bothered and wasted its time in dealing with dhobis and barbers and ladduwallas. It is not a Bill of that sort. It is a Bill which is intended to give protection with regard to Civil and Fundamental rights. (Jadhav 2013: I, 232)

Thus, the conceptual basis of the statute had to be clearly articulated—it was not dealing with 'trifles and piffles' but rather with 'civil and fundamental rights'—and the legislation had to articulate a constitutional vision of protecting citizens from discrimination from their fellow citizens. Ambedkar said, '[U]ntouchability is not merely a social problem. It is a problem of the highest political importance and affects the fundamental question of the civil rights of the subjects of the state' (Moon 2014: V, 139).[8]

[8] This insightful comment is still extremely valid if we consider the legislations which have been enacted to address the problems faced by those at the very bottom of the socio-economic hierarchy, namely those in manual scavenging. The two legislations are titled The Employment of Manual Scavengers and Construction of Dry Latrines (Prohibition) Act, 1993, and the Prohibition of Employment as Manual Scavengers and Their Rehabilitation Act, 2013. Both legislations in their title give little indication of the deep dignitarian harm caused by the caste-based practice of manual scavenging and the constitutional importance of the legislation; see PUCL-K (2019).

To actualize this vision, Dr Ambedkar in fact argued that the statute should move away from the language of untouchability and move towards conceptualizing the offence as perpetrated on the body of the Scheduled Caste person. Referring to Shri Kailash Nath Katju, who tabled the bill, he said, 'I don't know why he should keep on repeating Untouchability and Untouchables all the time. In the body of the Bill he is often speaking of Scheduled Castes. The Constitution speaks of the Scheduled Castes and I don't know why he should fight shy of using the word Scheduled Castes in the title of the Bill itself' (Jadhav 2013: 1, 231).

Dr Ambedkar then addressed the problems that had to be faced in enacting a law which, in its intent and character, was counter-majoritarian.

The first loophole that he pointed out was the compoundable nature of the offence which would ensure that the law remained a dead letter (Moon 2014: V, 236). He illustrated this point by referring to the Thakkar Bapa Committee Report on conditions of the Depressed Classes. He quoted from the report to make the point that

> the Untouchables were not able to prosecute then [their] persecutors because of want of economic and financial means, and consequently they were ever ready to compromise with the offenders whenever the offenders wanted that the offence should be compromised. The fact was that the law remained a dead letter and those in whose favour it was enacted are unable to put in action and those against whom it is to be put in action, are able to silence the victim. (Moon 2014: V, 234)

The second loophole, Dr Ambedkar pointed out, was with respect to the question of punishment. The punishment prescribed was imprisonment for a maximum of six months or a fine. He was scathing on the question of the bill fighting shy of prescribing a punishment commensurate with the gravity of the offence. He observed:

> My Honourable friend was very eloquent on the question of punishment. He said that the punishment ought to be very very [*sic*] light and I was wondering whether he was pleading for a lighter punishment because be himself wanted to commit these offences. He said, 'let the punishment be very light so that no grievance shall be left in the heart of the offender.' (Moon 2014: V, 236)

What emerged through the discussion on the Untouchability Offences Bill, 1954, was the lack of seriousness of the government in bringing into effect a law tasked with combatting a deeply entrenched, socially and religiously sanctioned system of beliefs. The only person who seemed to grasp the nature of this enormous task was Dr Ambedkar.

The law which was finally enacted—though it now had the title of Protection of Civil Rights Act, 1955—did not address the key concerns raised by Dr Ambedkar, that is, naming the subject of the offence as the Scheduled Castes, ensuring non-compoundability and adequate punishment.

What emerged so powerfully in the debate was the commitment of Dr Ambedkar to not just articulate the norm but also work on actualizing it. This meant working with the mechanisms of law and thinking through elements of procedure. When jurisprudence is meant to protect the interests of the oppressed it cannot just stop at norm development but should rather work with the technicalities of procedure to arrive at the best legislative design. It is this combination of attention to norm development as well as legislative design that characterizes an Ambedkarite commitment to the deployment of law as a strategy to counter caste discrimination.

Towards Crafting a Counter-majoritarian Law: The SC/ST Atrocities Act, 1989, and Subsequent Developments

The gaps pointed out by Dr Ambedkar in the Untouchability Offences Bill, 1954, were only rectified in the SC/ST Atrocities Act of 1989, a full 34 years after the Protection of Civil Rights Act, 1955. The three aforementioned loopholes noticed by Dr Ambedkar in his comments on the Untouchability Offences Bill were redressed by this new Act.

First, the Act made a shift from the language of 'untouchability' to referring to it as an 'atrocity'. This Act made clear that what was being punished was no minor transgression but rather a serious criminal offence referred to as an atrocity.

The general terms in which the Protection of Civil Rights Act was crafted was converted into a specification of the forms of atrocities committed on SC/ST persons. The listing of the nature of offences perpetrated on the SC/ST population reads almost like an anthropology of the ways that caste discrimination and atrocities are perpetrated on the bodies and lives of the SC/ST population.

The offences range from those perpetrated on the body, such as forcing the SC/ST members to eat inedible substances or forcibly removing their clothes and parading them naked, to those which injured their dignity, as well as electoral offences and gender-based offences.

Second, the SC/ST Atrocities Act made offences under it non-compoundable, thereby addressing the concern that those who filed the case will not have the wherewithal to sustain a lengthy prosecution or withstand pressure from the perpetrator and go in for a compromise.

Third, the fact that the offences created under this Act were serious offences was apparent by a glance at the punishments section. Under this Act punishments were graded on a scale which moved from six months' imprisonment right up to death penalty.

However, in spite of these changes, the conviction rate with respect to offences under the SC/ST Atrocities Act is less than 1 per cent. This is largely due to the difficulties in implementing a law which in the ultimate analysis still goes against a prevalent public morality. As a PIL filed with respect to the implementation of the SC/ST Atrocities Act makes clear, there are many ways in which a counter-majoritarian law can be subverted in its implementation.[9]

This experiment in conceptualizing an ideal counter-majoritarian law continues with the latest avatar being the Scheduled Castes and Scheduled Tribes (Prevention of Atrocities) Amendment Act, 2015.[10]

[9] Some of these failures are listed below.

(1) FIRs are registered without reference to proper sections of the Act
(2) Charge sheets are invariably filed late
(3) Accused are not arrested and are allowed to roam free
(4) Investigations are often not done by the deputy superintendent of police but by junior officers, rendering acquittal on grounds of improper procedure
(5) Victims are forced to turn hostile on threats of economic and social boycott.

See Mangubhai and Irudayam (2008, 150).

[10] This was based on the Scheduled Castes and Scheduled Tribes (Prevention of Atrocities) Amendment Ordinance, 2014, passed by the UPA government. Some of the key features of the 2015 Act are:

- While the concept of social and economic boycott, which was stressed by Dr Ambedkar as being the key offence to conceptualize,

Limitations of the Counter-Majoritarian Approach

It was never Dr Ambedkar's case that one could craft a watertight counter-majoritarian law. While it was important to think through and work on key jurisprudential and procedural elements of such a law, it was clear to him that it would not be enough by itself.

> Rights are protected not by law, but by the social and moral conscience of society. ... But if the Fundamental Rights are opposed by the community, no law, no parliament, no judiciary can guarantee them in the real sense of the word. What is the use of the fundamental rights to the Negroes in America, to the Jews in Germany and to the Untouchables in India? As Burke said, there is no method found for punishing the multitude. Law can punish a single, solitary

---

found expression through Sections 4, 5, and 6 of the Protection of Civil Rights Act, 1955, the tragedy of the statute remained its minimal punishments, and hence its ineffectiveness. The 2015 amendment defines for the first time the offence of social boycott and economic boycott specifically and awards a significantly higher punishment for the said offences, thereby indicating a greater state seriousness in thinking of both social and economic boycott as offenses worthy of punishment.

- There is a chapter on the rights of victims and witnesses under Section 15 A which attempts to address some of the key problems faced in prosecution, including intimidation, coercion, and threat of violence, by making it the responsibility of the State to ensure protection of victims from intimidation and coercion.
- In the key definitional section under Section 3, it increases the number of offences which can be committed against SC/ST persons from 15 to 29.
- The offences against women who are SC/ST are also expanded in the ordinance to include under Section 3w(i) 'touching a woman belonging to the SC/ST tribe knowing that she belongs to the SC/ST, when such act of touching is of a sexual nature and is without the recipients consent'; it also criminalizes under Section w(ii) the 'use of words, or gestures of a sexual nature towards a woman belonging to a SC or ST knowing that she belongs to a SC or a ST'.
- The dignity offences are also elaborated in greater detail including offences of 'garlanding with footwear or parading naked or semi naked', forcibly committing on SC/ST acts such as 'removing clothes from the person, removing moustaches, painting face or body or any other similar act which is derogator to dignity'.

> recalcitrant criminal. It can never operate against a whole body of people who are determined to defy it. Social conscience is the only safeguard of all rights—fundamental or non-fundamental. (Jadhav 2013: I, 222)

The history of the implementation of these laws might support this opinion of Dr Ambedkar. The way procedure in the SC/ST Atrocities Act has been deployed to circumvent its protections is a strong indictment of the difficulties faced in implementing counter-majoritarian laws.

A case study of the acquittal in the Tsundur massacre[11] as well as the Laxmanpur Bathe massacre[12] shows the challenges of ensuring justice through the coercive power of the law when the might of organized society is against it. However, the narration of the failures of a counter-majoritarian legislation is not to disavow or reject such efforts but rather to say that a counter-majoritarian legislative effort must be supplemented by other efforts to challenge the caste hierarchies of Indian society.

Dr Subhash Kasinanth Mahajan v *State of Maharashtra*: Defanging the Atrocities Act?

The legislature has made consistent progress in refining a counter-majoritarian legislation ever since the enactment of the Constitution. However, this progress is now being put in jeopardy by a two-judge-bench decision of the Supreme Court which has made the initiation of proceedings under the Act by the filing of an FIR that much more difficult. The court held:

> Accordingly, we direct that in absence of any other independent offence calling for arrest, in respect of offences under the Atrocities Act, no arrest may be effected, if an accused person is a public servant, without written permission of the appointing authority and if such a person is not a public servant, without written permission of

[11] The acquittal by the Andhra Pradesh High Court has now been stayed by the Supreme Court. See http://www.newindianexpress.com/states/andhra_pradesh/SC-Stays-Acquittal-of-56-in-Tsundur-Case/2014/08/01/article2357490.ece, last accessed on 20 June 2017.

[12] *State of Bihar* v *Girija Singh and Others*, Death Reference no. 5 of 2010.

> the Senior Superintendent of Police of the District. Such permissions must be granted for recorded reasons which must be served on the person to be arrested and to the concerned court. As and when a person arrested is produced before the Magistrate, the Magistrate must apply his mind to the reasons recorded and further detention should be allowed only if the reasons recorded are found to be valid. To avoid false implication, before FIR is registered, preliminary enquiry may be made whether the case falls in the parameters of the Atrocities Act and is not frivolous or motivated.[13]

The layers of scrutiny set in place before an arrest can be made under the Act in effect defangs it. As the history of past legislations under Article 17 makes clear, it was always a struggle to operationalize a counter-majoritarian legislation. By detailing a special procedure now for registering an FIR and making an arrest under the Atrocities Act, the judgment in effect renders the operation of the Act nugatory. Prior to this judgment, even though conviction rates were low under the Atrocities Act, the fact that arrest was possible and bail was difficult made the symbolic threat of the law a bit more real. The achievements of this legislation are now threatened by a judgment which shows no historical appreciation of caste violence in India and no sense of the long history of legislative and constitutional efforts to redress caste-based discrimination and violence.

The judges quoted Ambedkar to make the point that 'castes are anti-national. In the first place because they bring about separation in social life' and then went on to state that 'it is necessary to express concern that working of the Atrocities Act should not result in perpetuating casteism which can have an adverse impact on integration of the society and the constitutional values'. In a perverse conclusion, the judges decided that the reason for casteism was the Atrocities Act as the legislation was prone to being misused by the filing of false complaints (see also Doddahatti 2018; Nawsagaray 2018).

The fact that a judgment of the Supreme Court chose not to engage with the documented history of caste violence in the country, the rationale for Article 17, and the history of legislative interventions to address caste discrimination before coming to its conclusions is a matter of serious concern. Both the Constituent

[13] *Dr Subhash Kashinath* Mahajan v *The State Of Maharashtra*, available at https://indiankanoon.org/doc/108728085/, last accessed on 16 May 2018.

Assembly in the form of Article 17 and the Parliament in the form of successive legislations have grappled with understanding the nature of caste-based discrimination and formulating a response to the same. If the only point that the judges could make about the Atrocities Act was that it perpetrated caste discrimination as it was a legislation subject to misuse, it speaks of an inability or unwillingness to understand the preambular promise of social justice and the commitment to protect the dignity of the individual. The judges ignored the fact that the Indian Constitution is perhaps the only Constitution to criminalize a social practice such as 'untouchability' and that the legislation which aims to fulfil the constitutional promise of Article 17 should be seen from that lens as well.

In fact, if the judges had engaged with the legislative history of the Article, they would have found a counter to their conclusion that the law was being misused. The judges cited data from the National Crime Records Bureau which indicates that in '15-16% cases, the competent police authorities had filed closure reports. Out of the cases disposed of by the courts in 2015, more than 75% cases have resulted in acquittal/withdrawal or compounding of the cases'.[14] The judges used this statistic, indicating that in a majority of cases there has been acquittal/withdrawal or compounding of cases, to infer the 'misuse of the law'.

Dr Ambedkar had indicated in his speech on the Untouchability Offences Bill in 1954 why the offences under that bill would get compounded. He referred to the Thakkar Bapa Committee Report on the conditions of the Depressed Classes to make the point that

> the Untouchables were not able to prosecute then [their] persecutors because of want of economic and financial means, and consequently they were ever ready to compromise with the offenders whenever the offenders wanted that the offence should be compromised. The fact was that the law remained a dead letter and those in whose favour it was enacted are unable to put in action and those against whom it is to be put in action, are able to silence the victim. (Jadhav 2013: I, 232)

As Ambedkar indicates, 'compromise' does not mean 'misuse', rather 'compromise' means that the Dalits do not have the

[14] *Dr. Subhash Kashinath Mahajan* v *The State Of Maharashtra*, available at https://indiankanoon.org/doc/108728085/, last accessed on 16 May 2018.

wherewithal to sustain prosecution. It is a blindness to this legislative and social history of the law which lead to erroneous conclusions on 'misuse'. The judges wrongly invoked Ambedkar to uproot, in effect, an Ambedkarite legacy. It is up to the Parliament to set right this judicial anomaly. A review petition was filed challenging the judgment. The Supreme Court, in review, held that 'we do not doubt that directions encroach upon the field reserved for the legislature and against the concept of protective discrimination in favour of downtrodden classes under Article 15(4) of the Constitution'.[15]

Fraternity: At the Limits of Positive Law

Dr Ambedkar was deeply inspired by the idea of liberty, equality, and fraternity as propounded in the French Revolution. Taking these ideas forward in the famous Mahad satyagraha on 20 March 1927, he asserted the right to equality by giving the call for Dalits to break the social prohibition of drinking water from a public tank in Mahad. In his speech, he explicitly saw the Mahad satyagraha as similar to the 'National Assembly in France [that] convened in 1789'. He said, 'Our Conference aims at the same achievement in social, religious, civic and economic matters. We are avowedly out to smash the steel-frame of the caste-system. ... Our movement stands for strength and solidarity; for equality, liberty and fraternity' (Moon, 2014: XVII, 62).

While the importance of the ideas of equality and liberty is self-evident, when it comes to the question of protecting the rights of the Dalit community, what is the value of fraternity? In the Constituent Assembly, Dr Ambedkar analysed the relationship of these terms.

> These principles of liberty, equality and fraternity are not to be treated as separate items in a trinity. They form a union of trinity in the sense that to divorce one from the other is to defeat the very purpose of democracy. Liberty cannot be divorced from equality, equality cannot be divorced from liberty. Nor can liberty and equality be divorced from fraternity. Without equality, liberty would produce the supremacy of the few over the many. Equality without liberty would

[15] See *Union of India* v *State of Maharashtra*. Available at https://indiankanoon.org/doc/90225896/. Last accessed on 20 July 2020.

> kill individual initiative. Without fraternity, liberty and equality could not become a natural course of things. It would require a constable to enforce them. (Lok Sabha Secretariat 1949, 979)

The relationship between equality and liberty is not a simple unilinear one, but rather a conflictual one. Emphasis on liberty could compromise equality, and emphasis on equality could compromise liberty (Narvison and Streba 2010). The insight that Dr Ambedkar provides is that it is only when fraternity has become a way of life that the conflict between the different interests that liberty and equality seek to promote can be resolved. Fraternity has received stepsisterly treatment when compared to her more famous kin, liberty and equality. In fact, 'fraternity' was even omitted from the precursor to the Preamble, namely the Objectives Resolution moved by Jawaharlal Nehru (Lok Sabha Secretariat 1946, 57–65). That 'fraternity' found its way into the Preamble owes a lot to the initiative of Dr Ambedkar. As chairperson of the Drafting Committee, he explicitly introduced 'fraternity' into the text of the Preamble.[16]

He expanded in greater detail on why fraternity was the key term in this trinity.

> Fraternity means a sense of common brotherhood of all Indians. ... It is the principle which gives unity and solidarity to social life. It is a difficult thing to achieve. ... [This is because in] India there are castes. The castes are anti-national. In the first place because they bring about separation in social life. They are anti-national also because they generate jealousy and antipathy between caste and caste. But we must overcome all these difficulties if we wish to become a nation in reality. For fraternity can be a fact only when there is a nation. Without fraternity, equality and liberty will be no deeper than a coat of paint. (Lok Sabha Secretariat 1949, 980)

The challenge of course is: How does one promote the value of fraternity? How can the law build a common culture where fraternity becomes a way of life? How do you build links between members

[16] As Ambedkar put it: 'The Committee has added a clause about fraternity in the preamble, although it does not occur in the Objectives Resolution. The Committee felt that the need for fraternal concord and goodwill in India was never greater than now and that this particular aim of the new Constitution should be emphasized by special mention in the Preamble' (Rao 2010, 510).

of different castes such that the feeling of difference ultimately dissolves? The answer to these questions is really an acknowledgement of the limit points of positive law. To achieve fraternity as a way of national being, one's endeavours will have to go beyond the law.

In *What Congress and Gandhi Have Done to the Untouchables* (1945, reprinted in 2017), Dr Ambedkar gestures towards a social space outside the law when it comes to the struggle to bring about social change. Talking about the work that the Anti-untouchability League, initiated by Gandhi, should do, he indicated the necessity of fostering what he called 'social intercourse'.

> I think the League should attempt to dissolve the nausea, which the Touchables feel towards the Untouchables and which is the reason why the two sections have remained so much apart as to constitute separate and distinct entities. In my opinion, the best way of achieving it is to establish closer contact between the two. Only a common cycle of participation can help people to overcome the strangeness of feeling, which one has when brought into contact with the other. (Jadhav 2014: I, 307)

Dr Ambedkar focussed on social contact because he was convinced that 'the touchables and the Untouchables cannot be held together by law, certainly not by any electoral law substituting joint electorates for separate electorates. The only thing that can hold them together is love' (Jadhav 2014: I, 307).

Of course, this idea of love is premised upon an acknowledgement of the legitimacy of the Untouchables' just demands. 'Outside the family, justice alone, in my opinion can open the possibility of love and it should be the duty of the Anti-Untouchability League to see that the touchable does, or failing that is made to do, justice to the Untouchable. Nothing else, in my opinion, can justify the project or the existence of the League' (Jadhav 2014: I, 308).

In Dr Ambedkar's writings one finds a clue that to achieve this change one needs to challenge prejudice in the intimate sphere.

> Do not be under the wrong impression that untouchability will be removed only by removal of a ban on personal meetings and drawing of water from wells ... it will remove untouchability at the most in the outer world, but not from the inner world. For that the ban on inter-caste marriage will have to be removed. Once that happens untouchability will vanish from inside the house. (Jadhav 2013: I, 97)

The question of inter-caste marriage as a solvent of caste appears forcefully again in 'Annihilation of Caste'

> I am convinced that the real remedy is intermarriage. Fusion of blood can alone create the feeling of being kith and kin, and unless this feeling of kinship, of being kindred, becomes paramount, the separatist feeling—the feeling of being aliens—created by caste will not vanish. The real remedy for breaking Caste is intermarriage. Nothing else will serve as the solvent of caste. (Jadhav 2014: II, 217)

Dr Ambedkar's advocacy of the concept of fraternity has important implications for contemporary India, not only with respect to challenging caste hierarchy but also other hierarchies in Indian society. The idea of fraternity is possibly even more salient in the contemporary era with the stoked controversy around 'love jihad' and the so-called 'anti-Romeo squads' in Uttar Pradesh.[17]

There have been serious and sustained attacks on fraternal ways of living by the Hindu right wing. Myriad examples of threat to fraternity due to the actions of the right wing are present in the human rights reports produced by the Peoples Union for Civil Liberties-Karnataka (PUCL-K), which document a series of attacks on social as well as romantic relationships between young people belonging to different religious communities in the context of Dakshina Kannada (PUCL-K 2009; 2012). What the right wing tries to curb using vigilante violence is not only love relationships across lines of caste and religion but also social interactions including visiting each other's houses on religious festivals, attending weddings, and socializing together whenever this is done across religious lines.

Using an Ambedkarite lens we need to understand love relationships and social interactions across lines of caste and religion as not just an exercise of the individual right to love and the right to association but really as an active promotion of the principle of fraternity. These relationships of love and association, formed across lines of caste and religion, are really nothing less than a people's action to implement the Preamble's promise of fraternity.

[17] See http://www.firstpost.com/politics/love-jihad-in-uttar-pradesh-bjps-latest-strategy-against-akhilesh-1678829.html and http://indianexpress.com/elections/uttar-pradesh-assembly-elections-2017/amit-shah-promises-anti-romeo-squad-to-protect-girls/, last accessed on 15 June 2018.

Constitutional Morality: Its Relevance in a Majoritarian Democracy

There are at least three references in Dr Ambedkar's corpus to the notion of 'constitutional morality'.

In a speech in the Parliament on the Constitution (Fourth Amendment) Bill, 1954, he notes:

> But as soon as Swaraj presented itself, everybody thought that there was the prospect of political authority passing into the hands of a majority, which did not possess what might constitutionally be called 'Constitutional Morality'. Their official doctrine was inequality of classes. Though there is inequality in every community or whatever be the word, that inequality is a matter of practice. It is not an official dogma. But with a majority in this country, inequality as embodied in their 'Chaturvarna' is an official doctrine. Secondly their caste system is a sword of political and administrative discrimination. (Jadhav 2013: II, 421)

In another speech titled 'Conditions Precedent for the Successful Working of Democracy' he identifies the observance of 'constitutional morality' as one of the 'conditions precedent'. In his judgement, the Constitution only 'contains legal provisions, only a skeleton. The flesh of the skeleton is to be found in what we call constitutional morality'. The framework of constitutional morality would mean that 'there must be no tyranny of the majority over the minority. ... The minority must always feel safe that although the majority is carrying on the Government, the minority is not being hurt, or the minority is not being hit below the belt' (Jadhav 2013: I, 291).

The most famous reference to the idea of constitutional morality was, of course, given by him in the Constituent Assembly while presenting the draft Constitution.

Dr Ambedkar quoted Grote, the historian of Greece, who had said:

> The diffusion of constitutional morality, not merely among the majority of any community but throughout the whole, is an indispensable condition of government at once free and peaceable; since even any powerful and obstinate minority may render the working of a free institution impracticable without being strong enough to conquer the ascendancy for themselves. (Lok Sabha Secretariat 1948, 38)

Dr Ambedkar went on to say,

> By constitutional morality Grote meant 'a paramount reverence for the forms of the Constitution, enforcing obedience to authority acting under and within these forms yet combined with the habit of open speech, of action subject only to definite legal control, and unrestrained censure sure of these very authorities as to all their public acts combined too with a perfect confidence in the bosom of every citizen amidst the bitterness of party contest that the forms of the Constitution will not be less sacred in the eyes of his opponents that in his own'. (Lok Sabha Secretariat 1948, 38)

He concluded:

> The question is, can we presume such a diffusion of constitutional morality? Constitutional morality is not a natural sentiment. It has to be cultivated. We must realise that our people have yet to learn it. Democracy in India is only a top dressing on an Indian soil which is essentially undemocratic. (Lok Sabha Secretariat 1948, 38)

Clearly, the idea of constitutional morality was a theme to which Dr Ambedkar returned again and again. What could Dr Ambedkar have meant in his repeated invocation of constitutional morality? Plausibly, the importance of the concept flowed from his own experience of advocating the rights of the Depressed Classes. He was acutely conscious that a democracy that was based upon a majority, which was no political majority but a communal majority, was deeply dangerous to the very notion of democracy itself.

As he put it:

> In India, the majority is not a political majority. In India, the majority is born; it is not made. That is the difference between a communal majority and a political majority. A political majority is not a fixed or a permanent majority. It is a majority which is always made, unmade and remade. A communal majority is a permanent majority fixed in its attitude. (Ambedkar 1945)

Pratap Bhanu Mehta, in one of the few academic engagements with the idea of constitutional morality, correctly identifies this important thrust in Dr Ambedkar's work.

> After all, the burden of Grote's great history of Athenian democracy was to defuse the criticism of Athens that popular sovereignty was a threat to freedom and individuality. Once popular sovereignty or the

> authority of the people had been invoked, who else would have any authority to speak? (Mehta 2010)

At its heart, Dr Ambedkar's notion of constitutional morality is a response to the particular conditions of India where majorities are often communal majorities and where minorities may not have bargaining power in the Parliament. If parliamentary representation only throws up communal majorities, where are the minorities to go? Would minorities not be at the sufferance of majority opinion which misunderstands democracy to be equal to popular sovereignty?

The first time the concept of constitutional morality, as propounded by Dr Ambedkar, found a contemporary public resonance was when it was cited by J. Shah in his celebrated decision in *Naz Foundation* v *NCR Delhi* ([2009] 160 DLT 277 [Del]) when the court ruled that Section 377 of the IPC was ultra vires Articles 14, 15, and 21.

The dilemma faced by the Delhi High Court was in crafting a judgment which would secure the rights of the LGBT community against the viewpoint of representatives of religious communities that homosexuality was against their religious beliefs and hence against public morality.

The court chose to sidestep the debate on religion and sexuality by arguing that it was not a relevant consideration at all. Even if a majority of the followers of a particular religion was against homosexuality and, by extension, the 'public morality' was against homosexuality, public morality would be superseded by 'constitutional morality'.

As Justice Shah put it:

> Thus, popular morality or public disapproval of certain acts is not a valid justification for restriction of the fundamental rights under Article 21. Popular morality, as distinct from a constitutional morality derived from constitutional values, is based on shifting and subjecting notions of right and wrong. If there is any type of 'morality' that can pass the test of compelling state interest, it must be 'constitutional' morality and not public morality. This aspect of constitutional morality was strongly insisted upon by Dr. Ambedkar in the Constituent Assembly.[18]

[18] *Naz Foundation* v *NCR Delhi* [2009] 160 DLT 277 (Del).

The implications of this line of thinking are profound for our very understanding of democracy in what is after all a diverse, plural, and hierarchical society such as India. While the *Naz* decision extended the life of the concept of constitutional morality to LGBT citizens, the power of the concept lies in its possible application to other 'unpopular minorities'. In a country coming to grips with brute majoritarianism, this call to constitutional morality—and by implication the understanding that brute electoral majorities do not mean that minorities of every strip and hue can now be effectively lorded over—is even more important.

* * *

This chapter has sought to argue that the legal concepts put forward by Dr Ambedkar are of great relevance today. We need to think of the failures of the SC/ST Prevention of Atrocities Act through a historical lens. The 'failures' have to be located in the context of Indian society and the dominance of the ideas of caste as law. The law of the State has to be understood as nothing less than a brave attempt to challenge societal hierarchies of over 2,500 years. In this context, both norm articulation and an attention to the details of procedure are very important. A key Ambedkarite idea is that legal activism cannot stop at norm articulation but must struggle with the difficult task of actualizing the norm in a deeply flawed society.

Perhaps the ideas of greatest relevance embedded in Ambedkar's legal corpus are the notions of fraternity and constitutional morality. In a deeply hierarchical society in which fellow feeling between persons belonging to different religions and castes is at a low ebb, the imperative is really to build that fellow feeling: what Ambedkar called fraternity and at other points love. It is really essential that fraternal relations be built through a politics of love. As such, acts of love between people across lines of religion and caste should be seen as nothing less than a people's action to build fraternity.

In a diverse and hierarchical society such as India, the notion of constitutional morality should be internalized by the judiciary which must play the role of ensuring that Indian democracy does not become the brute rule of the majority. It is the constitutional responsibility of the judiciary to ensure that majoritarian sentiments are kept in check through the morality of the Constitution.

In these days of a rising tide of Hindutva, it is integral that we go back to the Ambedkarite corpus and retrieve the key notions of fraternity and constitutional morality as a guide to a more constitutional future.

References

Books

Ambedkar, B.R. 2017. *What Congress and M.K. Gandhi Have Done to the Untouchables*. Delhi: Kalpaz Publications.

Choudhury, Soumyabrata. 2018. Ambedkar *and Other Immortals*. New Delhi: Navayana.

Hart, H.L.A. 2012. *Concept of Law*. Oxford: Oxford University Press.

Jadhav, Narendra, ed. 2013. *Ambedkar Speaks*, vols I–III. New Delhi: Konark Publishers.

———. 2014. *Ambedkar Writes*, vols I and II. New Delhi: Konark Publishers.

Kumar, Aishwary. 2015. *Radical Equality*. Stanford: Stanford University Press.

Lloyd, Dennis (Lloyd of Hampstead), and M.D.A. Freeman, eds. 1985. *Lloyd's Introduction to Jurisprudence*. London: Stevens and Sons.

Lok Sabha Secretariat. 1946. *Constituent Assembly Debates*, vol. I. 13 December.

———. 1948. *Constituent Assembly Debates*, vol. VII. 29 November.

———. 1949. *Constituent Assembly Debates*, vol. XI. 25 November.

Moon, Vasant, ed. 2014. *Babasaheb Ambedkar: Writings and Speeches*, vols V and XVII. Mumbai: Dr Ambedkar Foundation.

Narvison, Jan, and James Streba. 2010. *Are Liberty and Equality Compatible?* Cambridge: Cambridge University Press.

Rao, Shiva, ed. 2010. *The Framing of India's Constitution*, vol. III. Delhi: Universal Law Publishing.

Paper in Edited Volume

Baxi, Upendra. 1995. 'Emancipation and Justice: Babasaheb Ambedkar's Legacy and Vision'. In *Crisis and Change in Contemporary India*, edited by Upendra Baxi and Bhikhu Parekh, 122–49. New Delhi: Sage.

Mangubhai, Jayashree, and Aloysius Irudayam. 2008. 'Building a Subaltern Women's Perspective'. In *Challenging the Rules of Law*, edited by Kalpana Kannabiran and Ranbir Singh, 48–77. New Delhi: Sage.

Paper in Journal

Galanter, Mark. 1969. 'Untouchability and the Law'. *Economic and Political Weekly* 4, nos 1/2 (January): 133–70.

Nawsagaray, Nitish. 2018. 'Scrutinising the Mahajan Judgment, 2018: Misuse of the Prevention of Atrocities Act'. *Economic and Political Weekly* 53, no. 22. Available at https://www.epw.in/journal/2018/22/special-articles/misuse-prevention-atrocities-act.html. Last accessed on 20 July 2020.

Web Links

Ambedkar, B.R. 1945. 'Communal Deadlock and the Way to Solve It'. Available at http://www.ambedkar.org/ambcd/09.%20Communal%20Deadlock%20and%20a%20Way%20to%20Solve%20It.html. Last accessed on 15 May 2018.

———. 1990. 'Waiting for a Visa'. Available at http://www.ambedkar.org/ambcd/53.%20Waiting%20For%20A%20Visa.htm. Last accessed on 15 May 2018.

Balagopal, Kandapalli. n.d. 'Lecture on Caste and the Law'. Available at http://ia600606.us.archive.org/4/items/BalagopalOnHumanRightsMovementInIndia/3.casteAndLaw.mp3. Last accessed on 15 May 2018.

Bhatia, Gautam. 2016. 'Why the Uniquely Revolutionary Potential of Ambedkar's Constitution Remains Untapped'. *Scroll.in*, 14 April. Available at https://scroll.in/article/806606/why-the-uniquely-revolutionary-potential-of-ambedkars-constitution-remains-untapped. Last accessed on 16 June 2018.

Doddahatti, Bindu. 2018. 'Flawed Official Data Is Responsible for the Myth of "Misuse" of SC/ST Law'. *The Wire*, 10 April. Available at https://thewire.in/caste/flawed-official-data-and-the-idea-of-misuse-of-law. Last accessed on 16 June 2018.

Mehta, Pratap Bhanu. 2010. 'What Is Constitutional Morality?' *Seminar* 615, November. Available at http://www.india-seminar.com/2010/615/615_pratap_bhanu_mehta.htm. Last accessed on 1 January 2020.

Narvison, Jan, and James Streba. 2019. 'A Millennial Struggle for Dignity: Manual Scavenging in Karnataka'. Available at http://puclkarnataka.org/wp-content/uploads/2019/06/ManualScavengingReport_May-25-Final.pdf. Last accessed on 30 June 2020.

Peoples Union for Civil Liberties-Karnataka (PUCL-K). 2009. 'Cultural Policing in Dakshina Kannada, Bangalore'. Available at http://young-feminists.wordpress.com/2009/04/20/pucl-report-cultural-policin-gin-dakshin-kannada/. Last accessed on 1 January 2020.

———. 2012. 'Communal Policing by Hindutva Outfits, Bangalore'. Available at http://puclkarnataka.org/?p=672. Last accessed on 1 January 2020.

4

B.R. Ambedkar's Imaginations of Justice

ANTJE LINKENBACH

Babasaheb Ambedkar's Vision of a Just Society

Babasaheb B.R. Ambedkar does not lend himself to an easy categorization. Depending on the particular perspectives and concerns of the recipients he is seen as a dedicated activist and fighter for the rights of India's Dalits, as a politician and main drafter of the Constitution, as a religious reformer and follower of (his own version of) Buddhism, or as an academic and theoretical thinker. Yet, even as a scholar, Dr Ambedkar moved between various disciplines. His conceptual reflections and writings refer to the fields of law, economics, political and social sciences, as well as religious studies. Following both Marx and Buddha, Babasaheb Ambedkar felt the need to link theory and practice in order to not only explain but also *reconstruct* the world (Ambedkar 1987a, 443; emphasis added). The basic normative principle which he thought has the potential to guide practical action and bring about social change is the 'compendious' principle of *justice*: 'Justice has always evoked ideas of equality. ... If all men are equal, all men are of the same essence and the common essence entitled them to the same fundamental rights and to equal liberty. In short justice is simply another name for liberty, equality and fraternity' (Ambedkar 1987b, 25). In Ambedkar's understanding, justice includes all these other principles which 'have become the foundation for a moral order' (1987b, 25) and, therefore, stands out as a valid criterion and appropriate tool for judging right and wrong in the contemporary modern constellation. Moreover, justice acknowledges the human being as an individual being. It takes it at its end and holds 'the moral good ... to be something which does justice to the individual' (1987b, 22).

Following B.R. Ambedkar, for a society to be just, liberty, equality, and fraternity are the necessary preconditions. Additionally, he understands a just society as congruent with democracy (Ambedkar 1989a, 77),[1] because the latter provides the only adequate governmental framework. For Ambedkar, therefore, the ideal (just) society represents a complex social, political, and (religiously based) moral imaginary. Let me specify this.

Starting with *democracy*: A true democratic government is for Ambedkar a 'government by the people and for the people' (Ambedkar 1991, 444). To fulfil this ambitious promise parliamentary democracy is not sufficient—and he is convinced that the failure of Western European democracies has given proof of this. Parliamentary democracy has never succeeded to 'assure to the masses the right to liberty, property or the pursuit of happiness' as it 'has never been a government of the people or by the people', but in reality a 'government of a hereditary subject class by a hereditary ruling class' (1991, 446–7). Parliamentary democracy only focuses on liberty, not on equality, but political democracy cannot succeed without economic and social democracy—they are 'the tissues and the fibre of a political democracy' (1991, 447). In modern language we would say that Ambedkar precedes Nancy Fraser's request for 'parity of participation' in the economic, social, and political realm.

Babasahab Ambedkar seems to have been aware of the fact that democratic structures encourage civil society. In their capacity as members of civil society people struggle for human values, thus turning civil society into the 'conscience-keeper' of the political sphere with the ability to influence the course of the government in the long run (Rodrigues 2002, 34). Besides other institutions

[1] Ambedkar argues that fraternity is another name for democracy (1989a, 57). Elsewhere, he says that '[d]emocracy is another name for equality', and that '[p]arliamentary democracy developed a passion for liberty' (1991, 447).

such as political parties, unions, or associations, *religions* occupy a significant place in civil society as each religion upholds certain values and, thus, is the main source of morality. This leads to the next aspect.

Religion: Babasaheb Ambedkar's ideal society is not one without religion, although God and the transcendent have no place in it. Ambedkar seriously studied different religions as he saw their importance in upholding moral claims.[2] In his text 'Marx or Buddha' he makes a strong argument by saying that '[h]umanity does not only want economic values, it also wants spiritual values to be retained' and adds that '[m]an must grow materially as well as spiritually' (Ambedkar 1987a, 461). He came to the conclusion that only in the 'secular religion' of Buddhism the values of liberty, equality, and fraternity are fully realized, and he confesses: '[I]t cannot be too much emphasized that in producing equality, society cannot afford to sacrifice fraternity or liberty. Equality will be of no value without fraternity or liberty. It seems that *the three can coexist only if one follows the way of the Buddha*' (Ambedkar 1987a, 462; emphasis added). As far as the method of social transformation is concerned, Ambedkar dismisses violence and all forms of constraint, but favours the Buddhist non-violent way of altering dispositions, so that people 'would do voluntarily what they would not otherwise do' (Ambedkar 1987a, 461).

Sociality: Against the backdrop of the everyday experiences of Dalits, who constantly have to endure lack of respect and even humiliation, sociality—in the sense of community, solidarity, and fraternity—is at the very heart of Ambedkar's vision. He asks: what is essential for the constitution of a society, and answers: Men constitute a society because they have things that they possess in common, because they act together. It is not enough to have similar things or follow parallel activities as in a caste society; this does not bind people together into an integral whole. An integrated society is based on communication; 'Society continues to exist by communication[,] indeed in communication' (Ambedkar 1989a, 51). The caste society with its occupational segregation, denial of

[2] Srivatsan argues that for Ambedkar '[r]eligion is a social form of cultivating individual conduct through moral action. It is an absolutely necessary secular form of social existence through which the community ensures its sustenance, survival and prosperity' (2017, 101).

commensality, caste endogamy, and the overall idea of purity–pollution fosters an 'anti-social spirit' and prevents any attempt of opening up to the other, of communication and solidarity. It precludes fellow feeling, emotional imagination, and sympathy, especially with the deserving and the sufferer (Ambedkar 1989a, 51–8).[3] For Babasaheb Ambedkar, however, all these qualities are the fundament of sociality, of (what we would call) a functioning and cohesive social life. A cohesive society implies that the existing diversity of interests is consciously and openly communicated and shared. It, thus, presupposes mutual recognition and respect, and free and respectful interaction and dialogue between all members across differences.

If we position Ambedkar's social imaginary in the context of contemporary egalitarian theories and theories of justice, we have to admit that his ideas are in line with the most advanced of them. While John Rawls (1999) in his theory of distributive justice focuses on liberty and equality of opportunity but still gives recognition a rather marginal place, Nancy Fraser postulates a 'bivalent' conception of justice that 'encompasses both distribution and recognition without reducing either one of them to the other' (Fraser 1996, 30). She includes a moral and universalistic understanding of equality, which is voiced, for example, by Ronald Dworkin (1977), is inherent in Elizabeth Anderson's egalitarian theory (1999), and also underlies the work of Avishai Margalit (1998): Every person has the same moral values and because of that the core of equality is about *being treated as equals*. Applying this to the idea of a just society we have to claim that all members of a society should stand *in relations of equality and should be treated/treat each other as equals*. This is the basic demand of Babasaheb Ambedkar, with one difference: While in Fraser's approach the universal value of equal worth and dignity of human beings is philosophically grounded, Dr Ambedkar's ideas are based on (Buddhist) religion.

[3] Ambedkar's focus on sociality shows his familiarity with American pragmatist theory, especially with John Dewey's work. For an analysis of Ambedkar's pragmatist background, see Fuchs (2001 and 2019); concepts such as communication, fellow feeling, and sympathy refer back to representatives of Scottish enlightenment such as David Hume and Adam Smith.

Promises of the Indian Constitution and (the Long Way to) Constitutional Morality

In the introduction to her book 'Tools of Justice' Kalpana Kannabiran claims that 'the Indian constitution gives voice to counter-hegemonic imaginations of justice' (Kannabiran 2012, 1). This statement refers to the far-reaching promises this Constitution makes to its citizens, especially to the deprived sections of society. The promise of *JUSTICE* (*social, economic, political*) is the subject of the Preamble of the Constitution of India. In addition, the Preamble promises *LIBERTY* of thought, expression, belief, faith, and worship; *EQUALITY* of status and of opportunity; and to promote *FRATERNITY*, assuring the dignity of the individual and the unity (and integrity) of the nation.

The following parts of the Constitution expand on its foundations voiced in the Preamble. They address the equal right of *Citizenship*, and the *Fundamental Rights*, which include the right to equality, to freedom, the right against exploitation, the right of freedom of religion, and cultural and educational rights. The right to equality is particularly important as it contains Article 15, prohibition against all forms of discrimination, demanding special provisions for SC/ST, Article 16 for equality of opportunity, and Article 17 abolishing Untouchability. The right to freedom cares (among other things) for life and liberty of the individual (Art. 21), while the cultural rights (Art. 29) demand recognition for minorities, that is groups with distinct forms of language, script, or culture. A quick view of the Fundamental Duties (IV A) reveals that, among other duties, the Constitution demands all Indian citizens 'to promote harmony and the spirit of common brotherhood amongst all the people of India transcending religious, linguistic and regional or sectional diversities; to renounce practices derogatory to the dignity of women' (51 Ae). To summarize, Ambedkar's vision of justice as equality, liberty, and fraternity seems very much mirrored in the Indian Constitution, which he was largely responsible for drafting. However, this is not the whole story.

In his speech to introduce the draft Constitution in the Constituent Assembly on 4 November 1948, B.R. Ambedkar raised concerns about whether the State administration as governing body will respect the constitutional form and function according to the 'spirit of the Constitution' (Ambedkar 1994, 60–1). He sees the precondition for 'the peaceful working of a democratic Constitution' in 'constitutional morality', a concept he took from George Grote, a classicist and historian of Rome. By quoting Grote, Dr Ambedkar explains 'constitutional morality' as:

> A paramount reverence for the forms of the Constitution, enforcing obedience to authority acting under and within these forms yet combined with the habit of open speech, of action subject only to definite legal control, and unrestrained censure of those very authorities as to all their public acts combined too with a perfect confidence in the bosom of every citizen amidst the bitterness of party contest that the forms of the Constitution will not be less sacred in the eyes of his opponents than in his own. (Ambedkar 1994, 60–1)

For Kalpana Kannabiran the idea of constitutional morality signposts the inauguration of a new social order in the subcontinent (Kannabiran 2012, 1), and Pratap Bhanu Mehta (2010) highlights the special significance the concept had for Babasaheb Ambedkar. Mehta argues that exceeding two commonly attributed meanings of 'constitutional morality', Grote brought forward a third and more important one. In common understanding, constitutional morality first refers to the *contents* of the constitution and, thus, to the morality *of* the constitution; second, it refers to the 'conventions and protocols that govern decision-making where the constitution vests discretionary power or is silent' (Mehta 2010, 2). The third way of understanding constitutional morality stresses the constitutional *form* and not a particular substance. It highlights 'formal elements' such as freedom and self-restraint, thus abandoning all (violent and non-violent) forms of revolutionary political action; recognition of plurality, which includes respectful management and adjudication of differences; and scepticism about authoritative claims to 'singularly and uniquely represent the will of the people' (Mehta 2010, 4), thus expressing concern for an open culture of criticism.

Ambedkar demands a culture of constant and consequent interrogation, possible only in a democratic environment that does not a priori claim to represent the will of the people.[4]

[4] It is 'Constitution's impulse that there should be no singularly authoritative arbiter of either popular will, or constitutional interpretation' (Mehta 2010, 5).

By stressing the formal aspects of constitutional morality, Dr Ambedkar points out that constitutionalism is basically a mode of association, 'a form of political organization sustained by certain ways of doing things' and 'not so much by objectives as by the conditions through which they were realized' (Mehta 2010, 6). A constitution for Ambedkar is not based on the relationship between concrete persons, but between abstract *personae* bound together by abstract rules. However, Babasaheb Ambedkar deeply knew that caste prevents the formation of a self that has the ability for abstraction and dissociation: to abstract from one's identity and belonging, to dissociate from one's views; 'to trust someone despite deep disagreement based on the knowledge that there is a shared agreement on processes to adjudicate that disagreement' (Mehta 2010, 6–7). Caste undermines the constitutional culture and morality. Caste embodies the principle of separation and, therefore, is opposed to the idea and praxis of association, cooperation, communication, and critique. In short: what is missing in a caste society is the ability to see in each person first of all a human being.

It is hardly surprising that Babasaheb Ambedkar was sceptical about the actual realization of constitutional morality in a caste-based society. Constitutional morality, he says, is not a 'natural sentiment' but has to be cultivated, especially in India because '[d]emocracy ... is only a top-dressing on an Indian soil, which is essentially undemocratic' (Ambedkar 1994, 61). The Indian Constitution consequently demands laws and provisions instrumental for the abolishment of caste, caste discrimination and violence, and caste-based disadvantages. With that the Constitution itself creates the conditions of possibility for constitutional morality—but in the light of its very high standards the realization might take a long time.

The Realities of Justice in Contemporary India

The lived realities of particular groups in India—Dalits, women, Adivasis—give striking evidence of the lack of constitutional morality nearly seventy years since Independence and the promulgation of the Constitution.

In her book *Justice and the Politics of Difference*, written from a feminist perspective and attempting to unravel injustices experienced by different social groups in the USA, Iris Young identifies 'five faces of oppression' and categorizes them as exploitation, marginalization, powerlessness, cultural imperialism, and violence (Young 1990). Although Young's categories are overlapping and probably not fully adequate to grasp all the nuances of the contemporary Indian situation, they seem to be helpful to identify and throw light on the different forms of oppression that Indian marginalized groups have still to endure. I will refer to these different forms of oppression in a very general way, not accounting for regional differences and merely indicating some and not expanding on the problems. I will refer to Dalits and Hindu women, paying attention to intersectionality; afterwards and separately I will briefly touch upon the predicament of the Adivasi.

Mechanisms of *exploitation* develop and function under particular conditions in the social, political, and economic structural set-up of a society. The basic condition refers to property relations and expresses itself in the exclusion of certain individuals or group of people from ownership and control of the means of production. In rural India land, respectively landlessness, is still the main marker of exclusion and exploitative relationships, and Dalits are usually those with no or only little property and, thus, forced to work as labourers on the fields of the landowning high-caste groups. Land reforms were not always effective. Sometimes the amount of distributed land was insufficient, sometimes the land was of bad quality, so that sooner or later farmers were driven again into the debt trap and ended up as (semi-)bonded labourers. Although urban spaces allow Dalits to transcend occupational barriers, many of those who live in cities are still found to be working in the informal, especially the service, sector and have to undertake polluting work.

Iris Young understands exploitation basically in terms of labour transfer, thus marginalizing the structural preconditions of such an exploitative mechanism. For her, exploitation indicates 'a steady process of the transfer of the results of the labor of one social group to benefit another' (Young 1990, 49). While this also applies to Dalit service castes, it grasps especially gender exploitation: 'transfer of the fruits of material labor to men and transfer of nurturing and sexual energies to men' (Young 1990, 45). In Indian society—as in most other hierarchical and patriarchal societies—marriage appears as the sociocultural institution that creates the possibility for such a form of material and sexual exploitation, which then is instrumental in creating dependency and strengthening gender inequality.

Again, in the Indian context the appropriation of women's labour in production and reproduction is most visible and severe in rural, agricultural areas; here, structural conditions such as the inability to actually control landed property hold women in an ongoing dependency on the husband and in-laws,[5] and the amount and arduousness of agricultural and household work contributes to their instrumentalization. Certain tasks in the household, such as fetching water, caring for the small children, and serving the male members of the family, are often the duty of young girls, who are so naturally socialized into the serving and caring role and do get no or only little time for education, leave alone leisure.

Marginalization and powerlessness are two interconnected forms of oppression and of crucial importance in the Indian context where they have a particular manifestation: both are the consequence of the social hierarchies of caste, which in turn intersect significantly not only with class but also with gender.

Many low-caste people, in particular Dalits, are often confined to lives of social marginality. Young's definition of marginality applies here: it means that these people are 'expelled from useful participation in social life and thus potentially subjected to severe and material deprivation and even extermination' (Young 1990, 53).[6] Marginality in India is mostly owed to caste stigmatization and discrimination, deeply interconnected with occupation. The majority of Dalits is still engaged in (polluting) manual labour—they work as landless labourers, tanners, scavengers, and sewage and toilet cleaners; a great number engages in the informal sector, for example as ragpickers and garbage collectors. Marginality also means powerlessness in all aspects of life: poor health, low education, experiencing humiliation and disrespect, and often culminating in physical violence. The powerless lack autonomy, authority, status, and a sense of self. They are denied participation and recognition, and all this mirrors in their overall social behaviour.

[5] I cannot discuss here the more recent legal developments in India such as the implementation of the Hindu Succession (Amendment) Act 2005, which allows daughters to become coparcener in their natal family. In many cases, this Act does not produce the desired effect because of structural conditions (patrilocality) and cultural prejudices and beliefs.

[6] Young's central criterion for marginalization is race in the United States of America.

Even the situation of those who profit from anti-discrimination policies is not without ambivalence. Critical scholars argue that, on the one hand, these policies are absolutely beneficial for the hitherto excluded section of the society but, on the other hand, improvements result in new fields and forms of marginalization. The education system is often mentioned as the prime example as it brings new orders of ranking and segregation in social relations (see, for example, Sukumar 2013). Stigmatization continues, for example, through welfare schemes in schools (free food, free learning material for Dalits), discriminatory treatment by teachers and professors, and inadequate housing (hostel) situation.

How does marginalization and powerlessness play out for women? In present times women—especially of higher status groups, but also some of the lower caste groups—have access to education, particularly in urban contexts. Women work, participate in politics and public social life, and may enjoy a certain extent of autonomy. However, the degree of freedom depends on the family setting and the determination and strength of the individual person. The cultural concept of Hindu womanhood is still a dominant part of the Brahmanical ideology and guides the attitudes and practices in the majority of families. Due to this concept, a woman's freedom can be extremely limited and she can be degraded to a subordinate position. This applies even more to low-caste women whose families belong to the Hindu fold. These women have not only to endure male domination in the family context but also to suffer disregard and disdain from higher social-status groups in the same way as the male Dalit would. However, because of their status as women and, therefore, naturally subordinate to males, they are more vulnerable and far more frequently the victims of physical and especially sexual violence.

Cultural imperialism, according to Young, denotes the 'universalization of a dominant group's experience and culture and its establishment as the norm' (Young 1990, 59). In Hinduist India the hegemonic interpretation and communication of cultural norms is grounded in Brahmanical scriptures and is still dominating the world view and life of many members of Hindu denominations even today. Of course, alternative interpretations always existed, especially those of the marginalized themselves, of reform groups, and in more recent times from social protest movements such as Dalit and women's movements. Yet, the Brahmanical norms are still very much accepted and even extend their realm of influence. Brahmanical hegemonic interpretations do not only legitimize the hierarchical social order but also the subordination of women and their segregation and exclusion from participation in most areas of social life.

The oppressive power of the Brahmanical hegemonial ideology is best to be captured in B.R. Ambedkar's argument for the conversion of Untouchables. He asks: 'Why should [the] Untouchables adhere to Hinduism which is solely responsible for their degradation? How can the Untouchables stay in Hinduism? Untouchability is the lowest depth to which the degradation of a human being can be carried' (Ambedkar 1989b, 412). And he concludes: 'That Hinduism is inconsistent with the self-respect and honour of the Untouchables is the strongest ground which justifies the conversion of the Untouchables to another and nobler faith' (Ambedkar 1989b, 412).

Violence, another face of oppression, is in all its different articulations a logical extension of the devaluation of Dalits as well as women. Young asks: What makes violence a phenomenon of social injustice, and not merely an individual moral wrong? She provides two answers: Violence is systemic, it is directed at members of a group simply because they are members of that group, and that '[v]iolence is a social practice. It is a social given that everyone knows happens and will happen again. It is always at the horizon of social imagination, even for those who do not perpetrate it' (Young 1990, 62). As far as Dalits are concerned, the stigma of impurity may lead to a de-humanizing treatment of this group even today. Denied full humanity they are in some regions and contexts excluded from participating in major activities of social life, which plays out especially in villages: Dalits are often not allowed to eat together with higher caste groups, marry members of higher status groups, enter temples, use the same water source, enter the kitchen of higher caste homes, and so on. Besides such forms of violence, Dalits who work as agricultural labourers or bonded labourers are maltreated, abused, physically attacked, beaten, and even murdered by landlords and higher-caste village members.

Dalit women have an additional predicament. With reference to the violence that took place during the Partition of India, Veena Das has argued that women's bodies were redefined as semiotic objects, they functioned as the 'signs on which the violent dialogue between men was conducted' (Das 1995, 70, 186). Das builds on Pierre Clastres, Franz Kafka, and Friedrich Nietzsche when she postulates that the body becomes memory through the infliction of pain. Violence exercised on the female body reminds the woman and her social environment of her subordination and dependency. In case of Dalit women this goes even further. They are not only subordinate to their husbands but also to all male members of higher castes. Sexually violated Dalit female bodies are memory in the sense that they give evidence not only of the inferiority of Dalit women but also of the inferiority of Dalit men and, thus, of the whole group.

Finally, I want to touch upon the predicament of India's Adivasis. They live under oppressive conditions too, but the context and reason for their marginalization and subordination are different as they are not based on the ideas and practices of caste but on the ideas and practices of race and stage of human development. Adivasis are concentrated in particular regions of India, have different colonial and post-colonial histories and religious allegiances, and follow traditional ways of life. Their current socio-economic and political situation within the Indian nation state has to be understood in this wider context. Many Adivasis still live in close relationship to the natural environment and are, therefore, immediately affected not only by the so-called development projects such as construction of hydroelectric dams, extraction of minerals, and large-scale industrialization but also by projects aimed at the conservation of nature. Many of these projects force Adivasis to sacrifice their land, forests, and water for the 'greater good', and with that their well-being and often even their cultural integrity. As a result, Adivasis have to face displacement and forced resettlement, and in most cases are insufficiently rehabilitated. Facing impoverishment, for many of them the only option is to move to the slums of the cities, try to make a living there, and only retain the memories of their previous ways of life. In the case of Adivasis, exploitation, marginalization, powerlessness, and violence predominantly occur under the mask of development, although land appropriation, deprivation, and displacement also happen in the name of sustainability and environmental protection. As in the case of Dalits, oppression of the Adivasis is basically caused by lack of recognition, not only of individuals or groups but of a whole way of life.

The main reason for this neglect and lack of recognition of Adivasis by the non-tribal world seems to be the fundamental difference between the Adivasi life world and the modern conditions of life. Adivasis have a different way of relating to nature; they also have different views regarding property relations, sociality, gender, the place of humans within the cosmos, and development or progress. Because of these differences tribals were and are still classified as inferior, primitive, savage, barbarian. Adivasis are seen as representatives of an earlier stage of life, a primitive past, and for many they do no longer have a legitimate space in the world as it is today. Adivasis have to be kept in dependence and bondage, or they have to be converted and civilized, or they simply have to vanish.

Concluding Remarks

B.R. Ambedkar was a visionary, and Arundhati Roy in her introduction of a new edition of Babasaheb Ambedkar's *Annihilation of Caste* calls this important essay a piece of utopian thinking (Roy 2014). She places it in the tradition of anti-Brahmanist movements, and especially relates it to the subaltern Bhakti poetry of Kabir, Raidas, or Tukaram and their imagination of a city without sorrow and humiliation, liberated from the bonds of Brahmanism; in short, a city of love. Ambedkar, according to Roy, imagined a *city of justice*, and saw the only hope for Dalits and the suppressed classes in modernity, liberalism, industrialization, and urbanism. For her, Babasaheb Ambedkar's vision is clearly opposed to Gandhi's nostalgic village utopia celebrating the 'uniquely Indian pastoral bliss' (Roy 2014, 49). However, Roy's very brief evaluation of both utopias sounds slightly superficial and requires a more nuanced analysis. Simply saying that both utopias were somehow right and 'grievously wrong' (Roy 2014, 49)[7] is not enough. Roy does not, for example, sufficiently emphasize that Gandhi's programme of village reconstruction never seriously challenged

[7] While Gandhi was right in his critique of development, he overlooked injustices in the village. Ambedkar, who saw the village as a 'sink of localism, a den of ignorance, narrow-mindedness and communalism', was blind with regard to the environmental and social consequences of urbanism, modernism, and industrialization.

the basic evil of Indian society, namely caste—and exactly that was the target of Dr Ambedkar's work and vision. On the other side, she overlooked that Babasaheb Ambedkar had difficulties to acknowledge that India is also home of non- or less hierarchical groups such as tribal minorities that cannot be classified as primitive or even criminal (Ambedkar 1989a, 52) but follow alternative and valid forms of life.

B.R. Ambedkar's vision was based on a euphoric trust in Western enlightenment and the idea of progress and social improvement through industrialization and urbanization. It obviously was not very different from the Nehruvian vision and the later post-colonial politics of development. Like Nehru, Dr Ambedkar did not anticipate the dangers of industrialization for the environment, people's health and well-being, unequal distribution of the benefits and burdens of development, and marginalization, especially of those populations which are still dependent on nature for their subsistence. Ambedkar, in the 1930s, was convinced that tribal populations live in a savage state and for their own benefit need to be civilized to change to a more 'honourable way of making a living' (Ambedkar 1989a, 53). He accused the Hindus for not having fulfilled such a civilizing mission (he draws a comparison with the work of Christian missionaries!) and saw the reason in caste society. 'Civilising the aborigines means adopting them as your own, living in their midst, and cultivating fellow-feeling, in short loving them' (Ambedkar 1989a, 53).

We see from today's perspective that the strange and derogatory passage on Adivasis in B.R. Ambedkar's text is nevertheless part of his general social imaginary: creating a cohesive and integrated—that is, non-hierarchical—society where people respect, love, and treat each other as equals, communicate freely, and join in the pursuit of common projects as well as the political project of building a nation.

How to put such a vision into practice? With the Constitution, Ambedkar established the *conditions of possibility* to create a just society, and the Directive Principles were meant as 'instructions to the Legislature and Executive' (Ambedkar 1994, 65) to implement laws and policies that can enforce justice with regard to all sections of society. However, the realities of (in)justice in India prove that this is not enough. What is still missing is the prevalence of constitutional morality. The latter requires, as Ambedkar himself knew, a fundamental change of 'philosophy of life' or 'outlook' of the ruling castes and classes. For Ambedkar, being a follower of Buddha, forcing people 'to do what they did not like to do' (Ambedkar 1987a, 461) was not an option; instead, he pleaded for peaceful forms of persuasion and political measures to counteract caste and gender hierarchies and discrimination. The history and successes of Dalit and women's struggles in independent India give proof that Ambedkar's strategies have at least started to produce the desired outcome. Many Dalits and women have succeeded in developing their own capabilities and building up self-confidence and self-esteem. They became visible and audible in the public space, for example, through literary engagement as well as social and political activism.

Altering attitudes deeply rooted in unjust cultural traditions and mindsets requires determination as well as patience. Babasaheb Ambedkar not only created a broad awareness of oppression and ignited the spark of a new life, he also provided important instruments for the struggle. However, the struggle itself has to be fought anew every day and by each and every person or group concerned.

References

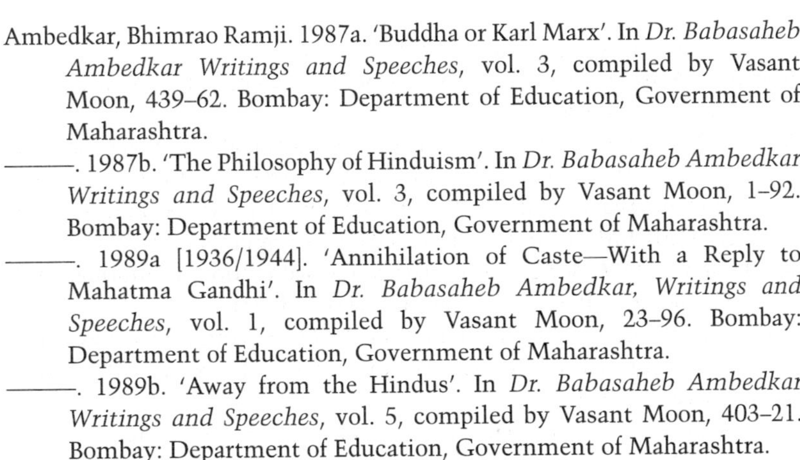

Ambedkar, Bhimrao Ramji. 1987a. 'Buddha or Karl Marx'. In *Dr. Babasaheb Ambedkar Writings and Speeches*, vol. 3, compiled by Vasant Moon, 439–62. Bombay: Department of Education, Government of Maharashtra.

———. 1987b. 'The Philosophy of Hinduism'. In *Dr. Babasaheb Ambedkar Writings and Speeches*, vol. 3, compiled by Vasant Moon, 1–92. Bombay: Department of Education, Government of Maharashtra.

———. 1989a [1936/1944]. 'Annihilation of Caste—With a Reply to Mahatma Gandhi'. In *Dr. Babasaheb Ambedkar, Writings and Speeches*, vol. 1, compiled by Vasant Moon, 23–96. Bombay: Department of Education, Government of Maharashtra.

———. 1989b. 'Away from the Hindus'. In *Dr. Babasaheb Ambedkar Writings and Speeches*, vol. 5, compiled by Vasant Moon, 403–21. Bombay: Department of Education, Government of Maharashtra.

———. 1991. 'Mr. Gandhi and the Emancipation of the Untouchables'. In *Dr. Babasaheb Ambedkar Writings and Speeches*, vol. 9, edited by Vasant Moon, 389–489. Bombay: Department of Education, Government of Maharashtra.

———. 1994. 'Draft Constitution—Discussion: Motion *Re*-draft Constitution'. In *Dr. Babasaheb Ambedkar, Writings and Speeches*, vol. 13, edited by Vasant Moon, 49–70. Bombay: Department of Education, Government of Maharashtra.

Anderson, Elizabeth O. 1999. 'What Is the Point of Equality?' *Ethics* 109, no. 2: 287–337.

Das, Veena. 1995. *Critical Events: An Anthropological Perspective on Contemporary India*. Delhi: Oxford University Press.

Dworkin, Ronald. 1977. *Taking Rights Seriously*. Cambridge: Harvard University Press.

Fraser, Nancy. 1996. *Social Justice in the Age of Identity Politics: Redistribution, Recognition, and Participation*. The Tanner Lectures on Human Values, delivered at Stanford University, 30 April–2 May 1996, 1–67. Avaliable at https://tannerlectures.utah.edu/_documents/a-to-z/f/Fraser98.pdf. Last accessed on 15 September 2017.

Fuchs, Martin. 2001. 'A Religion for Civil Society? Ambedkar's Buddhism, the Dalit Issue and the Imagination of Emergent Possibilities'. In *Charisma and Canon: Essays on the Religious History of the Indian Subcontinent*, edited by Vasudha Dalmia, Angelika Malinar, and Martin Christof, 250–73. New Delhi: Oxford University Press.

———. 2019. 'Dhamma and the Common Good: Religion as Problem and Answer: Ambedkar's Critical Theory of Social Relationality'. In *Religious Interactions in Modern India*, edited by Martin Fuchs and Vasudha Dalmia, 364–413. New Delhi: Oxford University Press.

Kannabiran, Kalpana. 2012. *Tools of Justice: Non-discrimination and the Indian Constitution*. London: Routledge.

Margalit, Avishai. 1998. *The Decent Society*. Cambridge, MA: Harvard University Press.

Mehta, Pratap Bhanu. 2010. 'What Is Constitutional Morality?' *Seminar 615: We the People, A Symposium on the Constitution of India after 60 Years, 1950–2010*. Available at http://www.india-seminar.com/2010/615.htm. Last accessed on 15 September 2017.

Rawls, John. 1999. *A Theory of Justice*, revised edition. Cambridge, MA: The Belknap Press of Harvard University Press.

Rodrigues, Valerian. 2002. 'Introduction'. In *The Essential Writings of B.R. Ambedkar*, edited by Valerian Rodrigues, 1–43. New Delhi: Oxford University Press.

Roy, Arundhati. 2014. 'The Doctor and the Saint, Introduction to B.R. Ambedkar'. In *Annihilation of Caste. The Annotated Critical Edition*, edited and compiled by S. Anand, 15–179. London and New York: Verso.

Srivatsan, R. 2017. 'Ambedkar's Framing of Religious Ideas'. *Economic and Political Weekly* 52, no. 33: 100–1.

Sukumar, N. 2013. 'Quota's Children: The Perils of Getting Educated'. In *Beyond Inclusion: The Practice of Equal Access in Indian Higher Education*, edited by Satish Deshpande and Usha Zacharias. New Delhi: Routledge.

The Constitution of India (as on 9 November 2015). New Delhi: Ministry of Law and Justice, Legislative Department, Government of India. Available at http://lawmin.nic.in/olwing/coi/coi-english/coi-4March 2016.pdf. Last accessed on 15 September 2017.

Young, Iris Marion. 1990. *Justice and the Politics of Difference*. Princeton, NJ: Princeton University Press.

5

The Significance of Rights and Rule of Law under the Indian Constitutional Framework

UMAKANT

Under the Indian constitutional framework, what was most important at the time of its drafting was to ensure a stable form of government with a clearly defined set of rules and regulations, not only to govern the country but also at the same time to maintain the country's unity and diversity. In other words, the other concern was to have a Constitution which could be sustained over a long period of time as per the changing needs along the way of the country's onward march. There was a consensus among the members of the Constituent Assembly about the need for an all-inclusive Constitution fully and fairly designed to promote and protect the needs and rights of people belonging to different castes and religious communities. Speaking on the means adopted by the Drafting Committee, Dr Ambedkar said, 'The means adopted were three: (i) a single judiciary, (ii) uniformity in fundamental laws, civil and criminal, and (iii) a common All India Civil Service to man important posts' (Lok Sabha Secretariat 1948; cited in Ambedkar 1994, 58). He further went on to say,

> One likes to ask whether there can be anything new in a Constitution framed at this hour in the history of the world. More than hundred years have rolled over when the first written Constitution

> was drafted. It has been followed by many countries reducing their Constitutions to writing. What the scope of a Constitution should be has long been settled. Similarly what are the fundamentals of a Constitution are recognized all over the world. Given these facts all Constitutions in their main provisions must look similar. The only new things, if there can be any, in a Constitution framed so late in the day are the variations made to remove the faults and to accommodate it to the needs of the country. (Lok Sabha Secretariat 1948; cited in Ambedkar 1994, 59)

The question that needs to be asked is this: Is the Constitution merely a document of rules, guidelines, and formalities that are required for a state's smooth functioning? This is certainly a question of paramount importance in a sense that it probes what the aims and objectives are of framing a Constitution for a newly liberated country where inequality, social divisions, lack of harmony, and fraternal relations had been the defining characteristics for a long time in its history? That such and other important questions relating to the nature of the State did bother the framers of the Indian Constitution is evident from the fact that Dr Ambedkar had a very strong opinion on these kinds of issues that could otherwise flare up a lot of confusion among the framers. Very categorically, he stated:

> The purpose of a Constitution is not merely to create organs of the State, but to limit their authority, because if no limitations are imposed upon the authority of the organs, there will be complete tyranny and complete oppression. The legislature may be free to frame any law, the executive may be free to take any decision; and the Supreme Court may be free to give any interpretation of law, it would result in utter chaos. (Lok Sabha Secretariat 1949, 1662; cited in Agarwal 1991, 13)

Such an opinion was certainly expressed to explain the purpose behind creating an orderly set-up which could smartly deal with different organs of the State in a balancing manner. 'The Indian Constitution may be summarized as having three strands: protecting and enhancing national unity and integrity; establishing the institutions and spirit of democracy; and fostering a social revolution to better the lot of the mass of Indians. The framers believed that the three strands are mutually dependent and inextricably intertwined' (Austin 1999, 6).

The Indian Constitution has matured over the years by overcoming several trials and tribulations. It cannot be looked at merely as a legal document underlining the basic philosophy or tools of governance; rather, it should be seen as a living document in the form of principles and guidelines depicting everyday realities of the country as a whole for a judicious functioning of the government and also for ensuring socio-economic and political justice to people at large. In *The Oxford Handbook of the Indian Constitution*, the authors have argued,

> [t]he Constitution has evolved through both partnership and contestation between different branches of government. The Supreme Court, may, on occasion, draw a red line through what legislatures can do; it can claim adjudicatory supremacy. But equally the legislature can deeply transform the shape of the Constitution, as it has done through a hundred amendments. Importantly, however, the Constitution is not solely shaped by duly instituted branches of government. Both legislatures and courts also respond to what might be understood as their readings of popular constitutionalism. There is a productive tension between the formal and legalistic understandings of constitutional law and the popular expectations and demands on constitutional law. As Ambedkar had envisaged, constitution is not just a noun; it is also a verb. It is co-produced by the collaboration and participants of different actors, where any claim to authority will always be contested. (Choudhry, Khosla, and Mehta 2016, 12)

The Foundation and the Nature of Indian Constitution

Adherence to a set of rules and regulations becomes quite an important element and also the founding principle on which any Constitution can work. In the absence of such principles and guidelines, a complete anarchical situation may emerge in different organs of the State and in the society at large. Speaking in the Constituent Assembly on 4 November 1948, Ambedkar made reference to Grote, a Grecian historian, who had said:

> The diffusion of constitutional morality, not merely among the majority of any community but throughout the whole, is the indispensable condition of a government at once free and peaceable; since even any powerful and obstinate minority may render the working of a free institution impracticable, without being strong enough to conquer ascendency for themselves. (Lok Sabha Secretariat 1948, cited in Ambedkar 1994, 60)

By constitutional morality, Grote meant

> a paramount reverence for the forms of the Constitution, enforcing obedience to authority acting under and within these forms yet combined with the habit of open speech, of action subject only to definite legal control, and unrestrained censure of those very authorities as to all their public acts combined too with a perfect confidence in the bosom of every citizen amidst the bitterness of party contest that the forms of the Constitution will not be less sacred in the eyes of his opponents than in his own. (Lok Sabha Secretariat 1948, cited in Ambedkar 1994, 60)

Ambedkar also observed:

> While everybody recognizes the necessity of the diffusion of Constitutional morality for the peaceful working of a democratic Constitution, there are two things interconnected with it which are not, unfortunately, generally recognized. One is that the form of administration has a close connection with the form of the Constitution. The form of the administration must be appropriate to and in the same sense as the form of the Constitution. The other is that it is perfectly possible to pervert the Constitution, without changing its form by merely changing the form of the administration and to make it inconsistent and opposed to the spirit of the Constitution. It follows that it is only where people are saturated with Constitutional morality such as the one described by Grote the historian that one can take the risk of omitting from the Constitution details of administration and leaving it for the Legislature to prescribe them. The question is, can we presume such a diffusion of Constitutional morality? Constitutional morality is not a natural sentiment. It has to be cultivated. We must realize that our people have yet to learn it. Democracy in India is only a top-dressing on an Indian soil, which is essentially undemocratic. In these circumstances it is wiser not to trust the Legislature to prescribe forms of administration. This is the justification for incorporating them in the Constitution. (Lok Sabha Secretariat 1948, cited in Ambedkar 1994, 60–1)

The most defining characteristic of any constitution is the social, economic, and political foundation that it proposes to construct. This task was such a big challenge for the framers of the Indian Constitution that every effort was made by them to prepare a constitution which could turn the destiny of a newly independent country and its people at large and lead them on the path of egalitarianism and justice. Considering that this was such a gigantic task, it was but natural that the Constitution-makers opted for a unitary as well as a federal system of governance, taking into account the need for unity in diversity as the guiding force for the future political set-up of the country. In another sense this is also to state the fact that people should shun any diversionary means of achieving the goals for a united India. K. Maitra, thus, rightly quotes A. Stepan's observation:

> The Indian Constitution has been characterized as having a 'holding-together' model of federalism, as opposed to the 'coming-together' model associated with the US-style federalism. As an evidence for this Stepan refers to Ambedkar's comment in his speech to the Constituent Assembly while presenting the draft Constitution in 1949 where Ambedkar explicitly notes that the Constitution was 'designed to maintain the unity of India—in short, to hold it together'. Stepan further argues that given India's internal diversity—linguistic, religious and cultural—this 'holding-together' model allowed far more flexibility to the central government. (Stepan 1999, 22; cited in Maitra 2012, 313)

Dr Ambedkar wanted to ensure that the draft Constitution produced by the Drafting Committee suited the needs of the people. The committee itself had suggested certain amendments to improve the draft Constitution. However, taking into consideration the debates in the Constituent Assembly, Dr Ambedkar felt encouraged to say that the Constitution as drafted by the Drafting Committee was good enough to make a beginning. In his own words:

> I feel that it is workable, it is flexible and it is strong enough to hold the country together both in peace time and in war time. Indeed, if I may say so, if things go wrong under the new Constitution, the reason will not be that we had a bad Constitution. What we will have to say is that Man was vile. (Lok Sabha Secretariat 1948; cited in Ambedkar 1994, 70)

Essence of a Modern Constitution: Fundamental Rights and Directive Principles of State Policy

A modern Constitution without detailed provisions for protecting people's rights and dignity, and without the guiding principles for ensuring justice (social, economic, and political) would certainly turn out to be a failed exercise as it would be bereft of its commitment of a revolutionary transformation of its traditional society. The need for ensuring basic human rights for everyone irrespective of caste, creed, race, religion, region, language, and other considerations would go a long way in making constitutional and other required arrangements for establishing an egalitarian society based on the notions of liberty, equality, and fraternity. It has been rightly said by T.H. Green, 'It is the business of the State ... to maintain the conditions without which a free exercise of the human faculties is impossible' (Austin 1999, 50).

> The Indian Constitution is first and foremost a social document. The majority of its provisions are directly aimed at furthering the goals of social revolution or attempts to foster this revolution by establishing the conditions necessary for its achievement. Yet despite the permeation of the entire Constitution by the aim of national renascence, the core of the commitment to social revolution lies in Parts III and IV, in the Fundamental Rights and in the Directive Principles of State Policy. These are the conscience of the Constitution. (Austin 1999, 50)

It is essential that every individual should enjoy basic human rights, and the State must ensure such conditions though proper provisions in the Constitution itself. By putting into operation a set of Fundamental Rights the responsibility of the State increases as it becomes the guarantor and custodian of people's aspirations and needs as well as the enforcer of conditions for a positive environment for them to realize their noble aims. However, as there are no absolute rights, what must also be of equal importance are the Fundamental Duties along with reasonable restrictions to be imposed by the State to ensure safety and security whenever a threat arises.

Explaining this concept in the Constituent Assembly, Dr Ambedkar said:

> There can be no doubt that while there are certain Fundamental Rights which the State must guarantee to the individual in order that the individual may have some security and freedom to develop his own personality, it is equally clear that in certain cases where, for instance, the State's very life is in jeopardy, those rights must be subject to a certain amount of limitation. Normal, peaceful times are quite different from times of emergency. In times of emergency

> the life of the State itself is in jeopardy and if the State is not able to protect itself in times of emergency, the individual himself will be found to have lost his very existence. (Lok Sabha Secretariat 1948, 950; cited in Agarwal 1991, 7)

> In the Directive Principles, one finds an even clearer statements of social revolution. They aim at making the Indian masses free in the positive sense, free from the passivity engendered by the centuries of coercion by society and nature, free from the abject physical conditions that had prevented them from fulfilling their best selves. To do this, the State is to apply the precepts contained in the Directive Principles when making laws. These Principles are not justiciable, a Court cannot enforce them, but they are to be, nevertheless, fundamental in the governance of the Country. (Austin 1999, 51–2)

Directive Principles, which are given in the Constitution immediately after the Fundamental Rights, in fact, complement the latter. They aim at directing the State to ensure social and economic justice to individuals. Needless to say, the Directive Principles present a novel feature of the Indian Constitution. The only other constitution of a parliamentary democracy which embodies these principles is that of Ireland. The Directive Principles were criticized by members of the Constituent Assembly. They described them as 'only pious declarations having no binding force' (Lok Sabha Secretariat 1948). All this criticism was found to be superfluous by Dr Ambedkar because the Constitution itself had declared them as having no binding force.

Answering the charge, Dr Ambedkar said,

> If it is said that the Directive Principles have no legal force behind them, I am prepared to admit it. But I am not prepared to admit that they have no sort of binding force at all. Nor am I prepared to concede that they are useless because they have no binding force in law. The Directive Principles are like the Instrument of Instructions which were issued to the Governor-General and to the Governors of the Colonies and to those of India by the British Government under the 1935 Act. Under the Draft Constitution it is proposed to issue such instruments to the President and to the Governors. The texts of these Instruments of Instructions will be found in Schedule IV of the Constitution. What are called Directive Principles is merely another name for Instruments of Instructions. The only difference is that they are instructions to the Legislature and the Executive. Such a thing is to my mind to be welcomed.

Wherever there is a grant of power in general terms for peace, order and good government, it is necessary that it should be accompanied by instructions regulating its exercise. (Lok Sabha Secretariat 1948, cited in Agarwal 1991, 9)

Explaining it further, he said,

That it has no binding force is no argument against their inclusion in the Constitution. There may be a difference of opinion as to the exact place they should be given in the Constitution. I agree that it is somewhat odd that provisions which do not carry positive obligations should be placed in the midst of provisions which do carry positive obligations. In my judgment their proper place is in Schedules 3-A, and 4 which contain Instrument of Instructions to the President and the Governors. For, as I have said, they are really Instruments of Instructions to the Executive and the Legislatures as to how they should exercise their powers. But that is only a matter of arrangement. (Lok Sabha Secretariat 1948, cited in Agarwal 1991, 9)

On Special Provisions for Scheduled Castes and Scheduled Tribes

Dr Ambedkar was highly concerned about the welfare of the lowest of the low, which is why he was of the view that merely abolishing untouchability by law may not be enough to eradicate this menace, nor may it be enough to change the caste Hindu's attitude. Therefore, the Constitution must contain special provisions for their upliftment. The Constitution of India, adopted in 1950, is a total departure from the philosophy, norms, and traditions of the Hindu social order. The adoption of the Constitution was preceded by strong social, religious, and political movements by the Untouchables in the early part of the twentieth century against caste order and Brahmanism. The induction of these viewpoints was particularly facilitated by the nomination of Dr Ambedkar, who led much of the struggle against caste and untouchability as chairman of the Drafting Committee of the Indian Constitution.

The philosophic ethos of the Constitution proclaimed justice, equality, liberty, and fraternity to all Indian citizens, as against rights based on birth. Further, the democratic form of government with elected representatives also provided an opportunity for members of different sections to participate in decision-making on a common platform.

> A section of people in the Indian society were denied of certain basic rights since ancient times with the result they remained economically, socially and educationally backward. Because of the fundamental disparities between the Schedules Castes and Schedules Tribes as compared to other communities and the urgent need for special measures to uplift their status, a clear distinction has been made in the Constitution itself in respect of the SCs (Dalits) and STs (Adivasi).[1]

The Constitution emphasizes 'safeguards' for Scheduled Castes under the 'Special Provisions Relating to Certain Classes' in Part XVI of the Indian Constitution. The Constitution also provides for protection and promotion of their social, economic, educational, cultural, and political interests to bridge the disparities and to bring them at par with other sections of the society. In addition, many articles in Parts III (Fundamental Rights), IV (Directive Principles of State Policy), IX, IX A, and the fifth schedule of the Constitution are a measure of the constitutional concern and commitment towards them.

Constitutional provisions include general measures found in Equality before law (Art. 14), Prohibition of discrimination (Art. 15), and Protection of life and personal liberty (Art. 21). Social safeguards extended specifically to address untouchability and caste-based work and discrimination are found in Abolition of untouchability (Art. 17), Prohibition of trafficking in human beings and forced labour (Art. 23), Prohibition of employment of children in hazardous jobs, and so forth (Art. 24), and Freedom to practice religion (Art. 25). Economic safeguards are provided under the provisions of Articles 23 and 24 stated earlier as well as under Promotion of educational and economic interests of SCs (Art. 46 in Part IV of Directive Principles of State Policy). Educational and cultural safeguards are specified in the Provision for reservation (Art. 15 [4]) and that admission into educational institutions will not be denied (Art. 29 [2]). Employment provisions are made

[1] National Commission for Schedules Castes and Scheduled Tribes, Sixth Report, 1999–2000 and 2000–1, New Delhi, 8.

under Equality of opportunities (Art. 16) and Claim to services and posts (Art. 335). Political representation was based on a compromise between Gandhi and Ambedkar: Reservation of seats in Parliament and state legislatures (Art. 330, 332). Monitoring of the safeguards provided under the Constitution and all other provisions and policies is also provided for by Setting up commission (Art. 338).

In addition, some of the legislations of general nature have greater relevance to Dalit communities: The Untouchability Offences Act, later reformulated as the Protection of Civil Rights Act, 1955, and Rules, 1977; The Scheduled Caste/Scheduled Tribe (Prevention of Atrocities) Act, 1989, and Rules, 1995, and now Amendment Act and Rules, 2016; Bonded Labour (System) Abolition Act, 1976; Employment of Manual Scavengers and Construction of Dry Latrines (Prohibition) Act, 1993; the new Prohibition of Employment as Manual Scavengers and their Rehabilitation Bill, 2013; Devadasi System Abolition Act in the states of Andhra Pradesh (1988), Maharashtra (2006), and Karnataka (1982); Child Labour (Prohibition and Regulation) Act, 1986; Minimum Wages Act, 1948; Equal Remuneration Act, 1976; and Land Reforms Act in different states.

Rule of Law: Due Process of Law versus Procedure Established by Law

The most significant part of the draft Constitution prepared by Ambedkar was that the State should not deprive any person of life, liberty, or property without the due process of law. These were adopted from the Fifth and the Fourteenth Amendments of the Constitution of the United States of America. Forty per cent of litigation in the US Supreme Court during the preceding half-century had centred around the interpretation of the expression 'due process', of which it had been said that in the last analysis it meant exactly what the courts said it meant in any particular case. No other definition was possible.

B.N. Rau, during his visit to the USA and other countries, had discussions with Justice Frankfurter of the US Supreme Court who was of the opinion that the power of review implied in 'due process' was not only undemocratic (because it gave a few judges the vetoing legislation enacted by elected representatives of the nation) but also threw an unfair burden on the judiciary (Kashyap 2010, 489). This view was communicated by B.N. Rau to the Drafting Committee, which introduced a far-reaching change in the clause by replacing the expression 'without due process of law' with 'except according to procedure established by law'. Later during debates, about 20 amendments were moved, each to replace the former phrase by the latter and the latter by the former. It was also said that such a provision would strip the court of its power to look into the merits and demerits of the ground on which the person was deprived of his life and personal liberty (*Constitution Assembly Bebates*: 7, 843).

At this stage, Dr Ambedkar added,

> I myself cannot altogether omit the possibility of a legislature packed by party men making laws which may abrogate or violate what we regard as certain fundamental principles affecting life and liberties of an individual. At the same time, I do not see how five or six gentlemen sitting in the Federal or Supreme Court could examine the laws made by the legislature and by dint of their own individual conscience or their bias or their prejudices be trusted to determine which law is good and which law is bad. It is rather a case where a man has to sail between Charybdis and Scylla and therefore I would not say anything. I would leave it to the House to decide in any way it likes. (Lok Sabha Secretariat 1948, 1000–1)

Under the Indian Constitutional framework, judicial review has been given a prominent place. The courts have the power to not only interpret the rights and legalities that are enshrined in the Constitution but also uphold constitutional values in the Indian body politic. S.P. Sathe observes:

> [T]he Indian Constitution expressly provides for judicial review in Article 13, clause (1), that says that all laws that were in force in the territory of India immediately before the adoption of the Constitution, in so far as they are inconsistent with the provisions containing the fundamental rights, shall, to the extent of such inconsistency, be void. Clause (2) of that article further says that the states shall not make any law that takes away or abridges any of the fundamental rights, and any law made in contravention of the aforementioned mandate shall, to the extent of the contravention, be void. The Constitution also divides the legislative power between the centre and the states and forbids either of them to encroach upon

> the power of the other. The courts decide whether a legislature or an executive has acted in excess of its powers or in contradiction to any of the constitutional restrictions on its power. Some members of the Constituent Assembly criticized the Constitution for being a potential lawyers' paradise. Others, like Dr. B. R. Ambedkar, defended the provisions of judicial review as being necessary. According to Dr. Ambedkar, the provisions for judicial review, in particular the writ jurisdiction that gave quick relief against the abridgment of fundamental rights, constituted the heart of the Constitution; the very soul of it. (Sathe 2001, 38–9)

★★★

After close to seven decades, a dispassionate evaluation of the Indian Constitution and its functioning presents a mixed story. It has certainly withstood several challenges of the task of nation-building that was bequeathed to it; at the same time, however, several things have remained non-starters. Sujit Choudhry, Madhav Khosla, and Pratap Bhanu Mehta claim:

> The greatest success of constitutionalism in India is now the promiscuity of the language of constitutionalism. Alexis de Tocqueville had suggested that in the United States political questions were often apt to become judicial questions. In India, by extension, a vast range of political, administrative, and judicial matters have become constitutional questions that are routinely brought to the courts. Both citizens and judges invoke constitutional values and doctrine not just when claiming rights, determining jurisdiction, or limiting governmental power. They invoke constitutional values in a variety of claims: from protecting ecology to allocating natural resources, redressing grievances against governments, and bringing ordinary tort claims. Indian constitutional law is interesting precisely because it has constitutionalised so much of Indian life. (Choudhry, Khosla, and Mehta 2016, 6)

On the other hand, it is also an undeniable fact that status quoism has maintained its stranglehold in society and the polity to such an extent that the inculcation of 'constitutional morality' in our political and public life, an important element in constitutionalism, has remained a non-issue so far. Its necessary role has always been kept aside. A.G. Noorani highlights the lack of attention paid to 'constitutional morality' and rues the fact that it still remains a non-issue in Indian polity and the society at large (Lok Sabha Secretariat 1948, cited in Noorani 2015).

Taking stock of the post-Constitution time in India, Upendra Baxi, a legal luminary, thus remarked recently:

> Ambedkar wished to 'annihilate the caste' system, 'restore the title deeds of humanity' to untouchables, and to liberate India from 'Dalit-hunting'—rape, arson, stripping and parading, plunder, killing, and massacre of untouchables. The constitutional order that he sculpted, he thought, would deliver us from that evil. We have now a system of reservations, a civil rights act, an atrocities act, and an abolition of manual scavenging act as late as 2013, and a plethora of statutory agencies and administrative devices. Surely, India reckons high for its GLP (gross legislative product), regardless of its GDP. Exuberant in normative law but feeble in real-life enforcement, a 66-year-old republic has not matched Babasaheb's poignant urgency for swift action against the social apartheid of the caste system and politics of production of social indifference. (Baxi 2016)

Despite several kinds of churning that have taken place from the time the Indian Constitution was promulgated and that the onward march continues to carry the baggage of contradictions that held sway at the beginning, the promise of an egalitarian society always remains the top agenda of the constitutional project. The functioning of a constitution must be evaluated taking into consideration the pluses and the minuses as well as the commissions and the omissions. There are three important elements in the human rights framework on justice, human rights, and governance that are worth mentioning here, namely (i) the need for a constitution and legislations; (ii) due diligence; and (iii) accountability. What we have is only the Constitution and a fairly large number of legislations, but we do not seem to practice due diligence and accountability in our society, economy, and polity. However, on a positive note, it could very well be concluded that in order to usher in the process of socio-economic and political transformation the provisions related to rights and rules of law remain not only as safeguards but also as the only hope for a better future wherein liberty, equality, and fraternity may be realized in their true forms.

References

Agarwal, Sudarshan, ed. 1991. *Dr. B. R. Ambedkar: The Man and His Message*. New Delhi: Prentice-Hall of India.

Ambedkar, B.R. 1994. *Dr. Babasaheb Ambedkar: Writings and Speeches*, vol. 13. Bombay: Department of Education.

Austin Granville. 1999. *Working a Democratic Constitution: A History of the Indian Experience*. New Delhi: Oxford University Press.

Baxi, Upendra. 2016. 'How Not to Recall an Icon'. *Indian Express*, 18 April. Available at http://indianexpress.com/article/opinion/columns/how-not-to-recall-ambedkar-2758030/. Last accessed on 15 July 2017.

Choudhry, Sujit, Madhav Khosla, and Pratap Bhanu Mehta, eds. 2016. *The Oxford Handbook of the Indian Constitution*. New Delhi: Oxford University Press.

Kashyap, Subhash C. 2010. 'Framing of India's Constitution—Select Documents'. *Reports of the Constitutional Advisor on His Visit to the United States of America*. New Delhi: Universal Law Publication.

Lok Sabha Secretariat. 1948. *Constituent Assembly Debates*, vol. VII, 4 November and 9 December.

———. 1949. *Constituent Assembly Debates*, vol. IX, 17 September.

Maitra, Keya. 2012. 'Ambedkar and the Indian Constitution: A Deweyan Experiment'. *Contemporary Pragmatism* 9, no. 2 (December): 301–20.

National Commission for Schedules Castes and Scheduled Tribes. Sixth Report, 1999–2000 and 2000–1. Available at http://ncsc.nic.in/pages/view/295-1999-00-and-2000-01-(english). Last accessed on 15 July 2017.

Noorani, A.G. 2015. 'Squandered Heritage'. *Frontline Magazine*, 26 June. Available at http://www.frontline.in/thenation/squanderedheritage/article7298390.ece?homepage=true. Last accessed on 15 July 2017.

Sathe, S.P. 2001. 'Judicial Activism: The Indian Experience'. *Washington University Journal of Law and Policy* 6, no. 29: 28–109.

Stepan. A. 1999. 'Federalism and Democracy Beyond the US Model'. *Journal of Democracy* 10, no. 4: 19–34.

6

B.R. Ambedkar and Indian Democracy

ANUPAMA RAO

> You are fighting for Swaraj. I am ready to join you. And I may assure you that I can fight better than you. I make only one condition. Tell me what share I am to have in Swaraj. If you don't want to tell me that and you want to make up with the British behind my back, hell on both of you.
>
> —Ambedkar (1942)

> The curse of untouchability is like a hydra-headed monster. You take away one of its heads, and two heads come out in its place. You remove it in one place, and it appears in another place. You try to cut it in one form and it appears in another form.
>
> —Sharma (1954, 706)

> There is not a single political party in India today, which has got on its programmes an item that the practice of untouchability should continue.
>
> —Deshpande (1954, 672–3)

B.R. Ambedkar (1891–1956) is best remembered for leading a powerful struggle for the rights and self-representation of the Untouchables, for his extensive writings on caste as a form of inequality and historical injustice, and for his enduring effect on trajectories of democratic justice and affirmative action policy as chairman of the Drafting Committee of the Indian Constitution. His conversion to Buddhism in 1956, just months before his death, was perhaps his most radical gesture of all: it constituted a rejection of Hinduism, the faith into which Ambedkar was born, as well as a powerful critique of Hinduism's persistent negation of Dalit humanity.

While there is extensive scholarship on M.K. Gandhi, there exists little by way of commentary and counter-commentary on Ambedkar's thought. Indeed, studies of Gandhi have witnessed something of a revival in recent years with the publication of a range of studies that address Gandhi in global as well as deeply vernacular contexts. One reason for the paucity of similar work on Ambedkar is the embarrassed treatment of caste both by scholars of anti-colonialism and by contemporary critics, many of whom prefer to believe that the 'caste question' was resolved through the institution of constitutional safeguards and a regime of affirmative actions in 1950. Another reason for the occlusion of caste is the view of caste as the unhappy burden of those who suffer its excessive embodiment, that is, Dalits and the lower castes. There are problems with the adulation of Ambedkar too: his iconization and the substitution of hagiography for critical engagement precludes attention to the enormity of his contributions to democratic thinking. Though he is a key global thinker for radical democratic thought and studies in the politics of recognition, Ambedkar's contributions have been elided from genealogies of Indian political thought and intellectual history.

My own work addresses Ambedkar as an insurgent thinker who challenged established modalities of thought and activism by drawing on political and ethical possibilities that were globally conceived, though they deeply engaged with forms of subaltern difference. I elaborate on this issue later. However, let me briefly propose an itinerary for insurgent thought by suggesting that it is a mode of engagement by which one might stake a claim to the universal from the position of subalternity; that this thought's 'insurgence' is predicated on its resolute rejection of any association between material deprivation and intellectual destitution. Thus, the claim to emancipated intelligence (and global thought-worlds) is crucial to insurgent thinking. Examples include: W.E.B. Du Bois's intimacy with Greek mythology and Latin liturgy; Jotirao Phule's imagined affinity with the Emancipation Proclamation (and figures such as George Washington and Marquis de Lafayette); and Ambedkar's insistence on locating subcontinental events with reference to European and universal history (for example,

Balkanization, the Holocaust, or the history of Roman law) in his quest for models of redress and reparation to respond to the hurtful history of caste and untouchability. Global connectivity between thought-worlds enabled commitments to critical thought and systematic critique as necessary precursors to subaltern resistance, while the imagination of subaltern equality was characterized by its defiant challenge to hegemonic history and exclusionary social structures. Fanon's conception of the 'wretched' and Ambedkar's recognition of the outcaste as *dalit* (lit. ground down, broken, shattered) were potent reminders of caste and colonial dehumanization, and ways to remake degraded subjects through a politics of radical humanism. We can challenge the persistent reduction of anti-caste thinkers into movement leaders by recognizing their commitment to the practice of critique and their efforts to build coherence, systematicity, and iterability—theoretical justification, in brief—for practices of resistance.

This chapter focuses on Ambedkar as a figure whose thought and activism transcend the divide of colonial/postcolonial history, which is typically framed around the dual axes of political partition and Britain's transfer of power, and argues that we attend to his powerful efforts to challenge a restricted conception of the caste question and the foreclosure of more radical conceptions of social equality in the aftermath of political independence. Ambedkar's efforts to recalibrate the relationship of the social to the political and his view of political agonism as central to public life are an enduring aspect of Indian democracy. Because Ambedkar's nationalism was deeply tied to his analysis of caste in Indian history, and because this account diverged so fundamentally from mainstream anti-colonial responses to caste, it is worth addressing his thought along two registers. Ambedkar's interventions have become salient (and consequential) in our time, though his interventions were often received with downright hostility and resistance when they were first proposed: a close, contextual reading of his thought would thus remain inadequate for explaining the afterlife of concepts and keywords that were set in motion by this radical thinker of caste annihilation. Therefore, what I propose is to engage in some combination of 'close' and 'far' reading that is capable of taking stock of the debates and interventions in which Ambedkar played a key role, while considering their implications for India's postcolonial democracy.

Ambedkar before 1940

Ambedkar's famous debate with Gandhi over separate political representation and the ensuing Poona Pact are typically associated with the former's emergence as a figure of national significance. To focus solely on the Poona Pact is to scant the immense intellectual labour that went into Ambedkar's efforts to redefine the Untouchable identity in the interwar period. Key among them was his effort to demarcate the Depressed Classes as a distinct group with separate interests, that is, as non-Hindus. In a series of representations before the Southborough and Simon Commissions, established to consider the extension of franchise and the functioning of diarchy respectively between 1918 and 1928, Ambedkar argued that the Depressed Classes constituted a distinctive third constituency (along with Hindus and Muslims) with the need for political representation.[1] Two broad arguments characterized Ambedkar's position on the representation of Depressed Classes between 1918 and 1928. The first was that any demand for separate representation ought to be a fallback option in the absence of adult franchise combined with reserved representation. The second distinguished the representation of Depressed Classes from separate electorate for Muslims and emphasized that the Depressed Classes were distinguished by the civic and economic disabilities from which they suffered. Ambedkar thus argued from the position of a theory of representative government based on adult franchise in making demands on behalf of a (heretofore) unrecognized constituency, the Depressed Classes.

The significance of this move is both subtle and significant. Ambedkar was laying claim to a universal right *to* politics through the demand for universal franchise while challenging the exclusionary systems of colonial nomination and, in the process, property qualification. Once universal franchise was accepted, it would be possible to emphasize the material deprivation and civic

[1] For the first time in 1911 the census contained three subcategories under the denomination 'Hindu': Hindus; Animists and Tribals; and the Depressed Classes or Untouchables. At the First Round Table Conference in 1931, Ambedkar and Raobahadur Srinivasan argued that the term 'non-caste' or 'non-conformist Hindus' was more appropriate than the insulting 'Depressed Classes'. However, the term was used until the current terminology of Scheduled Castes came into effect in 1935.

exclusion of the Depressed Classes as an alternative basis for special representation, rather than the prevalent colonial association of minority identity with religious difference. In effect Ambedkar, was calling for a shift from religion-based identity, which was the basis of colonial recognition for separate electorate for Muslims, to the contingency of class. However, this definitional shift also required viewing the franchise more expansively, beyond the institutional exclusions justified by the education and property qualifications, not to mention the colonial system of nominated representation. Universal enfranchisement was, therefore, crucial for reconceiving anti-colonial equality. Thus, at the Southborough Commission, Ambedkar argued that representation of the Depressed Classes was contingent on the extension of adult franchise. This was an important critique of colonial models of limited representation that articulated, and reproduced, upper-caste hegemony. Instead, (universal) enfranchisement could be used proactively to reveal potential constituencies or groups such as the Depressed Classes. Only then, Ambedkar suggested, could a subsequent reduction of the criteria of eligibility, that is, of the property (and taxation) qualification, enable substantive Depressed Class representation. In essence, a formal commitment to universal enfranchisement could open the door to policy measures to effect substantive equality for vulnerable minorities. In turn, Ambedkar argued that reserved or communal seats could enhance Depressed Class representation in the Legislative Council, but that communal electorates had a better chance of ensuring the selection of candidates who truly represented the community's interest.[2] For Untouchables, 'communal representation and self-determination are but two different phrases which express the same notion'.[3]

Ten years later, Ambedkar's representation to the Simon Commission marked a refinement of these arguments through a sustained critique of the Muslim separate electorate.[4] Distinguishing

[2] Supplementary written statement of B.R. Ambedkar in Ambedkar (1979: I).

[3] Evidence before Southborough Committee (Ambedkar 1979: I, 270).

[4] Ambedkar was labelled a 'British stooge' for agreeing to be a member of the Bombay Committee of the Simon Commission, which was boycotted by Congress and the Muslim League. He eventually submitted a book-length rejoinder criticizing the Simon Commission's recommendations. See Ambedkar (1982: II, 265–320).

the Depressed Class from the Muslims, Ambedkar described the former as 'educationally backward, that it is economically very poor, socially enslaved'.[5] As for Muslims, Ambedkar had argued before the Southborough Commission that Hindus could represent 'the *material* interests of the Mohammedans and vice versa'. Instead, material deprivation and social stratification united the Depressed Classes as an alternate constituency defined by a *class interest*: they required protection due to their low social and economic status, and weightage due to their small numbers.

The principle of weightage was first articulated in connection with the Muslim electorate not only to address the demographic growth of the Muslim constituency over time but to acknowledge their 'historical and political importance' as well. Instead, Ambedkar highlighted the socio-economic status of the Depressed Classes to demand similar measures for them. Representing the Bahishkrit Hitakarini Sabha, Ambedkar argued that weighted representation was 'literally showered upon a community like the Mahomedans holding a stronger and better position in the country than can be predicated of the Depressed Classes. The Sabha protests against this grading of the citizens of a country on the basis of their political importance'.[6] Ambedkar argued that if the position of Muslims as a demographic majority in Sind, Bengal, Punjab, and the Northwest Frontier Provinces was acknowledged, it would be clear that the Muslim-majority provinces were an 'ingenious contrivance' that 'involved the maintenance of justice and peace by retaliation'.[7] Hindu and Muslim minorities would be ruled by fear and anxiety since they could be held hostage for the behaviour of their co-religionists in other parts of the country: 'For if the Hindu majority tyrannized the Muslim minority in

[5] Evidence of Dr Ambedkar before the Indian Statutory Commission on 23 October 1928 (Ambedkar 1982: II, 465).

[6] Statement concerning safeguards for the protection of interests of the Depressed Classes as a minority in the Bombay Presidency and the changes in the composition of and the guarantees from the Bombay Legislative Council necessary to ensure the same under provincial autonomy, submitted by B.R. Ambedkar on behalf of the Bahishkrit Hitakarini Sabha (Depressed Classes Institute) to the Indian Statutory Commission, 29 May 1928 (Ambedkar 1982: II, 438–9).

[7] A report on the constitution of the government of Bombay Presidency, presented to the Indian Statutory Commission (Ambedkar 1982: II, 320).

the Hindu provinces the scheme provides a remedy whereby the Mohammedan majorities get a field to tyrannize the Hindu minorities in the five Mohammedan provinces. It is a system of protection by counterblast against blast; terror against terror and eventually tyranny against tyranny.'[8] Ambedkar was arguing that Muslims represented the principle of nationality, and not of political minority. This was prescient, but it was also politically potent.

During the 1930s, Muslim politics would articulate a position on nationality that challenged the politics of number—and the demographic calculus that had been set in place by colonial technologies of objectification, such as the census—and limited franchise. While majority and minority were enumerated entities within the nation, the nation form was organized around affective bonds, the feeling of commonality. Ambedkar's engagement with the distinction between a politics of minority and one of nationality organizes his *Pakistan or the Partition of India*, published in 1940. Here I want to underscore what was enabled through such a comparison. Ambedkar had focused on aggregating an as yet unrecognized minority, the Depressed Classes, through two sets of interconnected strategies: he argued that similar to Muslims, the Depressed Classes were minorities with a distinctive history, identity, and set of interests that set them apart from the Hindu community at large; next, he went further to argue that deprivation and social marginalization, rather than religious identification, ought to form the basis of minority identity. Indeed Ambedkar characterized the relationship between caste Hindus and Untouchables as a 'fundamental and deadly antagonism', and argued:

> The first thing I submit is that we [Untouchables, Depressed Classes] claim that we must be treated as a distinct minority, separate from the Hindu community: a distinct and independent minority. Secondly I should like to submit that the Depressed Classes minority needs far greater political protection than any other minority in British India for the simple reason that it is educationally backward, that it is economically very poor, socially enslaved and suffers from certain grave political disabilities from which no other community suffers. Then I would submit that, as a matter of demand for our political protection, we claim representation on the same basis as

[8] A report on the constitution of the government of Bombay Presidency, presented to the Indian Statutory Commission (Ambedkar 1982: II, 319).

the Mahomeddan minority. We claim reserved seats if accompanied by adult franchise.[9]

Let us extrapolate the immense significance of these efforts. If the Depressed Classes, Hindus, and Muslims could be said to constitute *three* distinct communities of interest, with the Depressed Classes forming 18–20 per cent of the population, then this third community disturbed the idea that only 'fixed permanent communities' existed in the political space. The Depressed Classes were defined by the principle of socio-economic status and material deprivation, rather than the primordial distinctions of religion. As a third community produced by the practice of power and inequality, the very existence of this community challenged the colonial obsession with Hindu and Muslim communities as primordial communities and corporate political actors. It also compromised Hindu majoritarianism. Increasingly, the Depressed Classes came to be defined as a community that Hinduism produced outside or apart from itself. Ambedkar had subverted the colonial discourse that equated religious community with constituency by suggesting a *fundamental* contradiction between Hindus and Untouchables.

Behind the historic confrontation of 1932 were a set of prior transformations in Ambedkar's strategic engagement with the political theory of representative democracy: this involved utilizing and enacting a shift from the discourse of universal franchise, to specifying the grounds on which political representation for the Depressed Classes could be justified, that is, through their separation from Hindus.

We will recall that Gandhi bitterly challenged the efforts at separate representation for the Depressed Classes at the Second Round Table Conference. However, Gandhi agreed to a compromise solution on the stalled question of minority rights, which would be decided by Prime Minister Ramsay MacDonald, though he had then embarked on a fast-unto-death (20–4 September) to challenge the provisions of the Communal Award of 16 August 1932. That award gave the Depressed Classes a separate electorate in areas where they were concentrated, in addition to a general vote. The Communal Award was a critical moment in the governmental

[9] Evidence of Dr Ambedkar before the Indian Statutory Commission on 23 October 1928 (Ambedkar 1982: II, 465). Ambedkar also submitted his own report to the (Simon) Indian Statutory Commission Ambedkar (1982: II, 265–320).

discourse on caste because it clearly marked the anomalous status of the Depressed Classes as a political minority whose identity was inseparable from their status as degraded Hindus. Its denouement, the Poona Pact compromise between Ambedkar and Gandhi, instituted reserved representation and an increase in seats reserved for Depressed Class candidates (from 71 to 148). The system of two-tier election allowed a primary election in Depressed Class constituencies, which would then produce a slate of candidates for whom a general Hindu electorate would cast their vote.

Like the text *What Congress and Gandhi Have Done to the Untouchables* (1945) that appeared a decade later, Ambedkar's incendiary text *The Annihilation of Caste* (1936) responded to the foreclosure of social equality that Ambedkar apprehended in the responses to untouchability as these developed in the final decades of the interwar period. A close reading of those texts falls outside the scope of this chapter. I merely mark here the discourse of negative or negated identity, that is, the position of the Depressed Classes as *non-Hindu*, that had come to occupy a central and defining place in Ambedkar's thought.

The Problem of Scheduled Caste Representation

In the 1940s, the discourse on Scheduled Caste representation fundamentally changed. (Indeed as is well known, the bureaucratic terminology for referring to 'Untouchables' had changed in 1935 from 'Depressed Classes' to 'Scheduled Castes' identified by a state-wise schedule.) In his speech of 20 August 1940 which offered India dominion status, Lord Linlithgow acknowledged the Scheduled Castes as a separate political constituency whose consent must be secured in the process of Britain's transfer of power.[10] Ambedkar was invited to join the Viceroy's Executive Council. As this invitation coincided with the launch of Congress's Quit India Movement, Ambedkar was accused of being an imperialist stooge.[11]

[10] 'Cabinet Mission and the Untouchables' (Ambedkar 1991: X, 539).

[11] This offer was made immediately after the Cripps Mission of March 1942. Linlithgow was antagonistic to Sir Stafford Cripps and threatened to resign when Cripps went off on his mission to India in March 1942. It is likely that Linlithgow's position reflected broader tensions within the British political establishment.

At the time, Gandhi argued, somewhat disingenuously, that though there was

> talk of the Hindus forming the majority community[,] Hinduism is an elastic indefinable term, and Hindus are not a homogenous whole like Muslims and Christians. ... In other words and in reality so far as India is concerned, there can only be political parties and no majority or minority communities. The cry of the tyranny of the majority is a fictitious cry. (Gandhi 1939)[12]

However, Lord Wavell continued as late as 1944 to argue with Mahatma Gandhi that the Scheduled Castes constituted a 'separate element in the national life of India'.[13] Yet, resistance to separate Scheduled Caste representation grew.

The focus on religious difference, rather than community inequality and exclusion, became political common sense, so much so that the Cripps Mission held that only religious minorities were entitled to separate representation.[14] Cripps's refusal to support Scheduled Caste demands for separate representation was described as a 'conspiracy of silence' between 'the Government, the Congress and even the Muslims'.[15] It was the immediate trigger for Ambedkar's establishment of the All-India Scheduled Caste Federation (AISCF), formed at a conference in Nagpur in July 1942.[16] The AISCF Working Committee even argued that Dalits were a religious minority and described Congress hegemony as leading to

[12] M. K. Gandhi, 'The Fiction of the Majority', *Harijan*, October 21, 1939, 312.

[13] 'Cabinet Mission and the Untouchables' (Ambedkar 1991: X, 538).

[14] Sir Stafford Cripps was a left-wing politician in Winston Churchill's War Cabinet, who came to India in March 1942 and offered Indian leaders dominion status after the war and eventual political independence if India supported the British war effort. Congress stopped talks with the mission and began the massive Quit India Movement after the demand for immediate self-rule was not met.

[15] Address by President Rao Bahadur N. Sivaraj, *Report of the Proceedings of the Third Session of the All-India Depressed Classes Conference*, held in Nagpur on 18 and 19 July 1942, 24.

[16] *Report of the Proceedings of the Third Season of the All-India Depressed Classes Conference,* held in Nagpur on 18 and 19 July 1942. A conference of the Samata Sainik Dal was held on 20 July 1942 along with the second session of the All-India Depressed Classes Women's Conference.

'the annihilation of our people as a political entity'.[17] Ambedkar strongly objected to the betrayal of the Cripps Commission, arguing:

> Up to the declaration of 8th August 1940 His Majesty's Government's view was that the untouchables were a distinct and a separate element and that they constituted so important an element that their consent was necessary for any constitutional changes that may be desired.[18]

Ambedkar noted that though the Scheduled Castes had enjoyed Muslim political support, the politics of Muslim nationalism now pitted Muslims against all other communities. He saw the Muslim League setting up 'a new equation of values ... that the Muslims, whatever their numbers, are just equal as to the non-Muslims and therefore in any political arrangement the Muslims must get fifty percent'.[19] The Muslim League had trumped number with nationality (Ambedkar 1990: VIII). The urgent task now was to find recognition for Untouchables as 'a separate element' in the national life of India. Physical separation was proposed through the establishment of Scheduled Caste villages, on government waste-lands and private lands, overseen by a government-established settlement commission.[20] Village committees would form the basic AISCF organizational units and provide funds through a tax on the constituents.[21]

This was out of synch with the political proclivities of other Dalit leaders. M.C. Rajah, chairman of the Depressed India Association

[17] Address by President Rao Bahadur N. Sivaraj, *Report of the Proceedings of the Third Session of the All-India Depressed Classes Conference*, held in Nagpur on 18 and 19 July 1942, 23.

[18] Address by B.R. Ambedkar, *Report of the Proceedings of the Third Session of the All-India Depressed Classes Conference*, held in Nagpur on 18 and 19 July 1942, 31–2.

[19] Address by B.R. Ambedkar, *Report of the Proceedings of the Third Session of the All-India Depressed Classes Conference*, held in Nagpur on 18 and 19 July 1942, 32–3.

[20] *Report of the Proceedings of the All-India Depressed Classes Conference*, 5. The demand arose again on 23 September 1944 at a meeting of the working committee of the AISCF in Bombay.

[21] Office bearers of the executive committee had to pay an annual fee of Rs 10, while members of the village, *taluka*, and district committee paid Rs 5 per annum. *AISCF Constitution*, January 1955.

and Ambedkar's most important rival, had demanded separate electorates all along. However, he issued a joint declaration with the Hindu Mahasabha demanding reserved seats for Depressed Class candidates, and noted that a separate electorate was only viable if the colonial government was the 'special protector of Minority interests'. Under changed political conditions, it was imperative that the Depressed Classes, who lacked an 'effective percentage', amalgamate themselves into the Hindu constituency, provided they got reserved seats (Ambedkar 1932). Apparently, constituencies could play the game of parity only if the colonial state adopted the role of ringmaster.[22]

Rajah's position apparently triumphed since the Scheduled Castes played no part in the critical Simla discussions of 1945.[23] The Cabinet Mission visited India from March to June 1946 to discuss the interim government and a new Constitution for India: Congress was identified as the chosen representative of all constituencies, except for Muslims. However, the Cabinet Mission Award of 16 May 1946 recognized three constituencies: General (this included Hindus and others), Muslim, and Sikh. While the Schedule Castes did not have separate representation, they would be accommodated within an advisory committee to the Constituent Assembly drawn from provincial legislatures.

This betrayal by the British government inflected the tone of Ambedkar's *What Congress and Gandhi Have Done to the*

[22] Important Chambhar leaders in western India supported the Rajah–Moonje Pact, showing the growing conflict between Mahar Ambedkarites and Chambhar supporters of the Congress. The famous cricketer P. Balu joined the Congress during this period, as did N.S. Kajrolkar. P.N. Rajbhoj, who played an important role in the Mahad and Nasik satyagrahas, embraced Gandhian politics by 1932 and supported the Rajah–Moonje Pact. Finally, G.M. Thaware, a Mahar leader from Vidarbha and assistant general secretary of the All-India Depressed Classes Association, who had initially supported a demand for separate electorates, now criticized Ambedkar's stance (Thaware 1932).

[23] The Simla discussion, held between 25 June and 14 July 1945, was organized by Lord Wavell, viceroy of India, to consider the shape of a 'transitional Government at the Centre representative of the main political parties', namely the Congress and Muslim League (Mansergh 1977, 39).

Untouchables, a vehement attack on Congress hegemony, published a few years before the violent onset of Partition. It was an extended reflection on the Poona Pact compromise as the root cause of the failures of the 1940s. Ambedkar wrote that the Communal Award had redressed the political weakness of the Depressed Classes by making Hindus dependent on their vote.

> The second vote given by the Communal Award was a priceless privilege. Its value as a political weapon was beyond reckoning. ... No caste Hindu candidate could have dared to neglect the Untouchables in his constituency or be hostile to their interests if he were made dependent upon the votes of the Untouchables. (Ambedkar 1990: VIII, 90)

Although it was animated by an enormous sense of betrayal, the text was among Ambedkar's most important engagements with political liberalism. Moving from his earlier focus on redefining the colonial category of minority so as to include the Depressed Classes as constituting a especially deserving group, Ambedkar now targeted Hindu majoritarianism and its political representative, the Congress, for reproducing caste hegemony *through* the franchise. His immediate focus was the defeat of AISCF candidates in the historic election of 1946, a result tantamount to accepting Congress as representing Scheduled Caste interests.[24] His broader

[24] Zelliot (2004, 198) suggests that Ambedkar's political duties as a Labour member of the viceroy's executive council might have caused him to neglect preparing his political party for the 1946 elections. The SCF polled higher than the Congress in primaries in Madras, Bombay, and the Central Provinces, yet the federation was soundly defeated during the 1946 elections, losing all 15 reserved seats in Bombay, 14 to the Congress and 1 to an independent candidate. This mattered because election results were the basis for participation in the Constituent Assembly. Again, in 1948, Ambedkar lost a bid for election to the Constituent Assembly from Bombay to a Congress Chambhar candidate, Narayan Kajrolkar, and in 1952, lost a seat in the Lok Sabha to another Congress Chambhar candidate, N.S. Kajrolkar. Thus, at a crucial political point, the Scheduled Castes found themselves without independent representation in the Constitution-making body, lacking crucial input into the structure of the national State. Ramnarayan Rawat's painstaking analysis of the historic 1946 election results confirms Ambedkar's critique of the Poona Pact in almost every detail: the two-tier structure of electing Scheduled Caste candidates worked almost always to the advantage of Congress (Rawat 2003).

concern, however, was with demarcating a distinctive Scheduled Caste interest within the field of liberal politics.

Ambedkar's analysis began with the Poona Pact provisions pertaining to the selection of Scheduled Caste representatives. This was a two-tier process where Scheduled Caste voters selected a group of Scheduled Caste candidates in a primary election in which only they voted. Later, they voted together with the general electorate to choose a Scheduled Caste candidate for the reserved constituencies.[25] Ambedkar argued that because caste Hindus could ultimately swing their votes towards a palatable Scheduled Caste candidate, the initial selection of candidates by Scheduled Caste voters, too, would be dictated by the unstated bias of producing a list of Scheduled Caste representatives who would be acceptable to the general (Hindu) electorate: Scheduled Caste interests were thus ultimately subservient to the political proclivities of the general constituency. Ambedkar noted that the system of reserved constituencies worked in favour of the Congress, which put up Depressed Class candidates in *both* reserved and general constituencies. This substantiated the Congress's claim that Untouchables were Hindus, and that the Congress represented a wide range of interests, including those of the Scheduled Castes. Without the separate electorate, which essentially transformed the principle of minority into a logic of (political) exception, the Scheduled Caste electorate remained a numerical minority subservient to Hindu interests.

Likewise, distributive voting weakened the self-representation of Depressed Classes. Ambedkar's argument against distributive voting focused on the skewed results of the 'one person, one vote' principle versus the aggregative logic of cumulative voting. For instance, if voters typically distributed their votes across five different candidates, the cumulative voting system recommended by Ambedkar aggregated votes so that the voters could show their preference for one or two candidates. Scheduled Caste voters who had been chosen in the primaries (as representatives of the Scheduled Castes) would then find themselves

[25] Qualifications for Scheduled Caste voters had been reduced to include literacy or previous performance of inferior village-servant duties. Government of India Bill, *Instruments of Instructions to the Governor-General and Governors*, 1935 (Zelliot 2004, 188).

confronting caste Hindu candidates on a more even, if agonistic, terrain.[26]

Ambedkar's critique of the electoral process and the Congress was interpreted to reflect his pro-British, anti-nationalist stance.[27] This effectively rendered his own efforts to position himself as *a nationalist critic of Congress politics* untenable. One Congress detractor declared *What Congress and Gandhi Have Done to the Untouchables* to be 'an incoherent jumble' without order or justification, determined to represent Gandhi and the Congress as 'wholly evil' (Santhanam 1946, 2). This author argued that the text was structured so as to refute the Congress's claim to represent the nation, and that there was an attempted step-by-step illustration of Hindu democracy as an oxymoronic concept. C. Rajagopalachari went further to argue that the Scheduled Castes had no claims on a separate democracy.

> The Scheduled Castes are evenly distributed all over India and are about ten per cent of the population. ... Thus distributed, they have to be part of the general population and cannot isolate themselves into a separate democracy. Nothing therefore follows from the argument even if conclusively proved that the Scheduled Castes do not stand behind the Congress and do not support its claim for political freedom. (Rajagopalachari 1946, 5–6)

Ambedkar's critique of the non-representative character of the Congress was thus a moot point since 'it may often be impossible

[26] Lani Guinier has made a similar point about cumulative voting in the contemporary United States of America. Accepting group interests as integral to the democratic process, Guinier argues that racist societies experience 'qualitative vote dilution', unrecognized due to the focus on the 'one person, one vote' principle (Guinier 1994, 7). As an antidote, Guinier suggests a system of cumulative voting where 'voters get the same number of votes as there are seats or options to vote for, and they can then distribute their votes in any combination to reflect their preference' (Guinier 1994).

[27] Omvedt (1994, 182–3) notes that between 1937 and 1940, communists began supporting the Congress, withdrawing support from Ambedkar's Independent Labour Party and Periyar's Self-Respect movement in the Tamil country. By 1948, the Communist Party of India's 'political thesis' described Ambedkar as an anti-national separatist and a pro-British opportunist. During the 1952 elections, Nehru was especially virulent in his criticism of Ambedkar and the Scheduled Caste Federation as 'communal' (Venkatarangaiya 1952, 32–4, 37).

to get minorities to agree to the claims for self-government which is majority rule even though the minorities be fully protected in their civil and political rights' (Rajagopalachari 1946, 8–9). Another text, K. Santhanam's *Ambedkar's Attack* (1946), also discounted the Scheduled Castes as a territorially dispersed minority. 'Whether there are 50 or 60 millions, it is of minor importance. I may point out that they are distributed almost evenly in all the villages of India. In each village they constitute a minority' (Santhanam 1946, 20). Santhanam was essentially arguing that a community without demographic concentration had to accept its status as a 'Hindu' minority. This was of a piece, of course, with the Congress's insistence on characterizing the AISCF as a communal organization. Ambedkar, not the Congress, was said to hold on to untouchability as a 'precious possession', resisting assimilation and integration. Scheduled Caste representation was also posed as a 'short cut' to political power for leaders who benefited from the safeguards enjoyed by their community (Santhanam 1946, 33–4).

In the course of time, the Poona Pact would be represented as having resolved the issue of political representation because it had settled the issue of the religious identity of the Depressed Classes. That is to say, while Ambedkar had foregrounded the interconnection between the 'religious' and 'political' aspects of untouchability in his efforts to endow the Depressed Classes with distinctive political value, the high politics of transition emphasized the political negligibility of the Dalits. Ironically, Sir Stafford Cripps acknowledged as much and noted that 'owing to the operation of what is known as the Poona Pact, they [Ambedkar's party] have been almost entirely excluded from the provincial assemblies'.[28]

Ambedkar continued to maintain that the political significance of the Depressed Classes derived from their status as an exceptional community defined by material and religious exclusion. He adhered to the view that the Hindu majority was a communal majority and not a political one, since it could not be 'made and unmade'. He had repeatedly tried to transform political discourse by naming the specificity of Dalits' oppression and their minority position, but separate representation appeared to be impossible for a stigmatized,

[28] *Lord's Debate on India: Text of Secretary of State's Speech*, GI, Home (Political), No. 51/2/1946, National Archives of India (NAI) (cited in the important essay by Bandhyopadhyay 2000).

territorially dispersed community. If political separation was a stymied project of the 1940s, Buddhist conversion replaced it. This project of radical self-making was enabled by Ambedkar's engagement with the political ethics of Hinduism and his radical reinterpretation of texts such as the Rg Veda and the Bhagavad Gita, which allowed him to focalize the lost worlds of Buddhist heterodoxy that had given way to Brahmanical hegemony.

Constitution and Postcolonial Transition

The last all-India census was undertaken in 1931 on the understanding that caste categories were attaining fixity as a primary identity and that national integration was precluded in the process. Reservations in educational institutions and public sector undertakings were envisaged as temporary measures to be renewed for a decade at a time. In addition, advanced caste groups were to be removed incrementally from the roster of groups eligible for quotas, culminating in a final 'de-scheduling' of Scheduled Castes and Tribes and Backward Class communities by 1981, the end of the Sixth Five-Year Plan. Today, however, members of Scheduled Castes, Backward Classes, and Other Backward Classes—all those entitled to some form of constitutional protection—together exceed 50 per cent of the nation's total population, even though the Constitution stipulates a 50 per cent cut-off for reservations. The *majority* of castes are defined as suffering from some form of social deprivation and 'backwardness'. Indeed, caste has taken on a class-like terminology, while the term 'class' has been interpreted by Indian law courts to subsume caste, now understood as but one indicator, if a significant one, of a group's socio-economic development.[29] What political practices develop around the fissure between a domain occupied by citizen-subjects and beneficiaries of caste privileges, and another by a majority that is defined as historically discriminated? What happens when policies of equalization, usually viewed as temporary and exceptional measures, become normative mechanisms of social integration? Does the legislation of caste identity enable new engagements with the State?

[29] *Balaji* v *State of Mysore* was one of the first cases in which caste came to be defined in this dual manner, All India Reporter [hereafter *AIR*] (1963), *Supreme Court Cases* [hereafter *S.C.*], 649.

The strains become clear when we examine these processes as the effects of a founding tension in the Indian Constitution. Foreshortening what was for Western democracies a contentious, incremental process of franchise expansion, India immediately enabled her illiterate and impoverished masses to participate in the political process through universal enfranchisement. Franchise is juxtaposed with an acknowledged long-term history of differential community rights and persistent, complex forms of ritual and cultural inequality. While 'the people' do appear in the Indian Constitution in their general aspect as citizens of a sovereign nation state, they are more often named in their particularity marked by class, caste, and religion. The putative equality of Indian citizens proceeds by detours through particularity. In the aftermath of Partition, Muslims lost their status as the model minority, giving up the separate electorate 'in the national interest' (Austin 1999). From the Constitution's distinctive focus on social and economic equality came a new category of persons, the poor. Caste, however, was at the very centre of constitutional commitments to social justice. Both a traditional category and a social evil, caste was to be excised from the body politic at all costs.

The Scheduled Caste citizen was given a distinctive identity between 1947–55 through constitutional protections that equalized her status with regard to other citizens of the republic. These included the abolition of untouchability by Article 17 of the Indian Constitution, followed by the institution of protective laws and affirmative action policies. With the nation aligned with the Hindu community in the years leading up to and following Partition, State protection of Dalits' rights as minority rights was placed on new footing through the institution of civil rights and the secularization of Hinduism. It is well known that Ambedkar's efforts to reform the Hindu family and intimate relations floundered not only because of the deep-seated resistance of the Hindu family to reform but also due to social prejudice against a *Dalit* law minister who sought to change *Hindu* law.[30] Ambedkar's efforts to transform caste into a civic disability and a form of socio-economic backwardness found greater success, but they did

[30] The *Constituent Assembly Debates* record encounters where Ambedkar's caste identity is either addressed frontally or through circumlocution.

so indirectly and through his more diffused 'influence' over the Constitution as a whole.[31] The reservations regime inaugurated a specific form of legal exception, what Marc Galanter calls 'compensatory discrimination', that marked out a very special place for the Scheduled Castes in the constitutional vision. This vision heuristically divided social space into two zones: one governed by the market principles of competition and putative merit, and one populated by those who suffered historic discrimination and became the objects of State intervention.

The Indian Constitution is the ultimate guarantor of citizens' rights through acts of equalization via positive discrimination for socially marginal and deprived populations. Quite simply, these moves anticipate a significant transformation of civil society by the State: whereas a liberal democracy commits to the sanctity of specific procedures believed to guarantee unbiased outcomes, the Indian Constitution specified a desired outcome and instituted policies to bridge the gulf separating the ideal of social equality from present conditions. Granville Austin, a major historian of the Indian Constitution, noted long ago that the Indian Constitution was an awkward and incendiary document: awkward because the federal structure and the administrative mechanisms by which the nation was administered had been established by the colonial Government of India Act of 1935, while the constitutional spirit emanated from the Objective Resolution of the December 1946 Assembly Session which called, among other things, for constitutional safeguards for vulnerable communities. Austin notes that the Constitution 'may be seen as having three strands: protecting and enhancing national unity and integrity; establishing the institutions and spirit of democracy; and fostering a social revolution to better the lot of the mass of Indians' (1996, 6). Those aspects of the Constitution that signal its historic role in effecting political transition appear in the discretionary powers of the State to bring about a social revolution, even at the risk of foreclosing other

[31] This is not the place to undertake a careful reading of Ambedkar's role in the Constituent Assembly, whether in the Minorities Committee of which he was a part, his remarkable erudition on the topic of comparative constitutionalism, or his interventions in the Drafting Committee. For an argument about Ambedkar's centrality to India's constitutional vision, see Jaffrelot (2005, 106–18).

fundamental rights—for instance, the right to property. Noteworthy in Part III of the Constitution is the abolition of untouchability under Article 17, while Articles 15(2), 23, and 24 articulate rights relating to the prohibition of discrimination on grounds of religion, race, caste, sex, and place of birth. Ambedkar argued that the most significant feature of the fundamental rights is that these rights are justiciable—that is, secured by the right to move to the Supreme Court for their enforcement—under Article 32. The force of Ambedkar's interventions is reflected in the 'protective discrimination scheme', or the reservation policy of the government, that is envisaged under certain provisions of Part III but more significantly by those elements of Part IV of the Constitution, in the Directive Principles of State Policy, that address the constitutional mandate to ameliorate the condition of the Scheduled Castes, Scheduled Tribes, and Other Backward Classes.

There are a number of consequences that follow from the conflict between a liberal conception of fundamental rights (such as the right to private property and personal integrity) on the one hand, and the alignment of personal freedom with freedom from social discrimination on the other: this conflict structures the very conception of 'fundamental rights' and animates the contentious consequences that follow. Another set of contradictions is evinced by the articulation of 'directive principles', which cannot be enforced by the courts as procedural law but that nonetheless organize the social imaginary. Thus, the division between Fundamental Rights and Directive Principles also enacts a divide between procedural and substantive law insofar as the Directive Principles articulate the principle of popular sovereignty and the capacity to hold law responsible to the demands of justice. Efforts to secure the Directive Principles have also enmeshed the courts in a number of contentious political battles. One might argue that a major consequence of the anti-colonial context in which a republican democracy was imagined is that the substantive equality that Constitution makers such as Ambedkar aimed for also requires active policy intervention. Nor should it be surprising that it was the demographic majority, which lacked social privilege, that became the target of redress and reparation.

The first front of caste equalization was the secularization of Hinduism. Article 26 of the Constitution guarantees that castes, viewed here as (religious) sects, have the right to exist, to maintain their own religious and charitable institutions,[32] and to manage their internal affairs. Similarly, Article 30 gives religious and linguistic minorities the right to establish and administer educational institutions of their choice. However, Indian secularism is also committed to religious equality, and seeks to balance the rights to religious practice against the commitment to religious equality. Article 25(2) (b) opens Hindu temples to all Hindus, placing at odds the rights of sub-sects and the right of equal access to religious institutions by all caste individuals.[33] In fact, the commitment to caste equality blurs the boundary between religious and secular rights. Lawmakers and courts have implicitly acknowledged their right to intervene in and reorganize religious practice (Bhargava 1998).

The second front of equalization is democratization through caste, insofar as equality has been specified as *equality between castes*.[34] What legal historian Marc Galanter has called compensatory discrimination is 'very much a domestic product, produced with little guidance or borrowing from abroad' (Galanter 1984, 361); it is a unique kind of civil rights law which takes caste as a class-like structure of deprivation and impoverishment. Untouchability is singled out in this framework through a series of exceptional legal measures that reflect Dalits' distinctive place in the political unconscious. There are three categories of reservations: (1) in legislative bodies, government service, educational institutions, and milder forms in housing and land allotment; (2) such programmes as

[32] An important case challenging Article 17 via Article 26 is *Chinamma* v *D.P.I.*, AIR 1964 Andhra Pradesh 277. For judgments arguing that Article 26 permits excommunication rights, see *Chinamma* v *D.P.I.*, AIR 1964 Andhra Pradesh 277; *Venkataramana Devaru* v *State of Mysore*, AIR 1958 *S.C.* 255; *Sarup Singh* v *State of Punjab*, AIR 1959 *S.C.* 860; and *Saifuddin* v *State of Bombay*, AIR 1962, *S.C.* 853 (869, 873, 875).

[33] In *Sangannagonda* v *Kallangonda*, AIR 1960 Mysore 147, the court held that assigning varna status to individuals is neither religious discrimination nor denial of equal rights.

[34] Early cases, such as *State of Kerala* v *N.M. Thomas*, interpreted the equal opportunity intent behind a system of reservations to also require 'equality of result' where the free and fair play of market forces obtains. *State of Kerala* v *N.M. Thomas*, AIR 1976 *S.C.* 490 (from *ILR* (1974) 1 Kerala 549.

scholarships, grants, loans, health care, and legal aid for Scheduled Castes; (3) special measures, mostly legislative, to protect Scheduled Castes and Scheduled Tribes from practices such as bonded labour, untouchability, and land alienation. The presumed obviousness of the category of Scheduled Caste served as an exemplary means of defining those groups entitled to 'preferential' treatment by the State.

Finally, an elaborate set of criminal laws to punish the perpetrators of untouchability were also passed in tandem with affirmative action laws, starting with the passage of the Untouchability Offences Act (1955). Each amendment to this Act has called for more stringent punishments for the perpetrators of caste crime. So much so that by 1989, the Prevention of Atrocities Act had expanded the field of caste crime to include political, ritual, and symbolic acts. For instance, Section 3(1) placed humiliation—caste insults and coercion to eat or drink noxious substances—on par with denial of access to water sources, public property, and thoroughfares; sexual violence against Dalit women; economic dispossession such as land grabs and demands to perform bonded labour; as well as efforts to prevent Dalits from voting or holding political office. In fact, atrocity laws have defined untouchability as consisting of acts of violence and humiliation that assume equivalence between hurtful words and harmful deeds. As well, a complicated bureaucratic edifice has grown around atrocity legislation to monitor and manage instances of anti-Dalit violence.

The legislation of caste and its relationship to an expansion of democratic aspiration are central to any understanding of contemporary India.[35] Caste's constitutional legacy was affected by the longer-term politicization of untouchability as the paradigm for understanding extreme social inequality, as much its legislation by the Indian Constitution set the terms for future social and political struggle, and Ambedkar played a constitutive role in each case.

[35] Elsewhere I have argued that affirmative action policy and atrocities legislation have together enabled a re-politicization of the political field and have explored the ambivalent effects and paradoxical consequences of such measures for the project of caste annihilation and social equality (see Rao 2009, especially 163–81, 217–64).

In Lieu of a Conclusion

The making of a contentious Ambedkarite legacy appears to be forgotten when set against the current glorification of Ambedkar as a Dalit icon rather than an insurgent thinker. Instead, this chapter has tried to map the complex set of readings that are enabled when we engage with Ambedkar in 'his' time, but with the benefit of a retroactive reading that addresses both the question of *why* Ambedkar might have thought and acted as he did, and his continued relevance for understanding India's postcolonial democracy in a manner that transcends the specificity of his biography. To fully inhabit Ambedkar's insurgence requires working at the interstices of his intellectual biography on the one hand, and adopting strategies of critical reading on the other. It also requires carving out for anti-caste thought a distinctive space between its complex globality and its existential or embodied specificity. Most of all, it asks us to think against political foreclosures and recall forgotten possibilities, and give the 'what might have been' and the 'otherwise' a serious, scholarly glance.

References

Ambedkar, B.R. 1942. *Bombay Sentinel*. 28 April.

Ambedkar, B.R. 1932. *Bombay Chronicle*. 24 March.

Ambedkar, B.R. 1979–91. *Dr. Babasaheb Ambedkar: Writings and Speeches*, volumes I, II, VIII, and X. Bombay: Department of Education, Government of Maharashtra.

Austin, Granville. 1996. *The Indian Constitution: Cornerstone of a Nation*. New Delhi: Oxford University.

———. 1999. *Working a Democratic Constitution: A History of the Indian Experience*. New Delhi: Oxford University.

Bandyopadhyay, Sekhar. 2000. 'Transfer of Power and the Crisis of Dalit Politics in India, 1945-47'. *Modern Asian Studies* 34, no. 4: 893–942. Available at www.jstor.org/stable/313135. Last accessed on 30 May 2020.

Bhargava, Rajeev, ed. 1998. *Secularism and Its Critics*. New Delhi: Oxford University Press.

Deshpande, G.H. 1954. *Lok Sabha Debates*, 31 August. New Delhi: Lok Sabha Secretariat.

Galanter, Marc. 1984. *Competing Equalities: Law and the Backward Classes in India*. Delhi: Oxford University Press.

Gandhi, M.K. 1939. 'The Fiction of the Majority'. *Harijan*, 21 October.

Guiner, Lani. 1994. *The Tyranny of the Majority: Fundamental Fairness in Representative Democracy.* Foreword by Stephen L. Carter. New York: Free Press.

Jaffrelot, Christophe. 2005. *Dr Ambedkar and Untouchability*. London: Hurst & Co.

Mansergh, Nicholas, ed. 1977. *Constitutional Relations between Britain and India*, volume 7 of *The Transfer of Power, 1942–47*. London: Her Majesty's Stationery Office.

Omvedt, Gail. 1994. *Dalits and Democratic Revolution*. New Delhi: Sage.

Rajagopalachari, C. 1946. *Ambedkar Refuted*. Bombay: Hind Kitabs.

Rao, Anupama. 2009. *The Caste Question: Dalits and the Politics of Modern India*. Berkeley, California: University of California Press.

Rawat, Ramnarayan S. 2003. 'A Study of the Scheduled Castes Federation and Dalit Politics in UP, 1946–48'. *Modern Asian Studies* 37, no. 3: 585–612.

Santhanam, K. 1946. *Ambedkar's Attack*. New Delhi: Hindustan Times Press.

Sharma, D.C. 1954. *Lok Sabha Debates*. 31 August. Delhi: Lok Sabha Secretariat.

Thaware, G.M. 1932. *Salvation of the Depressed Classes Lies* in *Joint Electorates*. Nagpur: Hitavada Press.

Venkatarangaiya, 1952. *The General Election in the City of Bombay*. Bombay: Vora Press.

Zelliot, Eleanor. 2004. *Dr. Babasaheb Ambedkar and the Untouchable Movement*. New Delhi: Blumoon Books.

Part Two

Economic Justice

7

Development through Informalization and Circulation of Labour

The Emerging Anatomy of an Uncivil Society

VIJAY GUDAVARTHY

The mainstream economic theory on employment, labour relations, and development has approached these issues by drawing dualistic distinctions between traditional and modern, rural and urban, unorganized and organized, informal and formal, unskilled and skilled, and so forth, one suggestive of backwardness and another of development, one suggestive of inefficiency and another of efficiency, one suggestive of customary idiocy and another of rationally thought-out behaviour and choices, one suggestive of stagnation or subsistence and another of accumulation, growth, or expansion (Gudavarthy 2015). Policy interventions ought to quite clearly favour the change towards development. Firms and the nature of employment and labour relations are embedded in a complex interplay between social organizations, cultural beliefs and practices, political systems, nature of policymaking, legal and regulatory institutions, and so on. This implies that the mainstream theory assumes that in all these realms changes either do not affect development or simply complement it. It is only when such assumptions are made can the model be reduced into one where the economic force has an overriding influence over all other categories, such that wage differentials or other rational calculations around trade-offs concerning economic welfare become the sole influence at the individual and systemic levels in understanding and analysing development processes. Claims that any macro-policy intervention through a fiscal or monetary policy will only make things worse rest on the assumption that economic force alone has the ability to eventually get it right (Lucas and Sagent 1979; Friedman 1977). However, when contrasted with the development experience and policy approach especially over the past five-and-a-half decades of the Indian economy beginning with the 1960s, there has been a wavering yet incremental progress towards neo-liberal reforms (Gudavarthy 2003). This experience with respect to employment and labour relations has several puzzles and paradoxes to address and explain, against the backdrop of which one would have to be sceptical or even anxious about the over-optimism of policymakers in the ability of markets to self-regulate or in the 'positives' of a flexible but uncivil social regulation to cause improvements to the welfare or well-being of all in economies such as India (Bhadhuri 2005; Parry, Breman, and Kapadia 1999).

The distinction between formal and informal employment contracts and labour relations has been discussed in literature as suggestive of modes of surplus formation and appropriation. Informal employment contracts and labour relations seem to increasingly connote surplus formation through cost-cutting—that is, surplus generated in the realm of circulation—as against formal, which may suggest a mode of surplus formation consequential to enhanced productive powers of factors and, therefore, happens in the realm of technical relations of production. This significant distinction between accumulation through technical structures versus social structures seems to be emanating from qualitatively different economic, social, cultural, political, legal, and institutional structures (Harriss-White 2003; Gudavarthy 2005). Modes of appropriation in the case of informality emerge from existing social structures of inequality and uneven development, while in the case of formality they emanate from structures of production and their development. These differences have a pertinent connect with the need to think afresh the analytical framework of development with specific reference to the informalization of employment and labour relations. It will not be an exaggeration to say that despite a vivid qualitative difference that continues to exist between formal and informal employment (registered and unregistered labour) and labour relations on several counts, they seem to almost converge, especially in the organized modern manufacturing sector as well as across organized and unorganized enterprises, in the manufacturing sector. This has huge ramifications for both formal and informal institutions and institutional change, as well as for the nature of social relations. These, in turn, have consequences and implications for the construction and analysis of development.

While internationally, civil society–based organizations of workers in the industrial districts of Third Italy are seen as institutions articulating and protecting the interest of the workers, critical scholarship studying the Indian labour markets has suggested that Indian labour relations are entrenched in cost-cutting sweat shops because of the absence of civil social organizations. However, in the context of cost-cutting strategies that determine the nature of production relations between capital and labour, the relationship between these production relations and the social relations that arises in the absence of a civil society remains to be explored. The predominant forms of employment contracts and the emerging nature of labour relations are based on modes of organizing circular migrant workers. This organizational mode is coordinated through community-based social networks. The social networks, therefore, rely heavily on existing social and cultural structures. The community relations are, in turn, entrenched in grave inequalities and relations of domination and subordination operating on the basis of discriminatory and heterogeneous norms. Added to this, the mobility itself constitutes movement across sectors, regions, and social conditions. This mobility is constituted by influences of uneven development having consequences for notions of subsistence, given that places of origin have varying degrees of distress. Further, mobility has implications in terms of changes in social hierarchies and consequential new inequality of power as well as asymmetry in terms of access to authority in the place of destination. It is in the course of dealing with such levels of complexity that ideas and analytical categories developed by scholars such as B.R. Ambedkar and Antonio Gramsci, who have attempted to discern non-economic structures in the context of development, have immense insights to offer. Quite clearly, with reference to constructing the metrics and analytical frameworks of development, development processes in India are producing more puzzles for the development analysts. While on the one hand, as already mentioned earlier, there is a kind of convergence in the forms of employment contracts and the nature of labour relations, there is simultaneously a growing heterogeneity that is brought out by the qualitatively differing nature of mobilizations, mobility, and labour process experiences of different segments of the working populations. Under such circumstances, aggregation of metrics or generalized narratives of development is a mounting challenge in itself. The significance of micro-level studies looking into institutional and relational indicators is increasing and, without undermining its relevance or significance, the official data based on macroeconomic generalizations is more likely to be flawed and challenged. While in all fairness, efforts have been made to correct and improve the definitions and concepts used by official statistics, the nature of the challenge is not as much one of imperfect technique or inadequate conceptualizations. The nature of the challenge seems, instead, to be linked to the process of development itself, which appears to expand on heterogeneity and non-commensurability of employment contracts and labour relations, having more substantive consequences for what seems to be an emerging uncivil society engulfed in difference, domination, discrimination, and so forth—all of which contribute to the expansion of conflict rather than cooperation. Ambedkar's categories of caste societies as division of labourers on the basis of graded inequality could suggest non-economic and non-commensurable social stratifications and segregations in social, political, cultural, and economic relations. Gramsci, on the other hand, attempts by improvising the political economy's understanding of mode of production in the context of uneven but simultaneous development to explain the significant role that civil society and its production of culture and ideology has in the political economy. This framework does not, therefore, restrict the analysis to the role of the State and its domination but extends it to the role of civil society and its production of hegemony as an important social condition for the subjugation of the subalterns and accumulation. Invoking these frameworks in itself implies that the relevance of the fundamental normative criterion underlying the mainstream analysis of development of societies such as India needs to be questioned. It is this emerging complexity of the development reality that this chapter attempts to analyse by addressing the following questions:

1. On the basis of what observable indicators from the working and living conditions of labourers can the informal employment contracts and labour relations in the unorganized

manufacturing sector be seen to be converging with yet remaining heterogeneous in relation to those in the organized manufacturing sector?

2. How do the processes of informalization and circulation, and the modes of organization of workers and labour processes affect this converging yet heterogeneous environment?
3. Given the nature of the rural economy's conditions in the place of origin and the socio-economic background of the labour force participating in unorganized and organized informal employment, how can we conceptualize the diversification of employment and spatial mobility in terms of their developmental consequences?

This chapter tries to address these questions by comparing two groups of long-distance circular migrant working populations employed in Telangana, namely long-distance migrants especially from western Odisha working in the unorganized manufacturing sector of brick kilns and long-distance migrants from Bihar, Uttar Pradesh, and Odisha working in organized manufacturing enterprises (thermo-mechanical treatment [TMT] steel production). Both unorganized and organized manufacturing units are located in Ranga Reddy district. The data used for understanding the brick kiln workers is a result of surveys done both in Odisha and Telangana to understand the conditions of workers in the place of origin as well as the place of work. A household-level survey was conducted during 2014–15 by the author in Bahubal and Debripally villages of Balangir district wherein a sample of 34 migrant workers employed in the brick kilns were interviewed using a structured questionnaire. Further, a sample of 82 households working in 10 brick kilns located in Maheshwaram and Dundigal villages of Ranga Reddy district in Telangana state have been studied in the place of work. This information was updated through informants with respect to wage details current to 2018, while other conditions have remained more or less the same. For the study of informal workers employed in organized manufacturing, a survey was done in 2012–13 involving a sample of 192 respondents; it was updated in 2018 with specific focus on the strata of long-distance migrants. The survey in 2018 was conducted with a sample of 20 workers drawn from the study of a steel industry which predominantly employs Odisha workers but also employs workers from Bihar and Uttar Pradesh. A structured questionnaire and interviews have been employed as methods for gathering information in all these surveys. The data pertaining to a comparable set of questions and comparable groups of workers (long-distance workers) alone is used in this chapter. The purpose of this chapter, however, is to rely more on empirical observations to draw qualitative inferences about the non-economic institutional and relational implications and the overall direction of outcomes from a labour perspective for development analysis.

Structures of Employment: Segmentation versus Segregation in the Informal Economy

Nature of Employment Contracts, Conditions of Employment, and Labour Relations

Comparing the employment contracts of workers employed in brick kilns with those employed in organized manufacturing, we observe that the employment contracts in organized informal employment have a much higher heterogeneity than those in unorganized informal employment. Brick kiln activity is seasonal and workers are recruited by junior contractors, referred to as *chote* sardars, who are agents of licensed contractors, called sardars. Workers are recruited as groups of three or four members (usually belonging to the same household), referred to as *patri*, by paying advance amounts (often upto to INR 15,000 per person). The workers are accompanied by chote sardars who also act as supervisors at the worksite, although the worksite—in this instance, a brick kiln as a production unit—is owned by another agent, referred to as the *seth*. Sardars, in fact, operate through the chote sardars with the finances provided to them by the seths. The recruitment of workers happens between November and January, while the brick kiln manufacturing activity itself occurs from January to June every year. It is the variation in the timing of the recruitment (sometimes linked to cropping patterns) and the differences in the physical health and abilities of workers (often linked to the number and age of the members of a patri) that generate heterogeneity in the advance amounts paid to the patris, rather than there being any heterogeneity in the nature of employment contracts or skill sets per se. Heterogeneity also exists as a result of restrictions imposed on the contractors with reference to the number of workers each contractor is permitted to recruit per license issued. This regulation generates two sets of workers, namely those whose names are registered and those who are unregistered. An estimate by locally operating research groups and activists puts the total number of brick kiln workers migrating from the Koraput, Balangir, and Kalahandi (KBK) regions at 4.5 lakh. The official records, however, show a figure of 50,000 workers (Sengupta and Gudavarthy 2015). This implies that close to 90 per cent of the circular migrant informal brick kiln workers from Odisha are actually unregistered. The internal heterogeneity, thus, is not very grave.

In contrast, in the organized manufacturing sector, workers do not receive any advance payment of wages but do receive advance payments to meet transport costs in instances where they are recruited by contractors at the place of origin. This mode of recruitment, however, is a miniscule part of the total employment of informal workers in the organized manufacturing sector. It happens when a manufacturing industry is newly established and has begun to operate or when there is a significant expansion of an old manufacturing unit. The predominant form of recruitment is based on workers who come to industrial areas through social networks involving family members, relatives, friends, and so forth, and get employed with predominantly local (Telugu) contractors, but also non-local contractors, to work for manufacturing units. Amongst such workers who move with the information provided by their social networks, some get directly recruited by the management of the industry. While the workers recruited by the management or through contractors have only a temporary contractual status, it generates two other forms of employment contracts—with reference to unregistered workers employed by the management and unregistered workers employed by contractors. When these numbers are put together, we observe that registered and unregistered workers constitute two equal halves of the total workers employed by organized manufacturing industries, as stated by a manager (who has requested anonymity) of the steel industry that has been studied. The heterogeneous modes of recruitment and employment contracts have explanations not only in the ability of workers but also in the multiple circulation rhythms that ensure stability in the supply of labour and the political economy of the power relations between managements and contractors, for managements do not risk becoming completely dependent on contractors.

It is quite possible that workers engaged in the same labour process at the same time could be having very different modes of recruitment and employment contracts. The heterogeneity in the modes of recruitment and employment contracts has nothing to do with the nature of activities performed in the labour process by both registered and unregistered informal workers employed in unorganized as well as organized sectors. This heterogeneity, which has limited bearing on the technicalities in terms of the detailed division of labour within each of these sets of activities, could, however, have a bearing on natural differences that Marx talks about while describing the social division of labour. The category called 'natural' in the European context moved in the direction of equivalent economic values from abstract labour, but was also determined by socially defined subsistence rooted in 'natural rights', or as Marx puts it 'right against right' (Marx 1977, 225). If the differences in education levels, time required for learning skills, and experiences are insignificant and yet there is a wage hierarchy, such employment hierarchy cannot be attributed to efficient allocation by a competitive market based on technical factors or on the value of marginal product differentials, but must be treated as decisions based on management prerogatives (for instance, non-economic values such as caste or regional affinity, loyalty, and so on).

In such economies, technical difference may not be an overriding factor over organizing labour through institutions associated with the social division of labour, which are equipped to effectively screen workers on the basis of natural differences matching the demand-side requirements as a functionality. The category of 'natural' in such societies could be associated with graded 'socialized normals' of each group of workers with associated imaginations of subsistence, which, rather than being derivatives of abstracted labour and 'natural rights', are outcomes of non-modern rationalizations and social hierarchies of domination and/or hegemony. While the process as a phenomenon may seem like any other ordinary accumulation in its structural forms of production, the underlying social, cultural, and political developments of such a process can be very complicated. In what follows, formations of social division of labour among the informal workers within and across organized and unorganized sectors are discussed in detail. In both these sectors, overwhelmingly, workers migrating from Odisha are being employed.

Take, for instance, the labour process involved in TMT steel making. The first stage of production involves loading and unloading iron ore and coal from trucks, filling the ore into bags, and carrying these bags along with coal to the furnace site of production. The iron ore is then converted into a molten form, a process which is meant to remove adulterations referred to as furnace slag and expanded slag from the iron ore. Workers operating on the furnace, or *bhatti*, are called *bhariman* and work for 12 hours a day, with every 3 hours of activity followed by 3 hours of rest. A typical working day would, for instance, begin at 6 a.m. and there would be activity till 9 a.m., followed by rest between 9 a.m. and 12 p.m., followed by activity between 12 p.m. and 3 p.m., and so on, till 3 a.m. The typical day ends at 3 a.m., only to resume again at 6 a.m. It is during these rest hours that the labourers engage in other activities such as cooking and doing other household chores, shopping, and social interaction—including watching television, listening to music, talking to their families back in their places of origin over mobile phones, and so forth. This profile of rest-hour activities holds for all the workers, cutting across particular time rhythms. The labour activities follow these rhythms so as to prevent the workers from suffering dehydration and exhaustion caused by being exposed to extreme heat conditions at work.

The iron ore is then processed through what is referred to as pelletization, enabling the formation of hot molten iron, which is then poured into moulds. Pellets of sponge-iron while red-hot are then automatically moved to the induction furnace. Unlike the technology that such industries were employing in the past—which involved the production of ingots that were then sold to rolling mills as inputs—shifting the red-hot pellets of sponge-iron to a continuous casting and rolling mill in a vertically integrated production structure involves significant savings on energy use in terms of the usage of coal and costs on electricity use. The induction furnace process involves the combination of sponge-iron pellets with several other minerals to forms alloys, which are then put into funnels to form long rods. The red-hot rods are then removed from the machines and treated by a specific process of cooling that in turn leaves them with internal structural strength. Workers employed on the billet side and those on the funnel side have a time rhythm wherein for every 2 hours of work, they get 1 hour of rest, and this cycle continues for the entire 24-hour period, similar to the 3-hour cycle explicated in the previous paragraph. Some workers on the rolling-mill side are employed for 8 hours, extendable to 10 hours (for over-time wages are paid at the same rate as regular hour wages and not as per the legal stipulations of double the wage rate). The remaining categories of workers work continuously for 12 hours, which is the normal working day for informal workers in the modern manufacturing sector, especially in small- and medium-scale industries located in new industrial towns. In comparison to the time rhythms observed in the surveys conducted during 1999–2001 on workers employed in similar industries, the time rhythms of labour processes now have altered significantly. Earlier, workers were involved in 12 hours of continuous work with a shift system. On the basis of data gathered in January–February 2018, the existing time rhythm continues to involve an aggregate of 12 hours of work, but given that the body and mind of a worker do not get continuous rest beyond three hours over several breaks, the relationship of time rhythms to the stress-levels they impose on a worker's body needs deeper analysis. While the change is quite clearly linked to a capital-intensive and vertically integrated technological upgrade, it seems to have implications for the intensification of work that clearly suggests extremely strenuous outcomes in understanding the nature of work from a labour perspective.

These rods are then moved to an open arena where they are bound into sets by clamping a set of them together. These sets are then loaded and transported for final use. Such rods are used in buildings and other constructions, for instance in large irrigation projects, flyovers, and so on.

Heterogeneity in time rhythms and wage packages is much more in organized informal employment than in unorganized informal employment. This may not in itself be surprising if one assumes that the inter-labour process heterogeneities could well be a result of greater division of labour that is possible with the development of the organization of production. However, workers employed in particular activities are found to be moved within the firm from one activity to another depending on the requirement without there being any alteration in the pay package, leading to heterogeneous payments for the same activity to different workers in the organized manufacturing steel industry.

In contrast, in the unorganized informal employment at the brick kiln, a typical working day begins at 3:30 a.m. and continues until 10:30 p.m. with some breaks in between for food or other refreshments. The average working day ranges between 14 to 16 hours. This is the only time rhythm for all kinds of activities in the labour process, namely digging, mixing of mud, filling moulds, drying, and baking. The only exception is loading and unloading. Much of the activity is, however, measured in piece-wage terms rather than in time-wage terms. The average production per person is 1,000 bricks per day.

Heterogeneity in the modes of payment of wages and the wage-payment processes is equally significant. As already pointed out for the case of brick kiln workers, a typical patri consisting of three individuals is usually paid INR 45,000 in advance. As of January 2018, when the brick kiln work had just commenced, the going wage rate was INR 350 per 1,000 bricks. In addition, a weekly allowance of INR 300 was provided for food consumption. This amount, then, is also treated as additional wage against which work will be taken.

In modern organized manufacturing, the nature of employment contracts amongst informal workers affects the modes of wage payments. Workers hired on a daily contract—who receive wages on a daily basis—are different from registered and unregistered regular-contract workers whose wages, although calculated on a daily basis, are paid once every month. This happens for the reason that workers in most of these informal employment modes do not have sick leaves. If they get sick and cannot attend to work, their wages get cut. Even in organized modern manufacturing, weekly food allowances of up to INR 500–1,000 per week are paid, but this amount gets deducted from the monthly wage. Quite clearly, the worker can retain no savings which can supply him with adequate liquid cash at hand to engage in cash transactions.

The wage-payment process, in turn, has its own peculiarities. Wages are not paid on the last day of the previous month or the first day of the new month. Workers receive their wages anywhere between the 15th and the 20th of a month for the work done in the previous month. This means that for every month's wages paid to the worker, 15 to 20 days of wage payments are always outstanding. This is done to prevent worker turnover.

Thus, while advance payments have led to one form of un-free labour relations among informal workers in the unorganized brick kiln sector, delayed and partial wage payments generate another form of un-free labour relations among informal workers in the organized modern manufacturing sector. Workers state that the delayed and partial payment is a strategy evolved by the contractors, initially meant to guard themselves against the defaults of outstanding payments to grocery shops that were making credit sale payments called *katha*s. While a part of grocery transactions continues to be on credit basis, the weekly food-allowance payments have now predominantly substituted this, and groceries, to a large extent, are now purchased for current payments. Katha-based customers are charged 5 per cent over the regular price, as opposed to the current transactions–based customers making purchases from the grocery shops. Despite the marginalization of katha transactions, delayed and partial wage payments continue as a strategy to control worker turnover.

As of January 2018, the wage rates for bharimans is INR 14,500, for the first hand (assistant to the bhariman at the furnace) is INR 14,000, for those employed at the pelletization and the rolling-mill side is INR 10,000–11,500 (however, some workers doing similar activities receive INR 8,500–9,000), and for those employed for loading and unloading activities is INR 7,500–8,000. The 15 to 20 days of delayed payments, cutting across activities, average to INR 10,400, which for 1,080 workers would be INR 1,12,32,000. The interest rate for the informal moneylending activity in the local economy is currently at 3 per cent per month, but there exists yet another moneylending activity where small quantities of money are lent to street vendors, shopkeepers, hotel owners, taxi owners, and so forth, who use it as their capital and by the end of the day repay the loan at 10 per cent interest per day. The contractor who receives money from the management for wage payments engages in delayed payments to workers and, in turn, puts this money into circulation in the local informal credit markets. A total of 1,080 workers are operating with 6 contractors. Together, these contractors are likely to make an additional income ranging between INR 1,68,480–1,68,48,000 from the informal credit markets in the local economy in the minimum delayed period of 15 days.

None of the circulating labour coming from western Odisha and getting employed as informal workers in the unorganized sector of brick kiln production has access to other social security–related protections, such as the employee's social insurance (ESI) or the provident fund (PF). Despite the many distinctions in the modes of recruitment or employment contracts of registered and unregistered labour, the denial of this provision is common to both. The living conditions of workers on the site of the brick kiln make the provision of ESI all the more imperative. It needs to be understood that brick manufacturing happens in erstwhile agricultural lands. The worksite, unlike a typical factory, has no roof. Workers are exposed to the sun, wind, and rain during the course of their work. The work is not intermittent but continuous in nature. The temperature in Telangana can soar up to 45 degree Celsius in the summer. Agricultural fields located in remote rural settings do not have access to safe drinking water. Usually, a small pond is created at the site of brick manufacturing in which the utensils used for food consumption are washed. The continuous reuse of this pond during an entire season of brick manufacturing eventually leaves it filled with floating rotten food refuse, stinking and extremely unhygienic for any use even indirectly linked to human consumption. Residences for workers are made up of tinned roofs, thatched roofs, or even polythene covers. On average, they are as small as 10 feet in length and breadth and 5 feet in height, with no ventilation, and often housing 2 or even 3 people together. That the workers have no safety gear or body protections and their residences are closely clogged structures without a bathroom or latrine facilities (the Swachh Bharat Mission hasn't reached this society) also implies that they are exposed to different kinds of insects and pests which are the vectors of a variety of communicable diseases, posing a danger not only to these individuals but to public health in general. Since their bodies are given very little rest and they consume poor-quality nutrition, the strenuous work makes this working population vulnerable to a variety of sicknesses. According to the sample surveyed at the brick kiln, it was common to have at least 14 minor accidents per season, and electrocution was the source of major accidents. While activity-related hazards are common at the brick kiln, the lack of first aid and the exposure of even simple wounds to a highly unclean environment usually makes the condition worse, sometimes heightening the risk and/or the recovery time. While the workers are allowed to have a leave per week, they are forced to work through the severe pain of their injuries. The condition is made much worse if the injuries are on the limbs (especially around toes, palms, and so on) that get exposed to wetness and are muddied while engaged in work. This is so because the seths are eager to recover the value of the advances that they have paid to these workers, and any time lost is a liability for them. Workers who slow down in their activity on account of sickness or injury risk inviting verbal abuse and physical assault to add to their miseries. The labour process and labour relations in practice are usually bereft of any sensitivity or humanity.

In comparison, an overwhelming majority of informal workers in the organized manufacturing activity (TMT steel production in this instance) also lack ESI and PF protections. However, their location closer to towns and the rhythms of their work allow private medical care to exist. Sometimes, a collusion between ESI hospitals and the contractors makes it possible for one worker to get medication on the ESI card of a fellow worker. Though at the risk of losing a day's wage, a leave is a possibility among these workers to rest and recover. Relatively speaking, although the workers are provided poor quality living spaces—15 feet by 10 feet and 7 feet high, without any ventilation, and shared between five workers on average—they are not exposed to the elements of nature as they live inside the premises of the factory and have access to toilet facilities and safe drinking water. Although the factory premises are very dirty with open streams of used water draining out, this seems as relatively nothing in comparison to the pool of stagnant water stinking with food refuge and swarming with flies, insects, pests, and worms right beside the workers' residences (which also had children in them) at the brick kiln.

Differences in the intensity of vulnerability within and across the unorganized and organized sectors need to be understood on the basis of multiple indicators of employment conditions, labour relations, and living conditions at work. Such quantifications can be developed into a systematic index to measure the improvements or deteriorations within sectors as well as the convergences and divergences across sectors. Against the backdrop of this vulnerability, we can analyse the meaning of the denial of access to social security protections such as the ESI and PF to various sections of the working population. Quite clearly, heterogeneity in the conditions of work and life has implications for the reading one takes of the well-being and welfare of working populations in both organized and unorganized sectors. The eventual representations of these readings are also affected by the intensity of the potential costs of seemingly similar denials. From the descriptions provided in the last few paragraphs, we can broadly surmise that on the basis of work timings, working conditions, housing, health risks, labour relations (especially in overseeing labour), and so forth, the conditions in organized modern manufacturing are relatively better than in unorganized brick manufacturing.

That employment forms and conditions of work and life are much more heterogeneous in organized manufacturing than in the unorganized sector may or may not pose a paradox in itself. What might come as a seemingly logical explanation is the aspect of possible differences in skill sets. If heterogeneity is a result of varying levels of education and skill, it could still be seen as a rational structure from a mainstream perspective. It would then be possible to reduce this unequal system of employment stratification to a simple incentive structure that can be explained as an effort–productivity–rewards hierarchy. However, these are hypothetical logical deductions, which are derivatives of an assumed rational behaviour of systems rather than an observed rational behaviour of systems, which require empirical verification. New Keynesian economists have recognized that systems cannot be rational under imperfect market conditions in terms of generating right price signals or the optimal allocation of resources, including factors such as labour. Going beyond this, political economy as well as the Ambedkarite approach recognizes the structural constraints to the rationalization of imperfect and less-than-rational systems that have explanations in institutional and social power–based differential norms. That price signals are derivatives of such power and contain no force to correct this power has substantive theoretical implications (Thorat and Newman 2010).

Paradox of Employment Immobility

Against the backdrop of the findings mentioned in the previous section, which to a large extent suggest that there is an overall convergence in terms of deterioration in the quality of employment and the nature of labour relations across the organized and unorganized sectors, it is clearly evident that these conditions remain differentiated and heterogeneous in favour of the organized sector. The obvious anticipation as a consequence to this differentiation is that the informal workers of the unorganized sector would be motivated to move towards organized informal employment, or towards better-quality employment and labour relations in general. We attempted to probe this as part of the survey. The findings are quite interesting.

From the total sample of brick kiln workers, 64 per cent of the households were already diversified but circulating between multiple livelihoods. 93 per cent of workers were experiencing circulation between farms and brick kilns. 26 per cent were circulating between farms and minor forest-produce activities. 35 per cent were experiencing circulation between brick kilns, farms, and rural non-farm (mostly construction) activities in the place of origin. Those experiencing circulation between forest and non-farm activities as well as those circulating into exclusively non-farm activities in the place of origin were 3 per cent each. Interstate mobility away from the place of origin was exclusively linked to brick kiln activity for 97 per cent of the households, this was the case for even those respondents who had over two decades of participation in employment that involved interstate circulation. In 3 per cent of households, represented by young educated youth, a mobility towards organized manufacturing industry was found. Considering that the farm sector is in deep distress and the conditions of employment and life at the brick kiln are horrific, one wonders why the sample's mobility away from brick kiln and farm labour is so low. Quite clearly, diversification is not an easy option.

On the side of organized modern manufacturing, all the workers surveyed made the observation that neither did they ever have anything to do with brick kiln labouring activity, nor had they ever come across a colleague who had earlier participated in it. Those employed in the organized modern manufacturing as informal workers, however, did experience some diversification and mobility between a range of activities; the overall figure of such participation was 36 per cent. From the total sample studied, 10 per cent experienced mobility between organized manufacturing activity and hotels. A relatively significant proportion of 20 per cent had experienced mobility between skilled construction and construction-related trading activity and organized manufacturing. Only one worker had experienced mobility between organized manufacturing and security guard activity, and another had earlier worked as a tractor driver for the activity of loading and unloading bricks for kilns. When asked why brick kiln workers never moved into manufacturing industrial activity, an overwhelming number of respondents ascribed the cause to the ignorance of brick kiln workers, which they further attributed to their social composition, that is, a large number of these workers belonged to the Scheduled Caste or Tribe backgrounds.

However, on being questioned why they themselves did not move away from the highly strenuous manufacturing activity towards other options such as hotels and being security guards, the respondents attributed the reason to a high expected cost of living or uncertainties in terms of the cost of such a mobility. On the other hand, they perceived that they understood manufacturing activity and the related pros and cons better. This might well be the case with the brick kiln workers as well. When asked about the poverty and misery of the manufacturing workers in comparison to local workers, the managers also responded similarly, attributing this to the backwardness of the states these workers were migrating from and inferring, therefore, that the long-distance migrant labour employed in informal organized manufacturing was an ignorant lot. Each segment of the labour market seems to think that the one below is more ignorant than itself, only because it finds itself higher up in the order. This mode of reasoning is what Adam Smith was perhaps referring to in his theory of moral sentiments, the gist of which is that people hold the aristocracy in reverence and socialize themselves into obedience not because the aristocracy has such abilities that deserve reverence but rather because the aristocracy has wealth and this wealth exists for very undeserving reasons. Quite clearly, the two circulating migratory informal labour networks are not merely segmented but almost segregated in regional and social terms. Could it be that the regional and social segregations are misrepresentations of underlying productivity differences attributable to levels of education and skill sets?

Amongst the brick kiln workers, we found that a significant proportion, 33 per cent of the sample of respondents, were illiterate. Of those who had formal education, 21 per cent, 37 per cent, and 9 per cent had primary, middle school, and metric levels of education respectively. 90 per cent of the respondents said they would require a week or less to learn the skills necessary to employ themselves at the brick kilns. In comparison, in the survey done in 2012–13 amongst the informal labour employed in organized modern manufacturing (especially in small and medium enterprises), 31 per cent of workers were found to be illiterate, and of those with formal education, 11 per cent, 11 per cent, and 38 per cent respectively had primary, middle school, and metric levels of education. Sixty-one per cent of long-distance migrants responded that the average time required to pick up the skills necessary to employ themselves ranges between a few weeks to less than 7 months. In the steel industry, which has had major technological upgradations towards a more capital-intensive and automatic, vertically-integrated production system, the learning time for workers has reduced and now lies within the range of 3 days to 3 months. Thus, on the basis of education or skill levels it seems highly unlikely that we can explain away the segregation of these circular migration networks. The claims, therefore, that the heterogeneities in recruitment, employment contracts, modes of payment, conditions of work and life, as well as organizational structures are rational outcomes on the basis of education or skills do not seem to be substantiated by empirical evidence.

The circulation of labour experienced and the specific paths of employment which workers tread in this course, being allocated to different types of labouring across the hierarchy of employment structures or activity roles, seem to be random and independent of educational qualifications, self-determined choice, or self-assessed ability of the worker to perform an activity (from the supply side or from the vantage point of the workers supplying labour). The allocation of workers in terms of the activities as part of the employment hierarchy also seems to be similarly independent of the time required to learn a skill at a micro level (from the demand side or from the vantage point of the labour process involved in the production). Therefore, the informally employed labour, which is always on a temporary basis in the course of their participation in the activities, could find themselves randomly at any level of employment hierarchy within this informal segment across time periods, independent of the strictly structured employment hierarchy determined by technical structures or a strictly secular upward mobility across the employment hierarchy. Technical structures do not seem to explain in any systematic form either the intra-industry segmentation or the inter-industry segregation within or between the organized and unorganized sectors that have been studied here. And this is despite the labour source areas being located in the same state of Odisha and the educational backgrounds of the workers also being similar.

These heterogeneities are not fallouts of an intensely competitive system which gets to the optimal allocation of labour through economic forces. Rather, the structure seem to require a non-technical explanation. The origin of particular networks of labour engaged in circular migratory streams is rooted predominantly in rural distress or lack of adequate employment at the place of origin, and the perpetuation of particular pathways of circulation labour is happening because these supply-side processes operate through personalized social networks.

The most significant characteristic of the brick kiln migration is that the basic unit of recruitment in this sector, referred to as a patri, already connotes that family and kinship ties are embedded inevitably in such networks. Information flows could go beyond family members as the source of information about the employment opportunity could be through neighbourhood relations. Eventually, thus, the entire supply catchments for brick kiln workers get identified with specific regions, villages, neighbourhoods, and caste groups. While for 53 per cent of the brick kiln workers the source of information about employment was either chote sardars or other known workers, 43 per cent got to know of it through their family, relatives, friends, and neighbourhood. There were no cases where the information flow was through unfamiliar persons. That the villages in India continue to be geographically structured on the lines of caste, especially for the poorest of the poor households, implies that these networks are the anchors for mobility. There is very little scope to diversify the nature of these social networks as they are likely to reproduce on the basis of highly personalized connections. Circular migration brought about by the structures of social economy and political economy reinforces such structures, and the possibility for diversification of employment is also constrained because the exploration of opportunities for diversification is a network-level function. Networks that remain highly personalized, therefore, offer very little opportunity for diversification nor for any significant socio-economic mobility.

There is a relatively greater variety in the network formations operating on the supply side of the informal labour working in organized modern manufacturing. With reference to information flows about work and certain forms of social protections, only 20 per cent of the networks are derived from highly personalized connections based in family and kinship. Another 5 per cent are rooted in neighbouring villages and not immediate neighbourhoods; networks are being formed among people who may not have known each other, although they could have been living in neighbouring villages. Among such structures of mobility, caste does get indirectly reinforced in characteristics that go to identify a social network. But a significantly large mode of network formation is offered when we find that 15 per cent of the network formations, information flows, and social protections have been formed between people who did not know each other before they reached their destination of work. Amongst such networks, about 5 per cent were formed because people hailed from the same state and, therefore, spoke the same language, while the largest proportion of the most impersonal formations is only 10 per cent. (This is the closest one can empirically get to the asocial imagery of the so-called economic agent, which is the best we can do around what can be seen to mimic the characterization of the modern times.)

The next best social network that may not be strictly rooted in family–kinship or caste structures but cannot escape regional or linguistic identities is one that is formed based on friendships, originating mostly in schools. This network presents itself as the most dominant, accounting for 60 per cent of the social networks, information flows, and social protections currently in operation among the informal labour employed in organized modern manufacturing.

Thus, more than marginal product differences, differentials derived from various levels of subsistence costs, which in turn open up different levels of cost-cutting, seem to better explain the structural formations. Evidence suggests that in the existing structure of the roles that the labour is performing, there seems to be no strict rational basis for stratification. The status of their activity in the hierarchy of employment in the labour process is measured by wages, time rhythms, and risk of accidents. In informal employment, unlike the assumptions made in the case of formal employment by mainstream theory, wages don't necessarily factor in all the costs. A very risky activity requiring the same time to learn in relation to other activities can be very low paid. The status of their activity may also be measured in terms of the technical parameters linked to the entry point, such as years of education, skills they know, or work experience in this segment of the labour market. Further, over the years, there is no observable process suggesting that this arbitrariness of matching the costs and rewards is being corrected to adhere to such rationality. It is possible, therefore, that this randomness of allocation of labour could link the arbitrary decisions of management to their control over the workers and to cost cutting, given the uncertainty-linked insecurity in terms of retaining the status within the stratification. The system, therefore, does not exhibit a need for a self-correction, nor is it seen as a market failure to seek any regulatory intervention for correction. The two circulating labour networks, that of the unorganized sector brick kilns and of the organized modern manufacturing sector, have remained segregated for over two-and-a-half decades of their functioning. This has huge implications for understanding the nature of interface between networks and markets on the one side and networks and formal and informal regulatory mechanisms on the other, both of which are supposedly bringing about rationalizations in allocations from economic and sociopolitical viewpoints respectively. The much eulogized step function of mobility in the informal sector and between the formal and informal sectors seems to be only a fable. The challenge, in a sense, is to explain the failure of the market as well as the State in being able to rationalize the behaviour of economic and social systems of organization. It is at this point that the understanding of both Monetarist/New Classical neo-liberals and New Keynesian reformers reaches a limit. Both these paradigms look to the mythology of competitive markets or the one that invokes the State's macro-policy regulations aimed at bringing about information, income, or interest-rate corrections to address market imperfections or failures, yet fail to appreciate the deeper structural processes that underlie these failures. Overwhelmingly, if the nature of accumulation in the economy, with reference to competition and the objectives of profit maximization at the level of firms, finds it to its advantage that the so-called imperfections and failures actually complement cost-cutting, done differently in different segregations and segmentations of employment, the system may not progress towards rationalization governed by an overriding economic force. Such an accumulation process, therefore, would not lead to improvements in the productivity of labour or in the incomes and consumption of such households, but to the expansion of rents to various middlemen and to their misrepresentation as profits derived from oppressive and uncivil relations of exploitation. The stratification of employment within and across the segmented labour market of the unorganized and organized sectors informal employment does not represent qualitative binaries in terms of employment and working conditions—one signifies development, while the other lacks it. The segmentation itself is a result of the socially and historically generated social networks used for mobility and recruitment, partially explained by the initial conditions of workers in the place of origin. Across the segments and the strata of employment within, while recognizing the significant relative differences in the conditions of employment and life—whether measured in standard terms of poverty lines or in terms of minimum wages, social protections, security of employment, and organization of labour, or even the ability to cope with contingent expenditure shocks or perpetual indebtedness—the differences are a matter of degree in miserable conditions that do not seem to improve over time in terms of the standard metrics. The social implications of such a system of supply and demand of labour warrants serious discussion.

Civic Entitlements and Civil Rights of Circulating Informal Labour; the Paradigm of *Daya*

In the course of our discussions with the informal workers employed in organized modern manufacturing, it was asked whether they could not find employment in their place of origin, and while this was the reason for them to move out of their villages, why did they have to move out of their state. There are industries located in towns closer to the villages that are the catchments from where people migrated to work in Kothur. However, the workers pointed out that the industries requiring similar skills which are located closer to their place of origin refused to recruit them. When asked for the reason, the workers stated that the managers of those industries thought of the local workers as lazy and non-cooperative. In our discussion with the manager of the steel plant in Kothur, a similar reason was given for not recruiting local workers by the unit from Kothur. But workers from Kothur, in particular, and from Ranga Reddy district and Mahabubnagar (known for the most hard-working Palamooru labour), in general, are circulating in employments which are equally (if not more) strenuous in the nature of activities. On pointing this out to the workers, it did not take them too long to say that they had not been chosen by the industry located closer to their place of origin because they would raise their voice against unfair practices if they were amongst their own people and closer to their villages. This was not possible here in Kothur, or such other places of work. That they accept meagre wages is linked to their miserable conditions in their place of origin, which leads to frugal imaginations of their subsistence, which further subserves efficiently the objective function of cost minimization. Misery is an asset that makes a group of workers the preferred lot from the demand side. In the various cost structures from the demand side, various subsistence structures from the supply side find their perfect matches to evolve into a well-ordered, functioning system of accumulation.

The disdainful employment so gained is a survival strategy directed towards subsistence and not gainful employment that delivers socio-economic mobility in any sustainable or tangible form. This is to least undermine the symbolic mobility and the value it in turn has in the social perception associated with migrating to urban spaces, particularly if the employment is in the organized modern manufacturing industry. This mobility is relative to its own socio-economic location and specific to the perception of the members of its own society rather than a mobility that can be measured in tangible and sustainable holistic, absolute, or structural terms.

It is interesting to observe that an overwhelmingly large proportion (70 per cent) of the brick kiln migrants drawn from the poorest of the poor households, belonging to most oppressed social groups such as the Scheduled Castes and Scheduled Tribes, and living in India's most backward districts (the KBK) do not have white cards (identifying these households as below poverty line). Although a special food security programme that provides a minimum of 35 kilos of rice at Re 1 a kilo is available to every household from such regions, the denial of white cards has serious implications for exclusion from several other government programmes meant to alleviate such households from conditions of dependence and vulnerability. While a large section of the informal labour working in organized modern manufacturing industries has white cards, they are being used by their families back in their places of origin. Despite having Aadhar cards, none of the workers are able to access the public distribution system (PDS) or any other government programme in the place of destination.

With respect to brick kiln workers, it is disheartening to observe that in both the place of origin and the place of destination, constitutional authority such as that of the sarpanchs in the Panchayats, far from playing the eulogized role of decentralizing power and democratization, find themselves as part of organizational modes that are anti-labour. In the place of origin, sarpanchs are part of village committees meant to monitor and regulate the behaviour of brick kiln migrant workers, and in the place of destination, the sarpachs are much closer to the farmer–seth collusions, having been party to the informal lease transfers of agricultural lands to the non-agricultural brick kiln use, while enjoying the subsidies and other benefits provided to agriculture. They are also often part of collusions promoting the illegal extraction of village tank clay-mud, usually reserved for improving the fertility of agricultural lands, for brick making. Similar is the fate of inter-state migrants working as informal organized manufacturing industrial workers who do not interest the local leaders as a constituency, since they keep circulating and do not have a voter registration in the place of destination. A large number of workers fail to vote even in their places of destination. In some instances, especially concerning the young first-time voters, because of being caught up in circulation, they fail to register themselves in the voters' list. Once their participation in the basic unit of representation and governance at the local level is taken away, this alienation only reproduces itself in other agencies, namely the labour commissioner's office, police officials, revenue officials, and so forth. The effect cannot be treated merely as a State failure in rationalizing the systems through equity, justice, and rule of law, rather it is one of a failed State, given that it is almost a rule rather than an exception that there is an active collusion of the state apparatus in perpetuating a variety of illegalities.

Inaccessibility to formal civil social institutions and concrete manifestations of the failure to rationalize the systems operating in interface with the employment and labour relations have grave implications. Some experiences of the workers go a long way to give deep insights into the nature of employment and labour relations amongst these sections of workers. The following paragraphs are excerpts from the press release that was given by a fact-finding team, of which the author was a member.

The fact finding team has inquired into a reported death of a brick kiln worker on 1/2/2014. Mr. Manoj hailing from Jogi Munda Village of Balangir district of Orissa died in suspicious circumstances on the 13th of January 2014. The worker has died while he was at work in a brick kiln owned by Mr. G. Madhava Rao. The team has interacted with a representative of the brick kiln who works as an accountant and who was present on the day, the death has taken place. The team also spoke to several workers who were also witnesses to the death of Mr. Manoj.

The representative of the brick kiln maintained that on the 12th night Mr. Manoj had got drunk and in the early hours of Monday the 13th of January Mr. Manoj has had a fight with his wife. The couple according to the brick kiln representative's version were hailing abuses at each other when the owner of the brick kiln visited the kiln. Having witnessed the scuffle between the duo the owner expressed his annoyance with the frequent fights the couple purportedly had which was affecting the work. Having been publicly rebuked Mr. Manoj was very upset and during the lunch break, Manoj's wife served him food and was sitting outside their settlement when Manoj as per the version of the representative of the brick kiln hanged himself inside the living space with his towel and within ten minutes Manoj reportedly died. The accountant narrates that on seeing co-workers crowded before the room in which Monoj is stated to have committed suicide, some workers brought Manoj's body outside the room. The owner is reported to have immediately called for a local RMP Dr. Suryanarayana to the brick kiln. On arrival, Dr. Suryanarayana declared Manoj dead. The owner of the brick kiln Mr. G. Madhava Rao is said to have then called for a distant relative of Manoj working as a tractor driver in another brick kiln owned by Mr. Venkat Rao. The accountant at the brick kiln stated that by 3pm on 13th of January the body of Mr. Manoj was cremated near the village lake.

The fact finding team tried to verify the veracity of the claim that Mr. Manoj had committed suicide based on material and circumstantial evidence.

The fact finding team has found that the room in which Mr. Manoj and his wife were staying had a tin roof barely 6–6½ feet high resting on a single rod passing through from the middle of the roof. There was in addition to the central rod on which the whole weight of the roof rested, another stick projecting out towards the rear end of the room. This wooden log was hardly an inch thick and was projecting in an awkward manner. This wooden log was projecting from a height which was at least half a feet less than the roof height itself. Further, while a large portion of the log was actually tucked into supporting the rear end of the roof, the actual free projection on which Mr. Manoj had purportedly hanged himself was further less by half a feet. This material evidence raises several doubts. The actual height from which Mr. Manoj is suggested to have hanged himself, using a cloth which in turn has been described as being longer than a usual towel. Manoj was a well-built person of over 5½ feet height and weighing a little over 60 kgs. When Manoj was reportedly found 'hanging' his feet were actually touching the ground. The projection of the log at a height of 5½ feet and the awkward and unstable position of the log could not have supported the entire weight of the body hanging with its feet above the ground while being suspended by some length with the towel. Had hanging been the cause of death, the reported time span during which the act of hanging happened was in a span of ten minutes. When the body was found hanging, the tongue had not protruded out suggesting lack of forceful strangulation.

The fact finding team has further probed into the circumstances of the death. On Saturday the 11th of January, the report of the total number of bricks made by each patri was submitted to the owner Mr. G. Madhava Rao. Mr. Madhava Rao having ascertained the details of the output, came to the brick kiln on Monday. He was upset that Manoj and his wife were not performing as much as he expects them to perform. A furious Mr. Madhava Rao entered first into an argument and then physically assaulted Mr. Manoj. The assault took place between 8am–9am on 13th of January following which Manoj collapsed and died. After which wife of Manoj was asked to wait outside the room they were staying in at the site while Manoj's body was carried into the room and later a scene of suicide was created and Manoj was declared dead.

Having said that some workers have actually carried the body of Manoj out, the representative of the brick kiln who was present at the sight [sic] initially identified two co-workers—one of whom was part of Manoj's patri and another who was a tractor driver as the workers who brought the body out. Both the workers however denied this and while the co-worker belonging to Manoj's patri said that he was actually making bricks at that time, the other worker stated that he was driving the tractor and was not present at the scene. While Manoj and the co-worker belonged to same patri, there was no way this worker could have been working alone while as claimed by the accountant, Manoj had come to have his lunch. Once the co-worker denied having brought the body out, the accountant took the name of one Mr. Adu Sahu as the person who brought the body out of the room. Adu Sahu however reportedly left the brick kiln to accompany Manoj's wife back to their village after Manoj was cremated. Workers were visibly fearful of associating themselves with the event in any manner.

Why are the workers so fearful in narrating the event and associating with the retrieval of the body of Mr. Manoj from his room? Why was a police case not registered? Why did the owner or the

RMP Dr. Suryanarayana not report what was a medico-legal case? Why was the body not sent for post-mortem? Why was the body so hurriedly cremated? Where was the need to burn even the cloth which was found at the scene of the incident?

There is a basis therefore to believe that Manoj's death was not only unnatural but was in fact not a suicide but a murder/homicide following physical assault or battering. The fact finding committee finds that even after several days have passed since the incident the police is blissfully unaware of this death. Police has not shown any interest in probing this case. Even if it were a suicide (which it seems it is not) it is the duty of the police and the local administration to take the necessary steps to conduct a proper investigation and ascertain facts. This is a gross negligence of their duty. This gives room for doubts about a possible nexus. Such doubts could affect the credibility of the police and the local administration. At least now, the police and the local administration including the labour inspectors, the collector's office have to wake up. The fact finding team demands that the local administration and the police order/conduct a fair and impartial investigation into the suspicious death of Mr. Manoj.

In January 2018, it was found that there had been no progress in this case and it had, in fact, been closed. The activists on the ground stated that the victim's family had refused to speak up, fearing repercussions. There are several such instances of physical violence and brutality, along with sexual violence against women.

With reference to the economic processes operating in such spaces of uncivil social relations where the oppressed members of a society do not muster the courage to speak up against some of the gravest forms of atrocities, they can hardly be imagined to come close to any normal, rational system in terms of a claim to value. When we reached Bahabal village in the Balangir district of Odisha to carry out our survey, we came across a respondent, Krupadhar Naik (22), who was very excited following his return from the previous season's brick kiln work in which his seth had rewarded him with an Atlas bicycle for his hard work. With 1,000 being the average number of bricks produced by an individual per day, the total number of bricks produced by a worker during 6 months of employment from January to June is approximately 1,80,000. As against this average, this patri of workers (consisting of his own family members) seemed to have averaged 3,05,000 bricks. As a reward, the worker had received a bicycle worth about INR 3,500. We began to calculate and demystified this reward. Against the usual average product, 3,05,000 bricks meant that he had actually produced 1,25,000 bricks in excess of the norm. The going wage rate during the time was INR 250 per 1,000 bricks. At this rate, the contractor should have paid the worker a wage of INR 31,250. The reward, in fact, meant that the worker had been duped of INR 27,750.

Cases of verbal and physical abuse involving informal labour employed in organized modern manufacturing are relatively insignificant. However, the experience of uncivil social relations takes other forms. Employers have defaulted on paying the wages of 25 per cent of these workers, and most of such cheating cases have gone unreported.

The case of Anukul Naik (23) from the Kendrapada district of Odisha, currently working in a battery manufacturing unit in Kothur, is similar. At his previous employment where he worked as a mason at a construction site in the Hitech city of Hyderabad, the contractor defaulted on the payment of wages, following which the workers went to the police station to report. However, they were spoken to harshly by the police officials and were driven out of the police station. He expressed his resentment over the government officials not treating poor people as equal citizens. In another formal institution–related experience, Anukul Naik stated that while he was working in the battery company in 2010–11, labour inspectors visited the factory one day. Much before the inspectors arrived to ask the workers about the wage rates they were receiving, the contractor instructed them to say that they were receiving INR 120 instead of the actual figure which was INR 80 for an 8-hour working day.

The same worker, as we stood near his rented house, pointed to a heap of waste being dumped before his house by the local people and remarked:

> I don't like this, we are also human beings. Why should waste be dumped like this before where I live? But I cannot say this, because I fear I might upset the local people who might gang up against us. I remain silent about such things. Back in the village [in the place of origin] it will not be like this.

In another episode, Govind Barikh (40) from the Bhadrak district of Odisha, currently working in a steel industry where he has been employed since 2008, informed us that he met with a major accident in 2014 where his leg got crushed under a vehicle while he was on the job. His limb suffered permanent damage. While he was admitted to a hospital and his medical expenses were borne by the company, he was not paid any wages for the period during which he recovered. After his recovery, his was not in a position to perform the same activities that earned him his wages, therefore a significant reduction was made in his wages. He was unable to send home the remittances required to meet the expenses of his family, and consequentially his daughter had to quit her education to reduce the household expenditure.

Juna Dalai (26) from Ganjam village in the Barampur district of Odisha, currently working in a steel industry in Kothur, narrated to us two episodes from his experience. In 2013, while he was working at Kalik Steels located in Jalna, Maharashtra, he went out to shop at a local market at 3 p.m. On his way to the market, he was waylaid by a group of local youth who beat him up and robbed him of the INR 300 that he was carrying with him. Such is the condition, he said, that workers with such experiences cannot report such matters for the fear of repercussions.

He narrated an other episode, making a case for differential treatment against migrants. This incident occoured while he was working at Hari-Om, another steel company located in Jalna, Maharashtra, where the majority of workers were from Odisha. In the loading–unloading section one day, some material being unloaded by an Odisha worker inadvertently fell on the hand of a Marathi-speaking worker who hailed from a local village. In a fit of rage, the Marathi worker held the Odisha worker by his collar and slapped him. The Odisha migrant workers, being larger in numbers, ganged up on the Marathi worker and beat him up in retaliation. Eventually, the Marathi worker returned with a whole village, gatecrashed the factory and thrashed everybody. The Odisha workers settled their accounts with the factory's management, received their balance wages, and left the place.

Bilas Majhi (45), employed with a steel industry located in Kothur, stated that he made regular purchases from a grocery shop located opposite the factory he worked in. Towards the end of each month, his contractor deducted his grocery expenses from his wage and handed him only the balance amount. While he was aware that his contractor might be cheating by deducting more than the fair amount towards grocery expenses, he could not raise his voice and demand to see the accounts pertaining to these expenses, fearing repercussions. He said that such things would not happen if he were living in his place of origin.

The nature of employment and labour relations, social formations constituting the mobility of informal labour, and their institutional and social interfaces bring into question whether their mobility from rural to urban or peri-urban geographies, or from agrarian, rural activities to unorganized/organized manufacturing in itself can be taken as suggestive of development. We cannot perhaps hold this taken-for-granted hypothesis to be true anymore. That informal workers employed in the organized sector do not have severely uncivil experiences with high frequency such as the ones experienced by the unorganized sector workers is a distinction that remains.

* * *

This chapter conducts a comparative analysis of empirical data collected from two groups of circular migrants predominantly from Odisha and employed as informal labour, one working in the unorganized sector of brick kiln activity, while the other in an organized modern manufacturing activity. A convergence is observed on several indicators of working and living conditions. However, informal employment in the unorganized sector is definitely distinct from that in the organized sector. This distinctness comes through in the form of the fact that the pathways of social networks supplying labour to the unorganized sector have remained segregated from those of the networks supplying labour to the organized sector. The basis of this distinction is not to be found strongly in technical differences represented by the educational background of workers or their skill sets required to perform the labour processes. The segregation of the social networks is explained by social compositions, levels of distress and interlocking of markets, nature of the social networks from the supply side, together with a general behaviour of units in both the sectors not to recruit local labour from the demand side. This in turn has caused systematic social displacement of people together with lack of competition in the labour market and regulatory failures with respect to enforcing labour laws has creating circumstances of uncivil social relations.

While this is the grave reality of the direction informal employment and labour relations are taking, the current government planned to introduce the Labour Code Bill on Wages 2015, Labour Code Bill on IR 2015, which has punitive measures including Rs 10,000 fine and 3 years imprisonment for trade union leaders, and the Small Factories (Regulation of Employment and Conditions of Services)

Bill, 2014, which involves withdrawal of 16 laws meant to protect the bare minimum standards of employment. Quite clearly, the direction of labour laws is in complete dissonance with reality and is likely to contribute to further accentuation of uncivil social conditions. One wonders as to whose interests such policymakers represent.

The aspirations of workers such as to be treated equally, with dignity, to seek procedural justice, to expect security to the money they own or to their body from physical harm, or to expect transparency about their own accounts being denied are manifestations of the all permeating uncivil social existence also of the informal workers working in the organized, modern, manufacturing industry and related circular mobility. The segregation between the unorganized and the organized informal workers and the segmentation within is not explained as much by technical differences or differentials in rewards as by forms of uncivil social experiences. Evolving appropriate indicators to measure and to build hierarchies of uncivil relations so as to have an index of uncivil relations in course of the unfolding development experience could be the direction in which research may have to look to for making meaningful development analysis of informal labour relations cutting across sectors. Can the shocking episodes of mob lynching, parochial politics, and tendencies of authoritarianism witnessed in contemporary times be corrected without the largest section of our nation, the informal workers, who depend on the material, social, and institutional foundations of civil social existence. This must be reflected upon by the policy makers who denounce such trends.

In course of approaching such peculiar structures of employment and labour relations we must understand that it would be a misnomer to believe that the processes operating among the labour engaging in inter-state circular migration for informal employment in unorganized and organized manufacturing activities behave in a well ordered and rational manner. To understand the development of uncivil social relations as complementarities to the cost-cutting modes of accumulation where standards and norms are set aside as rigidities and disincentives, one has to recognize the connect this process has with the social reproduction of the hierarchy of subsistence rooted in the miseries and vulnerabilities generated by levels of economic distress, social powerlessness, and political disenfranchisement. The challenge of analysing the interface between non-technical and non-economic forces underlying the production systems and accumulation—operating at a global scale on the one hand with non-modern, non-rational social formations of social organization of labour and on the other hand segregated into multiple universes—underlying the process of current development are better grappled by Gramscian and Ambedkarite analytical frameworks.

References

Bhadhuri, Amit. 2005. 'Joblessness'. In *Brazilian Journal of Political Economy* 25, no. 2 (98) (April–June): 45–59.

Gudavarthy, Vijay. 2003. 'Changing Policy Regime and Labour: A Case Study'. *Economic and Political Weekly* 38, no. 31 (2–8 August): 3261–70.

———. 2005. 'Migration, Vulnerability and Insecurity in New Industrial Labour Market'. *Economic and Political Weekly* 40, no. 23 (28 May–4 June): 2304–12.

———. 2015. 'Labour Movement in Globalizing India'. In *ICSSR Research Surveys and Explorations in Economics*, vol. 2: *India and the International Economy*, edited by Jayati Ghosh, 381–439. New Delhi: Oxford University Press.

Harriss-White, Barbara. 2003. 'The Workforce and Its Social Structures'. In *India Working: Essays on Society and Economy*. New York: Cambridge University Press.

Friedman, Milton. 1977. 'Nobel Lecture: Inflation and Unemployment'. *Journal of Political Economy* 85, no. 3: 451–72.

Lucas, R., and T. Sargent. 1979. 'After Keynesian Macroeconomics'. *Federal Reserve Bank of Minneapolis Quarterly Review* 3, no. 2 (Spring issue): 1–16.

Marx, Karl. 1977. *Capital*. New York: Vintage Books.

Parry, Jonathan, Jan Breman, and Karin Kapadia, eds. 1999. *The Worlds of Indian Industrial Labour*. London: Sage Publication.

Society for Labour and Development, Citizens Rights Collective, and Action Aid. 2017. *India's Labour Law Changes toward Advancing Principles of Rights, Inclusion and Employment Security*. Available at http://actionaid.org/sites/files/actionaid/e_book_indias_labour_law_final_1.pdf. Last accessed on.

Sengupta, Tathagata, and Vijay Gudavarthy. 2015. 'A Survey of Migration from Western Orissa to Telangana'. Report produced under the chairmanship of S.R. Sankaran (Rural Labour), NIRD&PR, Hyderabad.

Thorat, Sukhadeo, and Katherine Newman. 2010. *Blocked by Caste: Economic Discrimination in Modern India*. New Delhi: Oxford University Press.

8

India's Paradox of 'Hunger Amidst Plenty' Has a Name

Caste-Based Discrimination and Exclusion

JOSEPH THARAMANGALAM

> Democracy hasn't eradicated caste. It has entrenched and modernized it. This is why it's time to read Ambedkar. (Roy 2014, 37)

In all the measures used to gauge poverty, hunger, and human development (HD), India has had an exceptionally poor record. Despite some slow improvement in recent years (mostly attributed to the positive effects of such rights-based programmes as the Mahatma Gandhi Rural Employment Guarantee Act [MREGA] and the Food Security Act [FSA]), India's rank in the Human Development Index (HDI) of the United Nations Development Programme (UNDP) as of 2016 was 131 out of 188 countries (one rank down from the previous year), below most countries in East Asia and 41 ranks below China's 90. According to the Multidimensional Poverty Index (MPI), 55 per cent of Indians (some 633 million) were MPI poor (compare with China: 5.2 per cent, some 72 million). The Global Hunger Index (GHI) has continued to present an even more scandalous picture of India, now home to a quarter of all the hungry people in the world, with an exceptionally poor record in child malnutrition and mortality rates. This record has presented a paradox (puzzle to some) for a country touted as a rising economic powerhouse and arguably home to the single largest pool of educated and professional 'middle-class' people in the world. This chapter attempts to show that this Indian puzzle (Indian exceptionalism?) has something to do with India's historically entrenched system of exclusion as seen in the caste system and in caste-like exclusions meted out to the Adivasis, India's indigenous people. When we disaggregate the data by social groups, we see the large pocket of chronic poverty and endemic hunger as consisting disproportionately of the historically excluded groups, especially Dalits (or ex-Untouchables) and Adivasis (indigenous people or, literally, original inhabitants) who together make up one-third of India's population. They are officially called Scheduled Castes and Scheduled Tribes (henceforth SCs and STs).[1] This chapter proposes to examine the nature of this exclusion, focussing especially on the SCs (and to a lesser extent the STs), and the continuing and increasing gap between the upper castes/classes and the excluded castes/classes.[2]

The chapter is organized as follows. Part I after this introductory section provides a very brief overview of the entrenched nature of poverty, hunger, and social backwardness; the slow progress in HD; and how these issues are especially concentrated in the excluded classes. Part II attempts to examine the structures of exclusion (and unfavourable and enforced inclusion) that underlie these HD outcomes, and the processes by which these are maintained and reproduced, undermining the promises of liberal democracy. The chapter argues that these groups continue to be the victims of an entrenched system of exclusion and deprivation from livelihood resources, including land and knowledge; indeed, victims

[1] Note that the category of Scheduled Castes (SCs) does not include all ex-Untouchables or Dalits, but only those who are considered Hindus. Those who converted to Islam and Christianity have been excluded; those who are Sikhs or Buddhists were also originally excluded, but were added to the list later. Dalits, regardless of religion, probably make up about one-quarter of the Indian population.

[2] Even the World Bank (WB) has taken note of the significance of this structure of exclusion. Its report on this (WB 2011) focuses on three groups: SCs, STs, and women. While the exclusion of and the many ways of discrimination against all three are important to understand and factor in the dismal record with respect to such indicators as high maternal mortality rates, given the context of this volume, this chapter focuses on the first two (who are also generally physically segregated, unlike women).

of a system of structural violence. The explanation for the Indian puzzle lies largely in independent (and democratic) India's historic and continuing failure to seriously address the root causes of such systemic discrimination and exclusion as the highly unequal access to land and education. I attempt to examine why the numerous struggles of the backward classes,[3] the vigorous debates, and several policy initiatives (especially the reservation system) have produced only very modest benefits for the excluded groups, while the oppressive structures have actually become more entrenched and modernized. I argue that the historically entrenched burden on these excluded groups has ensured that whatever progress India has made—in economic growth, education, and health—could not trickle down to them, but has, in fact, increased the gap between them and the upper-caste/class groups. Unsurprisingly, the states which have achieved higher levels of HD and poverty reduction (for example, Kerala and Tamil Nadu) are also the ones which did address the issue more seriously in response to demands from relatively well-organized and robust movements of these deprived castes and classes. The last section of the chapter will provide a few concluding statements.

Part I: Who Are the Poor and the Hungry in India?

In understanding India's paradox of hunger amidst plenty it would be helpful to look at where poverty and hunger are concentrated, in a somewhat uniquely large and India-specific underclass. While this underclass itself is graded into many sections, as is all of Indian society (a structure best examined and explained by Ambedkar),[4] for purposes of our analysis and argument here we will focus only on two groups: the SCs and, to a lesser extent, the STs. However, even before focusing on these two groups we begin by referring to a measure regularly highlighted in the human development

[3] The term used for the disadvantaged low castes in pre-Independence India.

[4] This is best explained in his 'Annihilation of Caste', available in many versions over time, but best read in the annotated version edited by S. Anand and Kumar with a now well-known introduction by Arundhati Roy with the title, 'The Doctor and the Saint', her discussion of the debate between Ambedkar and Gandhi.

reports (HDRs)—the inequality adjusted HDI. According to UNDP (2016) India's low HDI value of 0.624 (contrast with China's 7.38), when adjusted for inequality, falls to 0.454, a loss of 27.2 per cent. This is a higher loss than even such notoriously inegalitarian societies as Brazil, which had a loss of 25.6 per cent the same year. No wonder that the reduction in India's poverty has also been unequal. As of 2004–5 the percentage of Indians living below its controversial poverty line was 27.5 per cent, but the figures for SCs and STs were 37.9 and 43.8 per cent respectively (WB 2011, Table II.2.1). The MPI (a more holistic measure of poverty that factors health and education besides living standard and uses 10 indicators) provides a far worse picture. As of 2010 (Alkire and Santos 2010), the percentage of MPI poor in India was 55.4 per cent, but the same for SCs was 65.8 per cent and for STs a whopping 81.4 per cent (UNDP 2010, 98). The *India Chronic Poverty Study Report* (Mehta 2011, 34) provides similar figures: '[O]ver 80% of the poor in the country now belong to socially disadvantaged groups like SCs, STs, the most backward castes among OBCs and weaker sections among the Muslims.'

An important point highlighted by the economist K.P. Kannan (2015), who made an extensive study of the impact of social exclusion on the incidence of poverty, is that in some of the richest and high-growth states with a high proportion of SCs and STs, poverty is concentrated almost exclusively among these excluded groups. He points to Punjab as a quintessential example and notes: '[P]overty in Punjab is now almost exclusively a problem facing the SCs (since there is hardly any ST community in the state). The situation is similar in Haryana as well.'[5]

[5] The GHI scores for 2017, released after this chapter was initially written, confirmed India's deplorable status; India now ranks 100th out of 119 countries (the higher the number, worse the hunger), ranking worse than every country in Asia except Pakistan and Afghanistan, and at the high end of the group considered 'serious'. The report once again highlighted how India's hunger was driven by exceptionally high child malnutrition. Unfortunately, it is becoming unpopular in India even to raise such a serious issue in today's hyper-national political context. When the opposition Congress Party leader Rahul Gandhi referred to the latest GHI data, the ruling party spokesperson and cabinet minister Smriti Irani accused him

India's record of healthcare and health outcomes also presents an equally dismal picture. A recent article in the medical journal *The Lancet* reported that India has 17 per cent of the world's population, and has more deaths of children aged five and under—over 12 lakhs a year—the highest in the world. It also has a poor record of tackling cases of tuberculosis, diabetes, chronic kidney diseases, and rheumatic heart diseases (as reported in *The Wire*, 2017). According to a Global Burden of Disease (GBD) study published in the same journal, India's health rank among 194 countries is a dismal 154, lagging behind not only China, as may be expected, but also all its poor neighbours in South Asia—including Bhutan—except Pakistan and Afghanistan. Once again, however, it is important to recognize the impact of exclusion: in most indicators of health (as also in education) there is generally a difference of 10 to 20 per cent between the general population and the SC/ST population. Let us take just the case of child survival—an important measure that indicates several underlying factors such as maternal health and literacy besides the state of healthcare in general. It is generally well known among the scholars in the field that the infant mortality rate (IMR) and under-five mortality rate (U5MR) figures are exceptionally high for India.[6] According to a recent article in *The Wire* (20 May 2017), India had the highest number of U5 deaths among all countries in the world; it was a staggering 1.2 million in 2015. Government of India (2011, 282) provides the disaggregated figures for social groups. As of 2005–6, the IMR for SCs stood at 66.4, for STs at 62.1, for OBCs at 56.6, and for Others at 48.9; the U5MRs for these four groups were 88.1, 95.7, 72.8, and 59.2 respectively—showing significant gaps between the excluded groups and the more privileged groups.

Similarly, while India's rural literacy rate was a low 67 per cent in 2007–8, the figure for SCs was 60.5; for STs, 58.8; for OBCs, 66.7; and for others (the upper castes), 76.9 (GoI 2011).

---

of 'maligning' the nation. See https://timesofindia.indiatimes.com/india/after-rahul-gandhis-poetic-taunt-smriti-irani-hits-back-with-a-sher/articleshow/61080174.cms, last accessed on 15 October 2017.

[6] See, for example, Amartya Sen's many writings, especially Dreze and Sen (2013, Chapter 6, 143–81).

Part II: Structures of Exclusion and Discrimination

We have already referred to the fact that inequality has a greater impact on HDI in India than in most other countries. A World Bank study (2011), already referred to, has further confirmed that India has among the highest levels of inequality in the world, on par with Brazil and South Africa, a fact hidden when consumption rather than income is used for the relevant calculations. Unlike in Brazil or South Africa where such inequality is the legacy of European colonialism, in India it is that of its indigenous caste system, a historically entrenched system of exclusion which is religiously sanctioned and has widely been practiced for millennia. At the bottom of this system of what Ambedkar called 'graded inequality' and exclusion are a number of castes of ex-Untouchables (also called Dalits, though the two are not exactly the same, as explained in footnote 1 of this chapter) who make up 16–17 per cent of the Indian population. A second excluded group, in many ways similar to the Dalits, is that of the Adivasis, most of whom traditionally are forest dwellers whose customary rights over forest resources have been threatened since colonial times and more so after Independence, a threat greatly aggravated during the neoliberal period that began in the early 1990s. The Scheduled Castes and Scheduled Tribes are so called because of their special status in the Indian Constitution that allows them certain provisions, including the system of reservations (affirmative action or protective discrimination) that guarantees them reserved seats in educational institutions, legislative bodies, and government jobs. The World Bank study about exclusion in India dealt with a third group—women. Their record of HD, education, poverty, malnutrition, and so on is far worse than that of men, which is mostly attributed to gender-based discrimination. While this is a major issue of concern and has been studied by eminent scholars such as Amartya Sen,[7] I will concentrate here on the first two groups (with a special focus on the SCs), given the context and focus of this volume.

I believe the concept of exclusion is reasonably well known, and that little can be gained by entering into an academic discussion about the concept and various conceptual distinctions of a sophistic

[7] Amartya Sen deals with this issue in many of his writings. See especially his article on India's 'missing women' (Sen 1990).

nature. It will suffice to make two points of clarification. First, a system of exclusion does not rule out, indeed inevitably enforces, varieties of unfavorable inclusion as regards services enforced on lower class/caste groups—such as the task of scavenging and street cleaning in the case of Dalits. It is for this reason that some analysts use terms such as 'graded' or 'unfavorable' inclusion (for example, Sen 2000). Indeed, it should be seen as a system of 'enforced' inclusion. Second, exclusion, especially in India, operates along multiple and interrelated dimensions, some of which may be deeply psychological, even 'spiritual'. For example, an 'Untouchable' is excluded from the domain of the 'human' and from that of 'sociality' or 'fraternity', one of the most fundamental concepts in the trinity of 'liberty, equality, and fraternity' that Ambedkar held up as the foundational principles underpinning India's new democracy. 'Fraternity' may be the most important of the three in the context of a caste system that kept Dalits outside its domain, thus also denying them basic human dignity and self-respect. Indeed, too many of them continue to be so excluded even today. Having provided these clarifications, let me hasten to add that the main focus of this chapter is exclusion from the most mundane and measurable vital resources and services—such as land and water, education and employment, and basic healthcare—that deprive the excluded from some basic capabilities.

It should be clear, then, that caste is inherently incompatible with modern democracy and its underlying principle of the inherent dignity and rights of the 'human person' regardless of such ascribed attributes as caste, race, or national origin—a fact that Ambedkar, the philosopher and legal scholar, understood and explained so clearly. His critique of Gandhi, who upheld the principle of differential rights, especially in his advocacy of hereditary occupations, was rooted in this understanding. Interestingly, in a lecture at Columbia University in 2012, historian Ramachandra Guha described caste as 'the most sophisticated, subtle and diabolical system of exclusion', even as his lecture aimed at 'reconciling Gandhi with Ambedkar'. He argued with many subtle twists that both Gandhi and Ambedkar contributed to reforming the caste system in their own ways (see Guha 2012).[8]

[8] Arundhati Roy (2014), more than anyone else, shows why such a comparison is fraught with difficulties for ordinary mortals, including scholars, since Gandhi had the status of a *Mahatma*, or great soul (a deeply

Dimensions of Exclusion and Unequal Inclusion

As discussed earlier, social exclusion has many dimensions. I discuss in this section what I believe to be among the most basic ones in determining people's life chances—access to the most vital livelihood resources and capabilities.

Untouchability

Untouchability is undoubtedly the worst form of exclusion invented by human beings anywhere, a form of human degradation that is worse than slavery. At its extreme, as it existed in Kerala, for example, the Untouchables were considered so impure that they became unapproachables and unseeables. The Untouchables were excluded from access to such vital livelihood resources as the village water tank, schools, and other public spaces.[9]

During the latter part of the colonial era and especially during the Indian nationalist movement there were many 'backward-class

---

spiritual man, according to Guha), whose thinking and actions apparently needed to be judged according to criteria beyond the purview of our common thinking and understanding. From everything we know—and despite the many changes in his thinking over the years—Gandhi supported the caste system, but one rid of untouchability. He visualized a system in which the scavenger and the Brahmin will continue to occupy their ancestral occupations but would enjoy equal social status and rewards, and this transformation was to be made not by the empowerment of the Dalits but by a 'change of heart' of the upper castes—a process of radical social change beyond the purview of any analysis by sociologists or historians. Anyone can see why Ambedkar, the scholar and social activist, had to resist such a tactic that would effectively pre-empt all attempts by the lower castes to 'educate, organize, and agitate' to achieve their emancipation. Having said all this, it must be acknowledged that Gandhi did influence many Indians to give up the practice of untouchability, and that it is less widely practiced today than before Gandhi's time.

[9] According to traditional caste codes or caste-based moral rules (Varnashrama Dharma), they are also excluded from access to all forms of sacred texts and religious knowledge, which are the preserves of the upper castes. The irony is that, excluded from the means to attain higher forms of enlightenment available to upper-caste Hindus and wallowing in ignorance, the Untouchables have little chance to escape being reborn as Untouchables in their next lives.

movements' organized by a variety of low castes, including the Untouchables, most prominently in south India and Maharashtra. While some upper-caste liberals were sympathetic to these movements, the leaders of the nationalist movement (mostly of upper castes), Hindu reformers, and the rising Hindu nationalists saw them as a threat to a unified nationalist movement and the consolidation of a Hindu majority in a new India. Gandhi, the shrewd politician and revered saint, dedicated himself to the cause of abolishing untouchability but opposed all kinds of militant movements of the backward classes and the Untouchables, promoting the cause of preserving a purified caste system sans untouchability. As already noted (in footnote 1 of this chapter), he set out to achieve this by urging the upper castes to 'change their hearts' and dedicate themselves to the service of the Untouchables. It is now left to historians to determine if Gandhi deployed his enormous popularity and 'sainthood' to hijack the movements of the low castes, spawning a new independent India that would continue to be cursed by the many evils of caste.[10] In any case, it was left to Ambedkar to pick up the pieces of these struggles—including his own—and to enact some basic constitutional guarantees and build an institutional and policy framework to redress the structural disabilities of these groups. Untouchability was legally abolished and provisions made for the now well-known system of affirmative action (reservations) for the SCs and STs. The potential empowerment of these groups was resented by the land-owning upper castes in many parts of India, and the backward-class assertion began to be met with increasing violence. India's lawmakers were moved to enact the The Scheduled Castes and Scheduled Tribes (Prevention of Atrocities) Act, 1989, but growing levels of these atrocities—some of them associated with newer causes (such as 'cow protection') espoused by the newly emboldened Hindu right—have become a regular feature of today's India.

There is evidence that despite being illegal, untouchability in its many forms is still widely practised in India.[11] It will suffice here

[10] It is in this context that the study of Ambedkar's writings—neglected for so long, as Arundhati Roy has convincingly argued—becomes more relevant than ever.

[11] In addition to studies by researchers, there are also periodical (often annual) reports by human rights groups that highlight caste-based discrimination and violence. See, for example, Human Rights Watch (1999) that focuses specifically on 'caste violence'.

to provide a few selected figures from a 2006 study that covered 565 villages in 11 states (Kadun and Gadkar 2014):[12]

1. 37.8 per cent Dalit students in India's villages are made to sit separately in government schools
2. 27.6 per cent Dalits in India's villages are prevented from entering police stations
3. 25.7 per cent of village Dalits are prevented from entering ration shops
4. 33 per cent of village public health workers refuse to visit Dalits homes
5. 14.4 per cent of village Dalits are not permitted to enter the Panchayat building
6. 12 per cent of village Dalits are forced to form separate lines at polling booths
7. 48.4 per cent of Dalits are denied access to water sources
8. 35 per cent of village Dalits are banned from selling produce in local markets
9. 47 per cent of village milk cooperatives prevent Dalits from selling milk and 25 per cent from buying milk

Instruments of enforcement of such regressive practices are brutal and effective, including periodical outbursts of violence, but most important is the *boycott* which denies recalcitrant deviants access to all livelihood sources in the village, including employment and food, forcing them to leave the village.

Land Ownership

Underlying all these, I argue, are the two fundamental and entrenched exclusions, those from access to land and to education. Despite all the changes in the past seven decades, these exclusions continue to determine the socio-economic status of the SCs and STs, together with their very visible presence in India's (indeed,

[12] This study draws on data from the SC/ST commissions report, New Delhi. A larger and book-length study by Shah et al. (2006) using similar data provides a more detailed analysis. The numerous village studies conducted by sociologists also document such practices. See, for example, M.N. Srinivas's (1976) classic depiction of a Karnataka village in the 1950s.

the world's) most deprived and excluded pool of poverty, hunger, malnutrition, and stunted and wasted children. First, it is well established, and perhaps self-evident (even to those who do not subscribe to historical materialism), that in agrarian societies the world over the major determinant of economic, social, and power structures has been the nature of ownership and/or control of land—the primary, if not the sole, means of production and livelihood. It is not accidental, then, that the emergence of newly independent post-colonial societies (the nation states) was accompanied by the 'peasant wars of the 20th century'—discussed in the classic work of Eric Wolf (1969), among others—and followed by some forms of land reforms and land redistribution.[13] They ranged from radical redistributions in socialist countries such as Russia, China, Cuba, and Vietnam to more modest, yet significant, redistribution programmes in Japan and other East Asian countries during the early post-war period. In India, too, land reform was very much in the promised agenda of the Indian National Congress with its slogan 'land to the tiller'. India (and the many Indian states) did debate the issue extensively, passing various legislations. However, the reality is that these efforts produced very little real change, especially from the perspective of the landless SCs and STs. Measures such as *zamindari* abolition and tenancy reforms largely benefitted upper-caste rich peasants; SCs gained little in the absence of any real land redistribution to the landless, while the STs continued their descent on the slippery slope of reforms as victims of newer forms of land grab and the erosion of whatever customary rights they had still retained. In Kerala (a state with among the lowest per capita availability of land and the highest percentage of landless Dalits), which enacted what were probably the most radical reform measures, the landless (some 90 per cent of Dalits) received ownership rights to their homesteads (10 cents or one-tenth of an acre of land). It was no mean feat in terms of achieving a measure of basic dignity and self-respect, as they no longer had to live and sleep in their houses on the sufferance of the landlords and under constant threat

[13] India was no exception to this pattern and saw numerous peasant movements and agrarian struggles during the colonial and early post-colonial period. See, for instance, Dhanagare 1983; see also my lengthy review essay that especially focused on Dhanagare's work in the *Journal of Peasant Studies* (Tharamangalam 1981).

of eviction. It is very important to note that even this very modest gain was achieved after decades of intense struggle (arguably also the best organized and most effective anywhere in India), finally consolidated under the leadership of robust and programmatic political (mostly communist) parties (Tharamangalam 1981, 1992, 2010).

Two further points need to be made before I close the issue of land relations. First is the intertwining of land and caste hierarchies in village India, a fact well documented by sociologists and anthropologists who have conducted intense fieldwork in India's villages. 'A crucial feature of caste,' says the eminent sociologist Srinivas (1987a), 'is its intimate linkage with production.' He clarifies the point further in his celebrated work on Rampura (1976, 10): 'There was a two-way relationship between landownership and caste rank. Traditionally, ownership of land conferred respectability and prestige, and this was translated into caste rank in course of time, and contrariwise, high ritual rank unaccompanied by landownership produced anomalous situations.' In fact, landownership is listed as one of the most important determinants of a 'dominant caste', a concept originally formulated by Srinivas and widely used by sociologists studying caste. Land ownership figures even in Srinivas's concept of *sanskritization*. Though this concept focuses on the ways in which lower castes imitate the lifestyles and cultural habits of upper castes in an attempt at social mobility (a process that Ambedkar labelled the 'infection of imitation'), the final success in achieving a higher status depends very much on their ability to assert their claim and get it accepted by the upper castes. This, in turn, depends on their economic and political power, of which landownership is a major factor.[14] How, then, do the SCs and STs fare in terms of landownership? Not surprisingly, some 70 to 77 per cent of SCs and as high as 90 per cent of STs (Roy 2014, Mohanty 2001) continue to be landless or near landless. Dalits,

[14] Srinivas also noted that education and occupational status were becoming more important in this process of upward mobility in a context in which land ownership may occupy a declining role in determining social hierarchy. More recent studies have confirmed the fact of such a trend. Nevertheless, no one denies that in Indian villages, where some 70 per cent of the nation's people and the vast majority of Dalits live, access to land continues to be the most important determinant of life chances and basic capabilities, of social status, and of power or the lack thereof.

with a population share of 17 per cent, made up 35 per cent of all agricultural households (Mishra 2001). The proportion of rural households without land was 45 per cent for India; this statistic reflected much higher in some states (Kerala: 79 per cent, Bihar: 77 per cent, Gujarat: 81 per cent).

A general point for consideration here focuses on the argument (an empirically testable generalization) that some effective form of land redistribution may be a necessary precondition for inclusive HD in societies burdened with historically entrenched systems of highly inegalitarian land relations. The most telling comparison here may be that between India and China.[15] As Amartya Sen has shown in several of his writings,[16] the two countries began their post-colonial development trajectory at about the same time in the early 1950s and at about the same level in terms of HD indicators, but, as already indicated above, they are in very different stages today with respect to the same indicators. While China made remarkably rapid progress in a short period in such areas as literacy, life expectancy, and child health and survival, India, with its exceptionally slow progress, lagged far behind. To take just the example of life expectancy (LE), by 1980—just three decades into their development paths—there was a gap of 14 years between the two countries. It is worth emphasizing that these achievements predated China's economic reforms, providing in fact a far better foundation for these reforms. What, then, were the factors that caused the difference in the trajectories of the two countries? For one thing, China's path was driven by extensive and successful public provisioning (now extended to previously excluded and newly empowered classes) of basic education, healthcare, and human security by a robust, revolutionary State committed to these changes, but the further argument advanced here is that these policies could be effectively implemented only after China had dismantled the structural base of its historical inequalities by eliminating the power of

[15] The comparison can be extended to many other countries—including those in East Asia and more radical socialist countries such as Cuba—indeed, even within India, the high HD states such as Kerala with the low HD states in north India. See Tharamangalam (1998, 2010) and the many works of Sen (especially 1999), and Dreze and Sen (2013).

[16] I have reviewed these in my examination of the two cases (Tharamangalam 2015).

the landlords and the warlords by effectively implementing radical land reforms and land redistribution measures (Tharamangalam 2015). By contrast, India's reform policies continued to be hindered and sabotaged by upper-caste landowning interests that had come to dominate the ruling Congress Party. Unlike China, India continued to carry the burden of its historically entrenched iniquities. As Dreze and Sen have noted, China could now move forward 'without the social problems and inefficiencies of highly unequal landownership and widespread landlessness, in sharp contrast with India' (2002, 121).[17] By the time China launched its neoliberal reforms, it had created the structural preconditions for more inclusive and sustained economic growth.[18]

Education

Another dimension of exclusion at the foundation of India's social structure has long been that from access to education and all forms of knowledge. Education and literacy have always had both intrinsic and instrumental values, and their roles have become more important in modern democratic societies for informed political participation as well as for human capital formation and skill-based occupations. No one perhaps understood this more clearly than Ambedkar whose well-known slogan for the excluded

[17] It is pertinent here to quote Srinivas regarding the failure of the early Bhakti movements to change the caste system. The Bhakti saints, he says '*do not seem to have taken note of the fact that as long as the mode of production remained unaltered, mere ideological attacks on the caste system would not change it*' (emphasis added; 1987a, 525). A similar argument has also been made by several social scientists that 'effective' and vibrant democracies too are associated with societies that have created similar preconditions. In many parts of India, traditional caste-based patron–client system has characterized electoral politics; many lower-caste clients are mobilized as vote banks for the dominant-caste patrons (Tharamangalam 2010; Kohli 2009; Breman 2015).

[18] As Sen has argued, the single-minded pursuit of a 'growth first' strategy in the post-reform period saw some reversals in China's human development momentum, but these reversals were reversed again as these negative consequences could not be ignored by a State and its policymakers who had become sensitive to any serious discontent from disaffected classes below (Tharamangalam 2015).

was: educate, organize, agitate. Having failed to empower Dalits through political assertion by means of what he conceived of as effective representation (as envisaged in the Communal Award he had negotiated with the colonial government), he finally turned his attention (using his position as the architect of the Constitution) to constitutional provisions and guarantees to improve the educational status of the SCs and STs through the system of *reservations*. This has had some beneficial effect in providing these groups greater access to literacy and education, even creating a class of educated professionals, intellectuals, and political leaders among the SCs and, to a lesser extent, STs. Yet, the educational achievements of these groups have been modest, lagging behind those of the upper castes, given the continuing—and increasing—gap in the opportunity structure. Indeed, the gap has been growing at an accelerated rate in the wake of the neoliberal reforms that saw an increased drive for privatization of an already inequitable education sector (as is also the case with healthcare).[19] For example, rural literacy rates of the SCs and STs (2005–6) were substantially below India's already low 77 per cent. The figure for SCs was 65.5 per cent and for STs, 58.8 per cent (GoI 2011). In the two decades after 1983 Dalit men registered a 39 per cent improvement in the attainment of post-primary education, which was still 17 per cent lower than the 56 per cent registered by non-SC/ST men. Similar was the gap between the improvement made by SC women and non-SC/ST women, 21 per cent versus 38 per cent (Das and Mehta 2012).

Dalit children continue to suffer various forms of discrimination. Rules of untouchability still apply in many places, especially in situations involving the sharing of food, water, and praying spaces. They also have to overcome other related barriers such as the lack of helpful guidance and role models, low self-esteem and achievement motivation, and above all, the contempt with which they are treated by *savarna* (upper caste, touchable) teachers. No surprise, then, that their dropout rates are high. In an issue brief prepared for the World Bank on the subject of poverty and exclusion of Dalits, Das and

[19] The gradual extension of reservations to the more resourceful and politically powerful OBCs (a process accelerated after the implementation of the recommendations of the Mandal Commission in the 1990s) may also have limited the opportunities for these groups. See Srinivas (1987a) on the conflicts of interest even among the low castes and how the more resourceful of them often grab bigger pieces of the pie.

Mehta (2012) provide some figures taken from the Indian government's Eleventh Five-Year Plan: about 74 per cent of Dalit boys and 71 per cent of Dalit girls dropped out of school between grades 1 and 10 (Das and Mehta 2012, 112). Another important factor underlying the differential educational performance and achievements of Dalit and upper-caste children is the different kind and quality of education to which they have access. While the latter patronize elite (often English-medium) private schools, Dalits attend the poorly run public institutions, which are also the hotbeds of the kind of discriminatory practices mentioned at the beginning of this paragraph. Among the many ironies in India, there is one that I have personally witnessed: upper-caste nationalist politicians (mostly of the Hindutva variety) oppose the teaching of English in public schools, even as they send their own children to often expensive English–medium private schools, including 'convent schools'—a term often used for schools run by Christian churches.

I digress a little to touch on a related issue, the puzzle of the widely noted neglect of primary education in India during the same period when the country made great strides in scientific, technical, and other forms of higher education spawning the now famous Indian middle class. One explanation for this neglect (and the massive failure in the promotion of basic literacy and elementary education) is that early planners pursued a misguided view that India needed to improve higher forms of education for rapid economic development. However, there is another explanation in which caste figures as a factor. A benign version of this view is that upper-caste Indians, following their habits of the heart, simply did not see the merit of educating the lower castes. A less benign version argues that the project of educating the low castes may have met with resistance from the upper castes who feared that such a project and the consequent upward mobility of the lower castes would jeopardize the control and management of their low-caste workers, dependents, and servants. Having done fieldwork in rural Bihar in the 1970s and observed such dynamics at work, I see some merit in this latter argument.

Dalit disadvantage plays out in the kind of work Dalit men and women do and the wages they receive. Being predominantly rural and landless, a majority of Dalits are casual labourers—over 41 per cent of Dalit men and 20 per cent of Dalit women in 2004–5—which shows only minuscule progress since 1983 (Das and Mehta 2012). The proportion of Dalit men in non-farm enterprises increased slightly from 11 to 15.6 per cent, while the corresponding figures for non-SC/ST men during the same period were 16.4 to 24 per cent. The casualization of labour, in conjunction with what has been called 'de-patronization' (the decline of whatever traditional protection that had been available to Dalits under the *jajmani* and other patronage systems), has created a crisis that Breman (1996, 2015) has referred to as 'footloose labour', a system of hunting and gathering for work.

It is noteworthy that returns to education, especially in terms of financial gains, also are lower for the SCs compared to caste-Hindus. And paradoxically, education appears to disadvantage Dalit men in rural areas, especially those with post-primary education, in a context in which employment, including that in agriculture, has not kept pace with the supply of educated Dalit men. A WB study noted that, in general, nearly 60 per cent of the wage gap between SC and general caste workers is caused by unobserved factors or cannot be explained by human capital endowments (2011, 20).

Finally, it is important to note that this structure is maintained not just by ideology and pollution rules but also by considerable violence. It is indeed a system of structural violence manifested by constant threats and periodic outbursts of physical violence employed by landowing upper castes threatened by changes in established relationships and also by the new assertion of some lower castes who dare to resist or retaliate.[20] 'Atrocities against Dalits'—ranging from murder, rape, and arson to such humiliating practices as parading Dalit women naked in the village and making the victims consume human excreta—are reasonably well documented. In her seminal essay on Gandhi and Ambedkar, Arundhati Roy provides data on such atrocities too; she notes, for

[20] Ambedkar has aptly described some features of direct and indirect violence that upholds the system. He writes:

> *That the Hindus most often succeed in pulling down Untouchables is largely due to many causes. The Hindu has the Police and the Magistracy on his side. In a quarrel between the Untouchables and the Hindus the Untouchables will never get protection from the Police or justice from the Magistrate. The Police and the Magistracy are Hindus, and they love their class more than their duty. But the chief weapon in the armory of the Hindus is economic power they possess over the poor Untouchables living in the village.* (Quoted in Roy 2014; emphasis added)

example, that every day more than four Untouchable women are raped by *touchables*.[21] India's parliamentarians regarded these practices as serious enough to formulate the 'Atrocities against Dalits' Act in 1989. While the effectiveness of the Act is disputed, Dalit activists insist that the act cannot be implemented without political pressure from below.

* * *

To summarize, it is clear that India's abysmal record in all the indicators of HD—poverty, hunger, illiteracy, maternal and child malnutrition, and so on—are rooted in the historically entrenched exclusion of three classes: SCs, STs, and women. Of these, this chapter has examined only the first in some detail. Three factors prompted my specific focus on caste as a major dimension of exclusion in India. First, this chapter has been prepared for a set of volumes on Ambedkar who, having experienced first-hand the social exclusion meted out to the Untouchables, contributed more than anyone else to the critique of caste and to India's constitutional and institutional provisions to address the issue. Second, unlike the STs and women, the situation of the SCs is rather unique to India.[22]

[21] Roy (2014, 11), who draws her data from the National Crime Records Bureau (NCRB).

[22] It is, in many ways, comparable to entrenched racism, as seen in the exclusion and discrimination against African Americans in the USA, and other similar practices elsewhere. It is noteworthy that when a UN conference attempted to deal with caste-based discrimination as similar to racism, India's upper-caste elite used all the resources at their command to oppose such a move. Notably, some 'eminent' sociologists who were deployed in this task argued somewhat disingenuously, using technical and anthropological material that caste could not be compared to race. They deployed such sophistry despite the clear fact that the UN used the phrase 'all forms of racial discrimination' and clarified in its first article that for the convention.

> the term 'racial discrimination' shall mean any distinction, exclusion, restriction or preference based on race, colour, descent, or national or ethnic origin which has the purpose or effect of nullifying or impairing the recognition, enjoyment or exercise, on an equal footing, of human rights and fundamental freedoms in the political, economic, social, cultural or any other field of public life.

Third, understanding and addressing caste-based exclusion and discrimination has acquired a new urgency in view of the fact that democratic India's constitutional provisions and policies (especially those of protective discrimination) have had so little effect in countering the nature of India's development process that is inherently non-inclusive, widening the gap between the privileged upper castes and the dispriviledged lower castes, especially Dalits.

Why has this structure of oppression and direct and indirect forms of violence continued even after seven decades of independence and democracy in India? Why have there been needless and preventable early deaths of so many, including the millions of children who die before reaching the age of five? What has caused the poverty and ill-health of so many SCs/STs, unmatched practically anywhere in the world, while most of India's neighbours in Asia—who had also suffered the same, if not more, impoverishment and socio-economic decline under colonialism—have all forged ahead with rapid progress in poverty alleviation and human development? Interestingly, this is all after over a century of backward-class movements, numerous organized struggles during the Independence movements, and after the life-long dedicated work of a Mahatma and saint for 'Harijan upliftment'. The answer is complex, but I believe we can identify some of the causes. Here, I invite the reader to consider the following:

1. Backward-class movements never became unified with national movements to exert the needed power to counter the influence of the upper castes who pre-empted such basic reforms as land redistribution and more effective provisions for Dalit education—except to a limited extent. It is not accidental that such provisions have had greater success in regions such as Kerala and Tamil Nadu where they were relatively better organized and more vibrant.
2. Some of these movements resembled those of earlier times (such as the medieval Bhakti movement) that caused the eventual creation of newer castes or quasi-castes. After all, do not the Ambedkarite Buddhists today resemble yet another caste-like community? As Ambedkar (like the sociologists who have conducted village studies) understood clearly, in a system of 'graded inequality' (and a 'division of labourers') in which every one of the many castes (in the hundreds in some regions) is at once oppressor and victim, except at the two

ends of the chain, it is probably the only oppressive system in the world that is practically insured against any uprising of a unified oppressed group. As many sociologists have pointed out, the system is resilient and adaptive, adept at accommodating some upward social mobility through such mechanisms as sanskritization (though there is a line at which this stops) and making room for the rising non-Brahmin 'dominant castes' when necessary. It deploys what Doninger called 'escape clauses' and what Slavoj Zizek, a Slovanian philosopher, called 'a panoply of tricks' to insure against rebellions from below (quoted in Roy 2014, 30n149). An understanding of this feature of caste may throw some light on the puzzle of why and how even the relatively successful Dalit-led movements in the largest Indian state of Uttar Pradesh (UP) (especially by the Bahujan Samaj Party (BSP), which captured power in the state for a short while) could accomplish so little for the Dalits. Kanshi Ram, the most influential politician to lead these movements, blamed the entrenched tradition of 'chamcha raj' which turned the Dalit leaders themselves into stooges in a patronage system. Though he did not mean to apply this to his own movement, it can be argued that even the BSP ended up being a hotbed of patronage politics that, in effect, eschewed any real empowerment of Dalits or the lower classes in general. Ironically, the state was subsequently swept over by the 'Modi wave' and is now under the rule of a controversial, saffron-clad Hindu sant (of the dominant and aggressive Thakur caste) under the Bharatiya Janata Party, an upper-caste-led Hindu nationalist group that has been aggressively wooing the SCs and STs with the aim of consolidating the numerical strength of the Hindu 'community' in an India where numbers have become increasingly important for any group to hold power. As Ambedkar would have predicted, 'atrocities against Dalits' have increased, often related to land and wage disputes but even in the service of newer causes, such as cow protection, that are becoming prominent in the wake of the 'saffron wave'.

3. The efforts of Ambedkar and other leaders of the backward-caste movements to consolidate these movements into one effective national movement were thwarted by upper-caste nationalists and reformers—a majority of them within, and

some hyper-nationalists of the RSS/BJP outside, the nationalist movement who appropriated their agenda. In this respect, Gandhi may have been the most powerful spoiler whose mahatma-hood allowed him the claim to be the sole representative of the oppressed classes and to effectively blackmail them and sabotage their efforts.[23]

4. In independent India, the measures that have had the best success in improving the status of the SCs and STs have, indeed, been those engineered by Ambedkar himself, such as rights-based measures and supporting institutional mechanisms of 'affirmative action' (reservations) guaranteed by the Constitution. Once the agenda of distributing land to the landless was practically abandoned, these remained the only means available to the SCs/STs to improve their status. They have had some positive effects, as we have observed, but their effectiveness too has varied from state to state, depending on the balance of actual power for their effective implementation in the face of numerous instruments possessed by entrenched interests to sabotage them (networks of patronage, corruption, keeping primary education in rural areas as a neglected field, and so forth).
5. To repeat a point made above, violence against the excluded has not declined but increased in recent years, much of it (especially the structural violence underlying the system) unseen by the liberal upper castes. Violence, of course, takes many forms, including social boycott and excommunication. It is pertinent to note a bitter irony here: Gandhi, the saint of 'ahimsa', used fasting unto death—the most potent weapon in

[23] Gandhi effectively blackmailed Ambedkar by his 'fast unto death' to sign the Poona Pact; his attempt to thwart the Vaikom Satyagraha in Kerala succeeded partially by forcing the non-Hindu participants as well as supporters from outside Travancore to withdraw from the struggle. Gandhi insisted that the whole issue was one of a family dispute within the Travancore Hindu community, and further that the upper caste (as the 'elder brothers') had to solve the problem. He, the *Mahatma*, though an outsider, was there to change the hearts of the upper castes. Periyar from Tamil Nadu was the only non-Travancorean who refused to withdraw (see http://www.sreenarayanaguru.in/content/narayana-guru-and-mahatma-gandhi, last accessed on 14 October 2017).

his arsenal and a highly coercive tactic—that left Ambedkar no option but to accept his prescription and sign the Poona Pact. There may be disagreement about whether this obviously coercive act was also an act of violence. In any case, whether the 'Communal Award' would have given Dalits the kind of effective representation and empowerment that Ambedkar expected from it remains somewhat speculative, but Ambedkar, the keen analyst of the caste system, clearly understood that an upper-caste-led project of 'Harijan upliftment' was destined to be a hopeless illusion. Remarkably, Gandhi justified the deployment of his ultimate weapon by arguing that he had to do this to pre-empt the violence that would have ensued in the Hindu society had the Communal Award been implemented. It appears that what he feared was not the violence against Dalits that we have been discussing but the violence of Dalits against the upper castes. 'Untouchable hooligans,' he said, 'will make common cause with Muslim hooligans and kill caste Hindus' (quoted in Roy 2014, 22). The irony continues as Hindu nationalists showcase, in India and abroad, the model of 'non-violence' as basic to Indian/Hindu culture even while the daily violence against these vulnerable groups continues to escalate.

6. Let me end with what I think is the most urgent question today as we celebrate the life and legacy of Mahatma Ambedkar: how, and through what means, must India's SCs and STs consolidate and unify the numerous movements scattered across the country to empower themselves to resist new forms of upper-caste-led fascism that seek to unite the Hindu 'parivar' (family) and vote-banks through instruments of co-optation and appeasement, even as the institutionalized violence against them becomes more entrenched. In my humble view, deep thinking and efforts along this line will be the best tribute to Mahatma Ambedkar.

References

Ambedkar B.R. 2014. *Annihilation of Caste*, edited and annotated by S. Anand and Kumar. New Delhi: Navayana.

Alkire, Sabina, and Maria Emma Santos. 2010. *India Country Briefing. Oxford Poverty & Human Development Initiative (OPHI)*

Multidimensional Poverty Index Country Briefing Series. Available at www.ophi.org.uk/policy/multidimensional-poverty-index/mpi-country-briefings/. Last accessed on 30 September 2017.

Breman, J. 1996. *Footloose Labour: Working in India's Informal Economy*, vol. 2 of *Contemporary South Asia*. Cambridge: Cambridge University Press.

———. 2015. 'A Footloose Scholar'. Interview with Jan Breman, *New Left Review* 94, (July–August 2015). Available at https://newleftreview.org/II/94/jan-breman-a-footloose-scholar. Last accessed on 5 October 2017.

Das, Maitreyi Bordia, and Saumya Kapur Mehta. 2012. 'Issue Brief'. In *Poverty and Social Exclusion in India*. Washington, DC: World Bank. Available at https://openknowledge.worldbank.org/handle/10986/26336. Last accessed on 30 September 2017.

Dasgupta, Manas. 2010. 'Untouchability Still Prevalent in Rural Gujarat: Survey'. *The Hindu*, 28 January. Available at http://www.thehindu.com/news/national/Untouchability-still-prevalent-in-rural-Gujarat-survey/article16839942.ece. Last accessed on 1 October 2017.

Dhanagare, D.N. 1983. *Peasant Movements in India, 1920–1950*. New Delhi: Oxford University Press.

Dreze, Jean, and Amartya Sen. 2002. *India: Development and Participation*. New Delhi: Oxford University Press.

———. 2013. *An Uncertain Glory: India and Its Contradictions*. New Delhi: Penguin.

Guha, Ramachandra. 2012. 'Reconciling Gandhi with Ambedkar'. New York Times , 21 March. Available at https://india.blogs.nytimes.com/2012/03/21/reconciling-gandhi-with-ambedkar/?_r=0_. Last accessed on 15 June 2017.

Heller, Patrick. 2000. 'Degrees of Democracy: Some Comparative Lessons from India'. *World Politics* 52, no. 4: 484–519.

———. 2007. 'Kerala: Deepening A Radical Social Democracy'. In *Social Democracy in the Global Periphery: Origins, Challenges, Prospects*, edited by R. Sandbrook, M. Edelman, P. Heller, and J. Teichman, 65–92. Cambridge: Cambridge University Press.

Human Rights Watch. 1999. *Broken People: Caste Violence against India's 'Untouchables'*. 1 March. https://www.hrw.org/report/1999/03/01/broken-people/caste-violence-against-indias-untouchables. Last accessed on 30 September 2017.

Government of India (GoI). 2011. *India Human Development Report 2011: Towards Social Inclusion*. New Delhi: Planning Commission, Institute of Applied Manpower Research.

Kadun, Pradeep B., and Ravindra D. Gadkar. 2014. 'Social Exclusion—Its Types and Impact on Dalits in India'. *IOSR Journal Of Humanities And Social Science* 19, no. 4 (April): 81–5.

Kannan, K.P. 2015. *Interrogating Inclusive Growth: Poverty and Inequality in India*. New Delhi: Routledge.

Kohli, Atul. 2009. *Democracy and Development in India*. New Delhi: Oxford University Press.

———. 2010. 'State and Redistributive Development in India'. *UNRISD Flagship Report on Poverty Project on Poverty Reduction and Policy Regimes, Country Study: India*, edited by R. Nagaraj. Geneva: United Nations Research Institute for Social Development (UNRISD).

Mehta, Asha Kapur. 2011. *India Chronic Poverty Report in a Dynamic Context: Towards Solutions and New Compacts*. New Delhi: Indian Institute of Public Administration.

Mishra, Srijit. 2001. 'Land Ownership Structure and Literacy among Scheduled Castes in Rural India: An Exploratory Data Analysis'. *Artha Vijnana Journal of the Gokhale Institute of Politics and Economics* 43, no. 1 and 2: 98–122.

Mohanty, B.B. 2001. 'Land among Scheduled Castes and Tribes'. *Economic and Political Weekly* 36, no. 40 (6–12 October): 3857–68.

NCSCS 1998.

Ramaiah, Avaathi. 2015. 'Health Status of Dalits in India'. *Economic and Political Weekly* 50, no. 43 (24 October): 70–4.

Roy, Arundhati. 2014. 'The Doctor and the Saint'. In *Annihilation of Caste* by B.R. Ambedkar, edited and annotated by S. Anand and Kumar, 1–134. New Delhi: Navayana.

Sandbrook, Richard, Mark Eldelman, Patrick Heller, and Judith Taichman. 2006. *Social Democracy in the Global Periphery: Origins, Challenges, Prospects*. New York: Cambridge University Press.

Sen, Amartya. 1990. 'More than 100 Million Women are Missing'. *The New York Review of Books*, 20 December. Available at https://www.nybooks.com/articles/1990/12/20/more-than-100-million-women-are-missing/. Last accessed on 30 March 2010.

———. 1999. *Development as Freedom*. New York: Oxford University Press.

———. 2000. *Social Exclusion: Concept, Application and Scrutiny*. Social Development Paper no. 1. Manila: Asian Development Bank.

Sen, Jahnavi. 2017. 'India Ranked 131 on Human Development Index; Inequalities Continue' *Wire*, 22 March. Available at https://thewire.in/rights/human-development-index-india. Last accessed on 25 December 2017.

Shah, Ganshyam, H. Mader, S. Thorat, S. Deshpande, and A. Baviskar. 2006. *Untouchability in Rural Bihar*. New Delhi: Sage.

Swamy, Arun R. 2003. *Hindu Nationalism: What's Religion Got to Do with It?* Asia-Pacific Center for Security Studies, Occasional Paper Series, March 2003. Available at http://apcss.org/Publications/

Ocasional%20Papers/OPHinduNationalism.pdf. Last accessed on 25 December 2017.

Srinivas, M.N. 1976. *The Remembered Village*. New Delhi: Oxford University Press.

———. 1987a. 'The Caste System and Its Future'. In *Dimensions of Social Life: Essays in honor of David G. Mandelbaum*, edited by Paul Hockings, 525–38. Berlin: De Gruyter Mouton.

———. 1987b. *On Living in a Revolution and Other Essays*. Delhi: Oxford University Press.

Tharamangalam, Joseph. 1981. *Agrarian Class Conflict: The Political Mobilization of Agricultural Labourers in Kuttanad, South India*. Vancouver: University of British Columbia Press.

———. 1986. 'Indian Peasant Uprisings: Myth and Reality'. *Journal of Peasant Studies* 13, no. 3: 116–34.

———. 1992. 'The Communist Movement and the Theory and Practice of Peasant Movements in South India'. *Journal of Contemporary Asia* 8, no. 2: 487–98.

_____. 1998. 'The Perils of Social Development without Economic Growth: The Development Debacle of Kerala, India'. Bulletin of Concerned Asian Scholars, 30, no. 1: 23–34.

_____. 2010. 'Human Development as Transformative Practice: Lessons from Kerala and Cuba'. Critical Asian Studies 42, no. 3: 363–402.

———. 2015. 'Amartya Sen in Beijing: Comparing Human Development in India and China'. In *Development, Decentralization and Democracy*, edited by A.N. Roy and George Mathew, 338–49. New Delhi: Orient Longman.

The Wire. 2017. 'India Ranks 154 Among 195 Countries in Healthcare Index. New Delhi'. 20 May. Available at: https://thewire.in/health/india-rank-healthcareindex. Last accessed on 25 December 2018.

United Nation's Development Program (UNDP). 2010. *Human Development Report* 2016. New York: UNDP.

———. 2016. *Human Development Report* 2016. New York: UNDP.

Welthungerhilfe (Concern Worldwide). 2016. 'India: Making Food a Right for All'. *Country Case Studies 2016*. Available at https://issuu.com/welthungerhilfe/docs/global-hunger-index-2016-ghi-case-s. Last accessed on 30 November 2017.

Wolf, Eric. 1969. *Peasant Wars of the Twentieth Century*. Norman, Oklahoma: University of Oklahoma Press.

World Bank. 2011. *Poverty and Social Exclusion in India*. Washington DC: World Bank.

9

Dalits Enter the Indian Markets as Owners of Capital

Adverse Inclusion, Social Networks, and Civil Society

ASEEM PRAKASH*

The caste system[1] has outlived India's Independence. While institutions of Indian democracy have given Dalits (Webster 1999, 76)[2] opportunities for sociopolitical progress, economic advancement remains a problem. There is also a view that half a century after Independence, with governance driven by Nehru's model of development and state protectionism, Indian society continues to be divided along the lines of caste with discrimination against Dalits,

* The author is thankful for the intellectual motivation and guidance provided by Barbara Harriss-White. The article was previously published in *Asian Survey* 55, no. 5: 1044–69. It is reproduced here with permission.

[1] Simply put, caste is a peculiar form of social stratification drawing its legitimacy from Hindu religious texts. The society is divided into four social classes (varnas): Brahmins, Kshatriyas, Vaishyas, and Shudras. Another group, now known as Dalits, was historically excluded from the varna system altogether, and its members were considered as 'Untouchables'.

[2] The name 'Dalit' is accepted as a political identity to describe the 'outcastes' (the ex-'Untouchables' in the Hindu religious order); they are referred to as Scheduled Castes in the official vocabulary of the colonial and post-colonial Indian State.

curtailing their social and economic advancement (Omvedt 2011, Panini 1996, 26–8). In the present context, some observers pin their hopes on globalization and a free market approach as means to bridge the gap between political equality and severe economic disparities between upper and lower castes (Prasad 2008, Ramaiah 2004).

This presupposes a view of the market as an impartial, level playing field where free agents can engage and compete for profits. It was expected that the emergence of modern economy and political institutions would also lead to a declining role for social identity in the social and economic spheres. Barbara Harriss-White finds confirmation of this view in the works of Western socio-economic theorists in the last 150 years (for instance, Marx, Weber, Veblen, Schumpeter, Myrdal, Akerlof, and North); Indian sociologists such as Srinivas and Madan; as well as prominent anthropologists such as Parry, Searle-Chatterjee, and Sharma (Harriss-White 2005). Kapur and his colleagues report that with the onset of globalization there has been a significant shift in the consumption patterns of Dalits, signalling higher social status, the waning of sociological practices of discrimination, and a secular shift in occupation. The authors note that these changes do not mean that caste has disappeared as a social construct; it is alive and has merely acquired a different form. It remains to be seen whether caste inequality will meet its end through the operation of the market or, conversely, whether the social dynamics will be reconfigured to exacerbate discrimination, albeit in a different way.[3] This, then, forms the key question for the present study. Toward this end, 90 Dalit entrepreneurs/owners of capital[4] from 13 districts across 6 Indian states were interviewed to collect information on their ventures (Table 9.1).

Through nuanced interviews, these entrepreneurs were asked to share their stories and experiences thus far as market players,

[3] Some Dalits strongly believe that markets are the panacea. Toward this end, several business people have come together and formed the Dalit Indian Chamber of Commerce and Industry with a vision to 'to instill the spirit of entrepreneurship among Dalit youth to develop business leadership, thus empowering them to walk in step with the world' (Dalit Indian Chamber of Commerce and Industry, available at http://www.dicci.org/about.html, last accessed on 4 February 2015).

[4] 'Entrepreneurs' and 'owners of capital' are used in this article as interchangeable terms.

Table 9.1 Dalit Business Persons Interviewed

State	City	No. of interviewees
Gujarat	Ahmedabad	8
Madhya Pradesh	Bhopal	10
	Hoshangabad	1
	Raisen	3
	Vidisha	1
Maharashtra	Aurangabad	9
	Mumbai	1
	Pune	10
Rajasthan	Jaipur	10
Uttar Pradesh	Agra	5
	Kanpur	13
	Lucknow	9
West Bengal	Hoogly/24 Parganas	10

Source: Author's field documentation.

charting their trajectory from wage worker to their current occupation. Each perceived that he or she had been in a position of disadvantage while operating in the market. Caste hierarchies continue to confer privileges on upper-caste businessmen, while Dalit entrepreneurs are expected to remain subordinate.

In the second part of this chapter we examine in detail the kinds of disadvantages faced by Dalit owners of capital in the market. There is a perception among Dalits that the precondition for rising in the market is the ability to enter the powerful informal social networks that drive market accumulation—networks composed of and controlled by upper castes—which Dalits are automatically excluded from by virtue of their low caste. Moreover, they feel that questioning the dominance of the upper castes or the Dalits' disadvantaged position would result in their complete exclusion from the market itself.

Given the significant bearing that the exclusion from social networks has on Dalit *adverse inclusion* in the market (elaborated on in the following segment), the next section elaborates on these social networks in terms of three aspects: normative, structural, and resource. Each has an effect on the others, and together they cement the adverse inclusion of Dalits. The *normative* aspect has to do with active attempts to safeguard the socio-economic domination by the upper castes of Dalits; the *structural* aspect refers to the inability of Dalits to form robust networks by consolidating various social groups; and the *resource* aspect pertains to the use of network resources in the market by upper castes to the detriment of Dalits.

The workings of these social networks based on caste lead us to probe whether caste is a uniquely Indian civil society formation. The fourth section takes up this enquiry by scrutinizing existing literature on civil society. The theories inform this chapter in their contention that civil society must also be viewed as a site of *accumulation*.[5] Therefore, caste, which must similarly be considered a social structure that facilitates accumulation, is a uniquely Indian form of civil society.

Accommodation and Rigidity: Adverse Inclusion of Dalit Entrepreneurs in the Markets

It is perceived by the Dalit entrepreneurs interviewed for this study that their position in the market is inherently one of disadvantage. Before proceeding, it would be useful to explain the concept of adverse inclusion in the market. Adverse inclusion is said to occur when persons occupying the lower rungs of the social ladder—in terms of race, caste, gender, religion, and so forth—reap lower returns on their capital investment than their privileged counterparts, regardless of the quality and prices of the goods and services they offer.

For instance, an Ahmedabad-based labour contractor made some observations that reflect the unfavourable conditions in which Dalit entrepreneurs are allowed into the market but remain highly restricted within it.

> The money in construction of the flats is invested by Patels and Baniyas [upper-caste traders], but people like me supply construction labour. ... There is no caste conflict in Gujarat. All conflict is over

[5] The transformation of investable money (surplus) into profit/surplus value (accumulation) requires a number of social and political institutions that exist *between* family and the State (that is, civil society). We claim that caste should be seen as a specific form of civil society that facilitates accumulation. For a detailed discussion, please refer to the section on 'Caste as Civil Society'.

> money. ... [Patels and Baniyas] never question my caste, but if I try and step in their shoes [by] managing my own small business, they will question my caste and ensure that I don't exist in business.

The labour contractor points out that entry into the market appears to be open to all players irrespective of caste.[6] However, Dalits come up against a glass ceiling in their efforts to reach higher levels of market-based accumulation. Having been accommodated as a junior partner, the contractor faces a wall foreclosing him when he competes for a position equivalent to his caste superiors, thereby indicating the inflexible nature of the market. There is a constant sense that if any such attempt is made, his caste identity would be invoked, he would be socially censured, and eventually his economic interests would be hampered.

There is a sense of paradox here as the market seems simultaneously permissive and restrictive. Were the market completely rigid, each player would be restricted to a certain predefined role, as per the structural principles that govern capital and in accordance with the traditional division of labour in society. There would be no tolerance, then, for workers—especially those sections of society that have historically been deemed such—to participate in the market as owners of capital. Conversely, a completely permissive market would attach no weight to a person's social position when it comes to entry into the market, acquisition, investment, or profit-making.

Contemporary sociopolitical factors render the notion of completely rigid market-based accumulation unrealistic—upper castes would impede full accommodation while lower castes continue to challenge their dominance. As a result, Dalits are allowed to enter and operate in the market, but on unfavourable terms. Table 9.2 delineates this oscillation between rigidity and accommodation, as faced by Dalits in the market.

Here are some of the ways by which Dalits are discriminated against in the market. Upper-caste employers create obstacles to prevent their Dalit employees from registering a prospective business and renting a work space, as well as from getting access to labour and credit. Then there are financial difficulties: high interest rates for credit, and a very high probability of loans being denied by formal institutions despite satisfactory paperwork. Dalit entrepreneurs find it harder to get supply orders from the outset.

[6] This is also noted in Kapur et al. (2010).

Table 9.2 Adverse Inclusion

	Nature of rigidity	**Nature of accommodation**
Market entry	Blocking registration by former Dalit employees	Paying bribes by taking informal loans at high interest rates
	Blocking labour supply by competitors	Bringing labor from a distant area at high cost
	Hardly any formal credit available to Dalits for small business; medium and big businesses are denied credit even when the paperwork is complete	
	Loan official tells them that they are not culturally adapted to business (read: they should serve the labour interest of upper castes)	Raising money through friends and relatives at high interest rates
	Denial of informal market credit	Availability of informal market credit at high interest rates
	Denial of physical space to do business	Conducting business from a makeshift office space
Market operations	Impediments to procuring initial orders	Long gestation period
	No extra time period allowed by the wholesalers to make payments for retail goods to Dalit retailers	Time period allowed at premium interest rates
	Competitors invoke and publicize the caste location of Dalits among the clients and buyers while facing tough market competition, especially in items like food where the mere touch of Dalits is expected to pollute the food items	Dalits sell the food items for less than market rate to attract customers or shift their business location to a Dalit-populated area

(Cont'd)

Table 9.2 *(Cont'd)*

	Nature of rigidity	Nature of accommodation
	Transaction cost is lowered for non-Dalits due to their access to local state officials who in turn give undue and often illegal concessions (in manipulating taxes and electricity bills) due to their caste and family ties. Dalits feel they don't have access to such contacts in the state apparatus	Transaction cost is relatively higher because of rent giving. Dalits feel that a caste or family contact in the state apparatus even lowers the terms and quantum of rent
	Upper-caste competitors use access to state to usher in non-competition. When the competition becomes intense, Dalits are often made to quit the market because of the adverse and illegal regulatory environment created deliberately by the state's officials on behalf of upper-caste market players	Surviving at minimum/low profit on the margins of the market
	Dalits get no help from upper-caste business peers in terms of additional labor or any kind of mechanical equipment for hire	Sourcing labor and equipment from outside at higher rates and transaction costs
	Upper-caste business peers threaten (at times with the support of the local state official) or indulge in actual violence to remove lower-caste competitors from the market	Selling retail products to upper-caste business peers at cost (who in turn sell to retail customers at profit), or moving out of the market

Source: Author's field documentation.

Wholesalers alter their terms when dealing with Dalit retailers, who, unlike others, are allowed no extra time to make payments. While it is fairly common among suppliers to extend support to their peers in case the latter manage to get a large order, such help, involving labour and machinery, is not extended to a Dalit supplier.

There are also discrepancies when it comes to the behaviour of local state machinery. Upper castes are allowed to bend the rules when it comes to taxes and utility charges, and are charged a small penalty for breaking municipal rules. Their unlawful support often even allows upper castes to criminally intimidate Dalit entrepreneurs who are perceived as potential competition.

The disproportionate effects of the influence exercised by caste-based social networks in the market are keenly felt by Dalits across the board—each Dalit entrepreneur covered under the present study attested to this. Let us now turn to how this process is orchestrated—how social networks operate and lead to the adverse inclusion of Dalits in the market.

Primacy of Social Networks: Dalit Perceptions of the Reasons for Their Adverse Inclusion

Social networks are the result of informal alliances among entrepreneurs to solidify their standing in the market against outsiders. The concept of the social network is useful to gain insight into the socio-economic dimensions of exchanges among market players.

To throw light on the issue of differential returns in the labour market, Nan Lin (1982, 1990) employs the idea of 'social resources', which are basically provisional and borrowed resources that are available thanks to close connections (immediate family) and indirect ties (friends of friends). Another useful idea is that of 'embeddedness', which highlights the importance of interpersonal relations and networks in creating knowledge and trust (Granovetter 1985). In situations where strong ties don't exist, it can still be possible to reach people through what Granovetter (1973) terms 'the strength of weak ties'. Taking off from this idea, Ronald Burt (1992) proposes the concept of 'structural holes' in the network that enable an individual to simultaneously tap into several mostly distinct networks. While these theories provide an important explanation for differential outcomes in the market, the focus here is on trust-based relationships. Given the empirical nature of the exercise, trust plays an important role in conveying information, as will be further discussed in the next section.

Social Structure and Social Networks

The respondents in our study feel that social networks are born out of specific markers of identity, such as religion, region, caste, and familial connections, and are reinforced by one's class position. These alliances are exclusive and exclusionary in nature: outsiders are denied entry due to deep-rooted social distinctions between them and higher castes, based on social discrimination.

In this light, one may find a resemblance between social networks and social structures (Radcliffe-Brown 1940). However, it is important to make a distinction between the two. When the social structure is viewed through the lens of social network, we understand the existing social relations, at a given point of time, which connect certain individuals together. The social network approach examines the short-term social ties forged in a market situation that are derived from a long-standing social structure. For instance, caste as an institution has long endured as a social structure. Despite undergoing considerable sociological and economic changes, it is still quite influential in determining how individuals connect with one another (Srinivas and Béteille 1964). In our context, caste is a long-standing social structure which translates into a particular social phenomenon when it connects different individuals and facilitates the formation of social networks. This social network is the object of our investigation.

To assess the operations of social networks that enable the accumulation of profits and lead to the adverse inclusion of Dalits, three key aspects of social networks have been identified: normative, structural, and resource.

Normative Dimension

The normative aspect of social networks consists of unspoken rules and norms observed and adhered to out of an implicit consensus. In the economic sense, a social network is said to be as strong as the sense of trust that prevails among its members. Where there is a sense of uncertainty, people feel the need to rely strategically on others. Being tactical, and born out of necessity, this trust is self-serving. The dynamics of a social network are such that members feel that it is in their own interest to adhere to its rules (Akerlof 1970, 1982). Trust is translated into converging economic interests of members when they conform to these rules and share information that in turn works to their advantage as well.

The underpinnings of the unspoken rules that govern social networks, however, lie not in economics but in the logic of social discrimination as ordained by the caste system. Society is segregated into distinct segments that are placed in a hierarchical relationship to each other. The 'other' then becomes either a superior or an inferior, depending on his or her position on the social ladder. Moreover, this becomes an all-pervasive difference as these hierarchies are maintained in the spheres of culture and politics as well as economics, thus forming a normative framework. Upper castes seek to legitimize their sense of superiority and entitlement along with the subordination of the lower castes, who are supposed to provide labour and other services for the economic advancement of upper castes. This can be clearly observed in the testimonies of Dalit entrepreneurs interviewed in the course of the present study.

For instance, a general merchant based in Lucknow, who used to be a sweeper, recalled an unpleasant comment made by a local government official: 'While I was taking charge of the shop that was allotted to me, the section officer told me that I had gone insane—I was dreaming of becoming rich; I would lose all my savings, since nobody would buy things from my shop.'

A similar experience was narrated by a laundry owner, also in Lucknow, about when he approached a bank for a loan to scale up his business:

> As soon as the officer learnt that I reside in Dhobi Katra [a ghetto of the community that has traditionally washed clothes, primarily for the upper castes], his behavior changed. He explained to me that I would be unsuccessful in managing a modern laundry and would lose all my money in the market. He further told me to continue with my washing activities on the river bank, along with ironing clothes. He went to the extent of suggesting that I should buy my son a new cart [for carrying and keeping clothes as well as ironing them] to iron clothes so as to augment my family income. You tell me, if my father and grandfather have washed clothes on the banks of the Gomti River, does that mean both I and my son also have to wash clothes there? I am pretty sure that if there was a friend of my own caste, or relative, he would have sanctioned the loan and would have been happy to see my progress.

The anger, pessimism, and disillusionment of the respondents are clear. There is a feeling of humiliation in being treated by officials as if Dalits cannot actually launch and run their own enterprises, and from being told that they should stick to their traditional occupations and not try to overreach them. The implication, according to Dalit businessmen, is that Dalits should restrict themselves to manual labour and leave other, more lucrative work to the upper castes. It is clear, in the second incident, that caste was seen to play a pivotal role in declining the loan. There is a sentiment that in such matters, results in the market depend on one's membership in social networks, which confer access to certain resources that can further one's progress in the market. The decisive role played by social networks can be seen even more clearly when upper-caste businessmen leverage their network resources to hinder persons they have previously employed from progressing towards managerial positions or entrepreneurial ventures (Table 9.3).

Almost 53 of the 90 respondents chose the sector they had worked in as employees to launch their entrepreneurial career. These respondents testified that their previous employers resented the loss of a worker trained by them and actually leveraged their social networks to thwart the entrepreneurs' attempts at entering the market. A total of 21 Dalit entrepreneurs reported that the former employers created hurdles in the registration of the new businesses, thereby prolonging the process; and 33 experienced trouble in sourcing credit from the local market because of people's unwillingness to upset their former employers, forcing the entrepreneurs to obtain capital at higher interest rates. While looking for a rented space to conduct their businesses, almost half the respondents were denied occupancy on one or more occasions. When it came to hiring employees, the troubles escalated substantially, as reported by 51 interviewees. The very real danger of having to face their upper-caste bosses' wrath was enough to override even caste/class affiliations. For more than half of the

Table 9.3 Market Impediments Created by Former Employers

Nature of impediment	No. of interviewees (N = 53)
Registration of their enterprises	21
Credit related	33
Physical location of economic unit	27
Getting workers	51
Procuring initial orders	53

Source: Author's field documentation.

interviewees, getting orders for goods or services in the beginning was also difficult.

Structural Dimension

There is also a structural aspect to social networks, which is born out of their normative dimension. Norms refer to an informal code of conduct that is generally expected of players in the market. Given the internalization of caste-derived norms of segregation and hierarchy, upper-caste market players tend to come together when it comes to their dealings with their Dalit counterparts in order to further their economic and labour interests. Generally, there are certain interlinked socio-economic practices that decisively work to the disadvantage of Dalit entrepreneurs. These are discussed in detail in the next paragraph.

The strength of the unspoken, exclusionary codes of behaviour is demonstrated when upper-caste entrepreneurs are willing to overlook their internal differences to maintain a united front against their Dalit peers. This can mean looking beyond sub-caste differences and across various sectors of trade and services. Upper-caste members also make it a point to connect with influential state officials in order to safeguard their interests. This behaviour is, in some ways, reminiscent of the concepts of 'strength of weak ties' and 'structural holes' mentioned earlier. While these resources are generally leveraged by upper-caste entrepreneurs during market transactions to gain the upper hand over their business peers during market transactions, their use becomes more marked when they are competing against their Dalit peers.

Ties between Dalit entrepreneurs and successful upper-caste owners of capital tend to be extremely feeble and seldom surpass one-to-one relationships (Figure 9.1). Such connections are, therefore, formed outside of the prevailing social networks, and the interaction between the two parties is characterized by an inbuilt hierarchy. The terms of engagement are determined by the upper-caste trading partner or client, usually to the Dalit entrepreneur's disadvantage. Meanwhile, upper-caste players consolidate their own positions in the market by coming together and forming social networks, with an eye to ensuring they retain the say in defining the terms of engagement with Dalit entrepreneurs.

Interestingly, Dalit entrepreneurs, on the other hand, have their own logic for accepting the position of inferiority doled out to them,

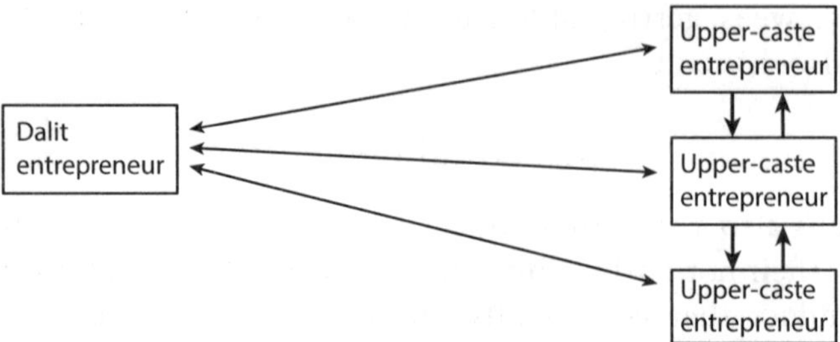

Figure 9.1 Dalit Entrepreneurs in Market Networks

Source: Author.

belying any simplistic logic of blind submission. Their compliance with the unfair terms set by their upper-caste peers is, in fact, a tactical move to ensure, at the very least, their entry into and survival in the market. There is a perception that any radical disruption or questioning of their adverse inclusion in the market could arouse hostility against them, or even threaten their very existence in the market. The idea, then, is to maintain their presence in the market and aim at accruing profits in the long run.

Resource Dimension

A social network's resource dimension refers to the functional domain of its normative and structural dimensions. Factors such as caste and ideological affinity that enable consensus on the normative framework for interactions between various social collectives allow upper-caste market players to forge a strong support base that includes their peers and representatives of local state authorities. Given this scenario, such social networks are not restricted to being economic interest groups, that is, peers in the market with overlapping economic interests and who are part of a similar trade or occupation. These networks are premised on determinants of social identity, that is caste, coupled with family, region, and so on.

Generally, on starting off in the market, an entrepreneur tries to tap into resource networks to propel a venture toward profitability. This section takes on the issue of why upper-caste market players are more successful in the market than their Dalit counterparts, by investigating the pool of resources that confer profits and accumulation.

In question are the material and other factors that entrepreneurs have at hand and can use to their advantage in the market. Much international research has dealt with businesses as independent bodies looking to gain an upper hand over their competitors by using external business organizations (Porter 1980) or internal resources and capabilities (Barney 1991). Other scholars have looked at enterprises in terms of their embeddedness in non-economic forces in the market.[7] The present study takes a similar stance as a larger body of work that has looked at the relatively low success of Dalit entrepreneurs in India in relation to their comparably positioned upper-caste counterparts, in the light of the social embeddedness of market connections (Throat 2006, Jodhka 2010). We discuss the contention of Dalits that their lack of access to network resources is what is behind their relative disadvantage.

Social Networks and Adverse Inclusion during Market Operations

To understand the impact of not having network resources at hand, we spoke to a number of Dalit entrepreneurs, who shared some of their experiences. For instance, a Pune-based entrepreneur who started a courier company talked about the challenges he faced.

> The really big orders for letter dispatch are given by big private companies. This is where I lose out. ... My work is much appreciated by my existing customers. However, I am not able to get big business orders for two reasons. First, I don't have any contacts in the big companies. ... Second, I am not in a position to do business with them as they release payments on a monthly basis and I don't have enough capital to wait for a month. I don't get credit from the market. Other franchises of DTDC [desk-to-desk courier] are controlled by Marathas and Gujaratis.[8] They have enough business friends and contacts in the market to avail credit and are able to do business with big companies.

In this testimony, there is a palpable incongruence between the normative and operational aspects of the market. The normative

[7] See notes 8, 10, and 11 of this chapter.

[8] Gujarati is a regional identity. However, it is again the upper castes of Patels and Kunbis that dominate this sub-sector.

structure of the market seems to suggest that people are free to enter and engage in the market to accrue profits. Hence, the courier-company owner expects that providing satisfactory services ought automatically to result in business growth. However, his inability to procure enough credit indicates that the market seems to operate on certain principles that make the going tough for anyone who is not a member of an influential social network. As he rightly understands, caste and region play a pivotal role in bringing in orders as well as enabling access to a range of resources that can help one fill large orders.

Similarly, a Pune-based entrepreneur who owns a brick kiln talked about the adverse consequences of his being unable to procure credit from his fellow kiln owners.

> I own one brick kiln. I don't have the resources to invest in a second one. All kiln owners usually help each other. I once got a very big order from a farm house at Khadakwasla. I was short by 50,000 bricks. None of the kiln owners helped me. I had to take credit from the open market at an interest rate of 12 to 14 per cent. Usually, brick kiln owners give credit to each other at 2 to 5 per cent. ... Mostly, I have to take credit from the open market for any big order I get. This lowers my profit and hence I am not able to invest in the second kiln.

The above testimony clearly highlights the frustrations of a Dalit entrepreneur doing business in a sector dominated by upper-caste persons who control the major chunk of business and credit flow. The Dalit entrepreneur is unable to succeed in the market due to the tactics employed by upper-caste competitors. The hostility of the credit market to the Dalit brick-kiln owner, in contradiction to the routine practice of all players in the sector sharing local resources, prevented him from being able to expand his market share.

Meanwhile, the case of a Vidisha-based entrepreneur with a handloom business and boutique goes to show that manipulating credit is not the only way that upper-caste networks can impede the operations of Dalits in the market: 'As per business principles, all handloom workshops release their labour for each other as and when required. Last March, I got a big order from Delhi. None of the workshops released their labour, and I had to get my order prepared from Hoshangabad and Bhopal at a higher cost'.

Caste-derived social networks, through their tight hold over labour supply, thwart the handloom-workshop owner's strategic

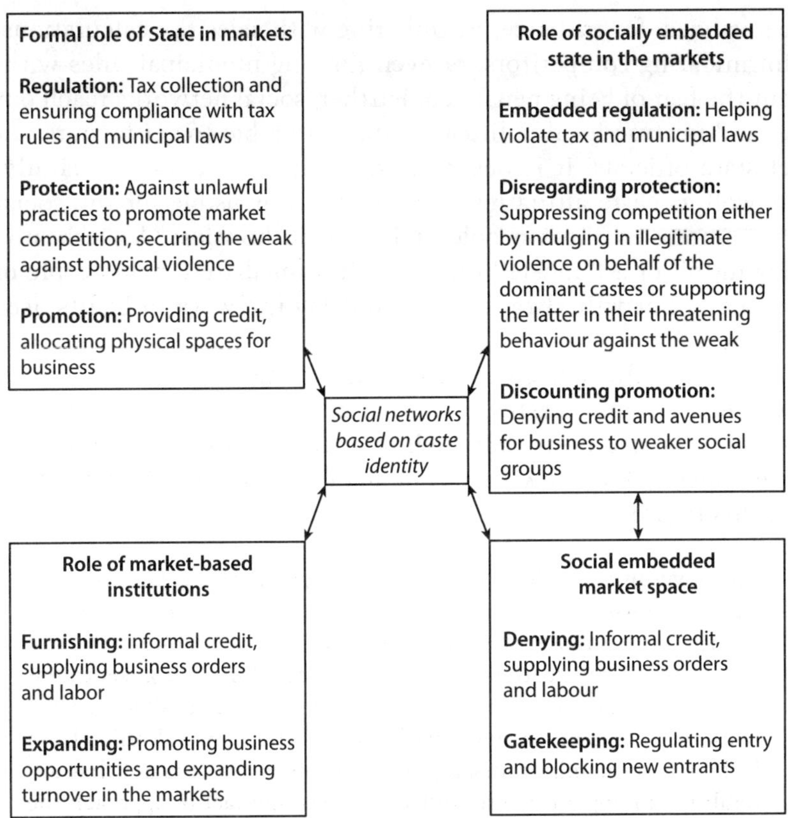

Figure 9.2 Social Networks, Resources, and Market

Source: Author.

attempts to make profits (see Figure 9.2). He recognizes the discriminatory nature of the labour regulations that clearly favour upper-caste entrepreneurs over players such as him. As a consequence, he is left with no choice but to tweak his strategy and revise the supply chain of labour, though this alternative does not yield optimal results.

Social Networks, the State, and Adverse Inclusion

Both Dalits and non-Dalits consider the State as the most powerful institution in the working of the economy. It is also a source of informal and often illicit power that can be used to tilt the balance in market exchanges and reduce transaction costs. Such power can be utilized, for instance, in tinkering with sales tax calculations, intimidating competitors, or even flouting municipal rules without the fear of being penalized. Further, social networks reach out to and nurture local political contacts in a bid to get favours out of state officials. It is observed by Dalit merchants that family[9] as well as caste affiliations are largely responsible for the social ties among business people and state authorities: 'A Deshastha Brahmin[10] or a Bhonsle[11] official will immediately help people of his caste but will always stall and delay the work of Dalits' (see Figure 9.2).[12]

While Dalit entrepreneurs acknowledge the heterogeneity within the upper castes, in terms of sub-castes and class divisions, it is also clear that such differences do not alter business outcomes. A Lucknow-based laundry owner shared his experience in this regard.

> The government offices predominantly operate through caste identity and rent-seeking. The social solidarity between the employees in the offices is rooted in caste identities—Baniya, Brahmin, Thakur, and so on. If the caste of the citizen approaching the government office is the same as that of the official, it is quite possible that the work will get done without any bribe or some minimal bribe. Even if there is some minor misalignment of sub-castes, it is not that difficult for an upper caste to find some social contact to approach the officials of a different sub-caste. Such social contacts invariably lead to a reduction in the size of bribe or rent.

The laundry owner claims that corruption and social relationships based on caste and sub-caste are most often what enable any dealings with government officials. His pessimism is apparent in that he takes both of these for granted. He is more bothered by the knowledge that he and others of his caste do not possess the requisite resources to negotiate with the bureaucracy and reduce the transaction costs, that is, in terms of time as well as money.

[9] As told to us by a general merchant in Lucknow.

[10] Deshastha Brahmins are a Hindu Brahmin sub-caste, mostly residing in Maharashtra.

[11] Bhonsles belong to the clan of Marathas, a dominant Marathi-speaking caste of warriors, commoners, and peasants.

[12] As told to us by a sanitary-goods shop owner in Pune.

Meanwhile, his upper-caste peers have no trouble accessing their social networks, even when the government official belongs to another sub-caste.

Dalit entrepreneurs, therefore, feel that family and sub-caste ties are largely responsible for the affinity between market players and the State, giving well-connected entrepreneurs greater access to state resources. Moreover, familial ties usually imply caste connections, given the close proximity between family and caste. Such caste-based familial ties have been observed to play a pivotal role in the attitude of local municipal officials towards illegal encroachments,[13] the requirement of licenses for trading in some goods,[14] administration of sales tax payments,[15] using the local police to coerce competitors,[16] and non-payment of taxes or electricity bills,[17] to name a few (see Figure 9.2).

While state resources can be used to minimize transaction costs, as the above instances demonstrate, there are other ways in which they can be instrumentalized to meet one's ends in the market. The State can regulate market operations to a large extent through 'non-competition' (Harriss-White 2001). As illustrated by the case of a Vidisha-based ironsmith, while social connections with state officials are a proven source of strength, the mere knowledge of familial ties with state officials is often enough to intimidate competitors.

> Two years ago during Diwali [a major festival], I tried to sell firecrackers.[18] The neighbouring shop, owned by Agarwal,[19] was also selling firecrackers. My sales were better. An employee in his shop came and told me to sell all my firecrackers to him at my procurement price. He threatened that his boss would lodge a complaint with the police. I was selling firecrackers without a license; so was he. But his license was his brother-in-law, who is a police sub-inspector.

[13] As told to us by a general merchant in Lucknow.

[14] As told to us by an ironsmith in Vidisha.

[15] As told to us by a leather-goods manufacturer in Agra.

[16] As told to us by a leather-goods manufacturer in Kanpur.

[17] As told to us by a teacher who runs coaching classes.

[18] Selling firecrackers is not his main business. It is a common tradition in India that during the festival of Diwali, all kinds of shops sell firecrackers for a quick profit.

[19] Agarwal is a surname used by Vaishyas/Baniyas, a trading caste.

It is clear that a less capable market contender, who also happens to hail from a lower caste, cannot succeed against upper-caste entrepreneurs while functioning informally in the 'free' market. In this context, state authorities take biased and often illegal measures that mean lower-caste entrepreneurs, despite managing to gain entry into and getting better results in the market—both using informal means—nevertheless could face heavy losses. This is the process by which the State brings non-competition into the market.

The State has often been known to illegally sanction the use of violence against Dalits at the behest of upper castes. An owner of an automobile repair shop shared his experience in this regard.

> Thakurs are the most powerful community in this area. They have considerable clout in local government, politics, and police, even though a majority of the population belongs to the Kurmi, Chamar, and Dhobi castes.[20] My old workshop was located just beyond Thakur Sahib's backyard. It was demolished by Thakur's men. I tried to stop them and a scuffle ensued. ... I was arrested and the local corporator [elected representative in the local municipality] facilitated my arrest. He won the election because of us [that is, Dalits], but he invariably helps the Thakurs. I have opened the shop at this new location now. I have lost all my old customers and am trying to establish relationships with new ones gradually. Eight years of effort in building a customer base has gone to waste.

This testimony clearly illustrates the sway held by upper castes over political and state officials, in a social capacity, which can be used to hinder Dalit business people's economic advancement. This is despite the sheer number of lower castes in the electoral fray.

The role of marriage alliances is also significant when it comes to consolidating upper-caste social networks. As an Aurangabad-based chemist was to find out, marriage, besides reinforcing social interactions among castes and sub-castes, can also be instrumental in driving official outcomes, with consequences for one's position

[20] Thakur is a Kshatriya sub-caste. Kurmis are, generally, a Kshatriya sub-caste (which has acquired some status in states such as Gujarat and Andhra Pradesh through the process of Sanskritization); the government classifies them as Other Backward Classes (OBCs). Chamars are a Dalit sub-caste. Dhobis are a Dalit sub-caste.

in the market: 'Pethe[21] and I started our medical shop together. Pethe's son-in-law is a surgeon at the Civil Hospital. This helped him secure a contract to supply medicines to the Civil Hospital ... and earn handsomely. Now he has invested his surplus to start a transport business.' On the other hand, a Lucknow-based owner of a laundry reflected on the lack of such social resources among Dalits.

> Our girls and boys marry within the community. All of us have a similar social status; all of us are destined to earn our livelihood by serving the rich and powerful. It does not matter whether we do petty business, or get employed in shops owned by upper castes, or work as labourers; the end result is the same. Which government official will marry a *dhobi*'s [clothes-washer's] daughter? Marriage alliances are always between people of equal social status.

Thus, Dalits, just like upper castes, generally marry within their own community, usually in arranged marriages. Dalits have almost no chance of finding a match from a higher caste; even if they sought to do so, such a possibility would not be supported by social or religious norms. Hence, their chances of being socially connected to state officials through marriage are negligible, since the latter almost always hail from higher castes. This has been confirmed by recent government reports, particularly with regard to mid-level and higher-level officials, as Table 9.4 makes clear. The bulk of the Dalit population is concentrated at the lower rungs, especially in the category of sweepers (a caste profession).

In providing a basis for informal alliances and social networks, therefore, caste becomes a tool to bypass the formal framework of the market. In the case of upper-caste business people, such relationships, whether horizontal (with suppliers, clients, and competitors) or vertical (with state authorities), end up reducing transaction costs.,oweverm tain observations that indicate ourable by in India.ts. This leads us to consider the key issue of whether caste is a u Such strategic alliances—formed on the basis of familial and caste ties, marriage, or interactions in social spaces such as temples, recreational spaces, or residential welfare organizations—are more often leveraged by upper castes, in the market and in the State, to make higher profits.

[21] Pethe is a surname found among Chitpawan/Konkanastha Brahmins in Maharashtra.

Table 9.4 Representation of Dalits in All Central Government Ministries and Departments

As of 1 January 1999			As of 1 January 2003			As of 1 January 2005		
Group	**Total employees**	**Scheduled Castes**	**Group**	**Total employees**	**Scheduled Castes**	**Group**	**Total employees**	**Scheduled Castes**
A	93,520	10,558 (11.29)	A	85,938	10,256 (11.93)	A	80,589	9,551 (11.9)
B	104,963	13,306 (12.68)	B	1,81,905	26,040 (14.32)	B	1,39,958	19,194 (13.7)
C	23,96,426	3,78,115 (15.78)	C	21,21,697	3,45,718 (16.29)	C	20,36,103	3,33,708 (16.4)
D (Excluding sweepers)	9,49,353	1,89,761 (19.99)	D (Excluding sweepers)	8,79,805	1,58,206 (17.98)	D (Excluding sweepers)	7,67,224	1,40,469 (18.3)
Sweepers	96,435	63,233 (65.57)	Sweepers	1,26,131	73,881 (58.57)	Sweepers	61,174	48,067 (59.2)
Total excluding sweepers	35,44,262	5,91,740 (16.7)	Total excluding sweepers	32,69,345	5,40,220 (16.52)	Total excluding sweepers	30,23,874	5,02,922 (16.63)
Total including sweepers	36,40,697	6,54,973 (17.99)	Total including sweepers	33,95,476	6,14,101 (18.09)	Total including sweepers	31,05,048	5,50,989 (17.74)

Note: Figures in parentheses denote percentages.

Source: National Commission for Scheduled Castes and Scheduled Tribes, Sixth Report, 1999–2000, p. 182; National Commission for Schedule Castes, First Annual Report 2004–5, p. 183; National Commission for Scheduled Castes, Second Annual Report 2005–6, p. 179.

Critical Features of the Role of Caste-Derived Social Networks

Let us identify certain salient features of caste-derived social networks, in light of how they favour the endeavours of a few dominant players in the market. The first point rests on caste as an institution conducive to an intermingling of social, economic, and political interests. Caste forms a conduit between the familial and the social at one end, and the State and the markets at the other, ensuring, in the process, the transference of views from one sphere to another. In other words, it gives aspirations born within the family/society continuum a voice in realms such as the State and the market. Such interpenetration between the State, the market, and civil society leads to the formation of a larger conceptual sphere where the interactions between these components give an institutionalized form to the disadvantage of Dalit market players. Caste, in this manner, plays an *exclusionary role* in the market.

In addition, caste is oriented toward enhancing the economic interests of the upper castes. It does so by somewhat replicating social hierarchies in the economic sphere, with the result that upper-caste entrepreneurs are positioned to set the terms of engagement in the market, whereby Dalits are made to operate on unfavourable grounds.

Then there are the *coercive* and *manipulative* aspects of caste, which refer to its strong-arm tactics, tiered structure, and need for strict adherence, all while caste itself remains unquestioned. This enables the privileged castes, by virtue of their membership in caste-derived social networks, to use the administrative and coercive power of the State to dominate the lower castes, potentially using violence with impunity.

The last feature of caste under discussion is collectivization. This implies that caste can transform personal aspirations into collective interests through a dialectical process whereby collective ideals of caste shape individuals, and individuals, by performing certain social activities, cement a larger world view. Caste-derived social networks can, therefore, be seen to play a range of functions in the realms of society, politics, and economics that further the accumulation of profits. This leads us, in the final section of this chapter, to consider the key issue of whether caste should be treated as a unique form of civil society in India.

Caste as Civil Society

Dalits view caste-derived social networks in the realm of markets as highly selective, coercive formations that confer economic benefits on those higher up the caste ladder. Caste is instrumental in consolidating individual interests and giving them a common platform. In this process, those in positions of power are able to set their own rules of engagement with Dalits as well as with the State and the market. Caste operates in a singular manner, quite independent of and indifferent to the State. The State, the market, and civil society become indistinguishable in that each is made to serve the collective interests of the powerful castes. In other words, the accumulative endeavours of upper castes are facilitated by caste-based networks. We contend that caste-derived social networks can be understood as civil society. What is the basis of this claim?

It may be useful to delve into traditional theories regarding civil society as a site of accumulation, while keeping in mind potentially contentious issues in the case of Dalits. One way to understand civil society in this regard is through the works of Locke, Adam Smith, and Hegel, and the points where their views seem to converge despite their varied ideological underpinnings. First, all of them consider civil society as a site of accumulation. This is the central point with which Dalits would agree, while differing with other insights on civil society coming from these authors.

Second, according to Locke and Hegel, the function of the State is to govern and safeguard the rights of citizens. Viewed in a favourable light, this would imply its role as a vanguard to uphold the social and economic rights of citizens. Contrary to Locke and Hegel, Smith argues that civil society is also expected to uphold the laissez-faire model of liberty. Let us elaborate these points. Dalit entrepreneurs seem to disagree with these views on the State.

Civil society, according to Locke, is the sphere where citizenship itself is conferred, and the basic rights to life, liberty, and property are obtained and legally enforced. Thus, this thesis lay the very foundation of liberal bourgeois civil society (Locke 1960). Hegel, on the other hand, takes a more detailed approach wherein civil society is seen as an intermediary between the family and the State (Hegel 1967, 182). Civil society is made up of people of various classes, constituted without any divine or political sanction, unlike the caste system or the allocation of classes by those in power (Hegel

1967, 206). However, civil society for Hegel is contradictory in nature. The contradiction is manifested in the increasing accumulation through the economic expansion of civil society, while at the same time the mass of people lack the purchasing power to enjoy the fruits of civil society (market), which in turn results in 'distress and dependence of the class tied to work of that sort' (Hegel 1967, 242). This analysis of civil society leads Hegel to call for an intervention by a universal State. In Smith's (2005) view, a distinction needs to be made between 'civilized society', which pertains to economic developments, and 'political society', the domain of the State. Civilized society is characterized by ongoing competition among self-governing entities—individuals and groups—engaging in economic relations in the market; it is best served by laissez-faire. It is because economic relations, as per Smith, are governed by the exercise of influence, rather than authority or trickery, that they constitute a 'civilized' society.

According to all three thinkers, civil society is the sphere meant for the realization of each person's attempts at accumulation. Moreover, it is the birthplace of inequalities which are born out of class rather than religion. The case of Dalit entrepreneurs differs in that their lack of privilege is determined by caste. Marx's perception is that the State is partial to the interests of the more powerful castes, unlike Hegel's universal State which intervenes in the dynamics of class while breaking down caste-based distinctions. Smith's conception provides no relief either, since the Dalits seek a State that brings rectificatory justice. While these conceptions clarify how civil society and markets cannot be viewed as entirely distinct entities, the notion of a State that operates independently of both would not be entirely satisfactory when it comes to the case of Dalits.

Marxist scholarship does, however, carve out civil society as an entity distinct from the State. Both the instrumental (Miliband 1969) and deterministic (Poulantsaz 1973, 1978; Bridges 1974) approaches to Marxism view the State as safeguarding the interests of the class in power. With the disintegration of feudal structures giving way to the capitalist state, civil society is born as a platform that protects the right to private property (Marx 1968) and encourages individual accumulation. The State, meanwhile, is expected only to selectively safeguard and uphold certain pursuits (Marx 1844).

It is useful to study the point where Gramsci makes a crucial departure from Marx's view of civil society, extending its scope beyond being merely a platform for accumulation in the economic sense to include political and cultural activities (Bobbio 1987, 148). Civil society, according to Gramsci (1971), is the site where the classes in power are constantly engaged in the process of acquiring the consent of the marginalized to maintain their power over them. The hegemony of the powerful, which is a product of both this consent and of might, is thereby born out of the overlap between civil society and the State (Gramsci 1971).

While their experiences of adverse inclusion in the market would bring Dalit merchants closer to the Marxist view that sees a collusion of civil society, the State, and markets favouring the upper classes, there may be certain departures. Dalits, for one, would appreciate the fact that there is no uniform class identity; there are a range of other markers such as caste which are pivotal to their experience. Dalit and upper-caste entrepreneurs may share a class identity, but the privileges of a higher caste allow the latter to leverage their social networks in the market as well as their relationships with state authorities—often in clear violation of laws—to their decisive advantage.

Another point of deviation pertains to the understanding of civil society itself, which Dalits view as a sphere of constant political tussle, contestation, and attempts to disrupt the privileges of caste, and not as a space for uncritical acceptance of the ideals of the State or sociopolitical and religious forces dominated by the higher castes. After all, the very fact that Dalit entrepreneurs manage to break into the markets and vocalize their adverse inclusion goes to prove their bitter knowledge of the operations of socio-economic and political structures that systematically shunt them into positions of disadvantage.

Basile and Harriss-White pick out this very gap in the understanding of civil society in India and turn their attention to the part played by civil-social organizations 'within the set of institutions underpinning capitalist accumulation' (2000, 3). In recognizing caste as an important part of the social structure of accumulation, they acknowledge that capitalism is not restricted to the market, which in turn cannot be equated with the economic domain, and instead look at the nuanced web of social institutions that accumulation is entrenched in. Subsequently, Harriss-White (2005) deals intensively with the operations of caste, religion, gender, and age as social institutions in the economic sphere, particularly in the local context. For Basile and Harriss-White, caste groups are dynamic institutions and are indeed a specific form of civil society, because they often take an organized form and articulate the interests—economic as well as political—of their members.

For our purposes, caste functions as a significant social institution that facilitates accumulation endeavours, especially by upper-caste entrepreneurs, by forging a conducive environment where persons and collectives can tap into formal and informal institutions to succeed in the market. It does so by aiding the formation of certain tangible relationships, bringing people into contact with others affiliated with 'diverse systems of enduring groups and categories' (Srinivas and Béteille 1964, 166) such as state authorities, religious groupings, business people, and caste-based organizations. Viewing caste as civil society throws into relief the dynamics of the formation of 'trust'-based relationships, sociocultural affinity, the use of religious and caste norms to sanction social inequality and penalize transgressors, and—in case of a serious threat—the instrumentalization of violence to uphold the socio-economic status quo.

This explains why people who even loosely share certain socio-cultural, economic, and political ideals are motivated to help each other in the market, assuming that they hold certain kinds of resources. This enables upper-caste merchants to consolidate gains by leveraging their state and informal contacts in the market, to the disadvantage of their Dalit competitors. The latter, meanwhile, are forced to transact on unfavourable terms in the market; they are threatened into unquestioning acceptance of an upper-caste domination, deviations from which could lead to being ousted from the market and could extend to physical harm.

***

This chapter contends that although Dalit entrepreneurs may be allowed to enter the market in India, they inevitably do so in a position of disadvantage. Caste, along with its accompanying factors, takes on a new form under capitalism, and thereby continues to contribute to discrimination. A variety of informal bodies are established that prevent any possibility of fair competition in the market between upper- and lower-caste players. This chapter locates the cause of the Dalits' disadvantageous market position in their lack of network resources, which are largely in the hands of upper-caste entrepreneurs. The latter, while allowing Dalits to enter the market, remain resentful of their presence.

In this context, it is important to interrogate Indian civil society to gauge whether caste is a specifically Indian form of civil society. While its role in the market does point toward its being considered thus—given its privileging of upper-caste entrepreneurs and promotion of their economic interests at the cost of their Dalit peers—it also goes to show the achievement of Dalit entrepreneurs, who have consistently fought against all odds to reach where they stand today.

References

Akerlof, G. 1970. 'The Market for Lemons: Quality, Uncertainty and the Market Mechanism'. *Quarterly Journal of Economics* 84, no. 3 (August): 488–500.

———. 1982. 'Labor Contracts and Partial Gift Exchange'. *Quarterly Journal of Economics* 97, no. 4 (November): 543–69.

Barney, J. 1991. 'Firm Resources and Sustained Competitive Advantage'. *Journal of Management* 17, no. 1 (March): 99–120.

Basile, Elisabetta, and Barbara Harriss-White. 2000. *Corporative Capitalism: Civil Society and the Politics of Accumulation in Small Town India*. Working Paper QEHWP S38, Queen Elizabeth House, Oxford.

Bobbio, Norberto. 1987. *Which Socialism? Marxism, Socialism and Democracy*. Cambridge: Polity.

Bridges, Amy Beth. 1974. 'Nicos Poulantsaz and the Marxist Theory of the State'. *Politics & Society* 4, no. 2 (June): 161–90.

Burt, Ronald. 1992. *Structural Holes: The Social Structure of Competition*. Cambridge, MA: Harvard University Press.

Gramsci, Antonio. 1971. *Selections from the Prison Notebooks*. London: Lawrence and Wishart.

Granovetter, Mark. 1973. 'The Strength of Weak Ties'. *American Journal of Sociology* 78, no. 6 (May): 1360–80.

———. 1985. 'Economic Action and Social Structure: The Problem of Embeddedness'. *American Journal of Sociology* 91, no. 3 (November): 481–510.

Harriss-White, Barbara. 2005. *India's Market Society*. New Delhi: Three Essays Press.

Harriss-White, Barbara, and Aseem Prakash. 2015. 'Social Discrimination in India: A Case for Economic Citizenship'. In *Indian Economy in Transition: Essays in Honor of C. T. Kurien*, edited by S. Jankarajan, L. Venkatachalam, and R. Maria Saleth, 294–326. New Delhi: Sage.

Hegel, G.W.F. 1967. *Hegel's Philosophy of Right*. Oxford: Clarendon Press.

Jodhka, Surinder S. 2010. 'Dalits in Business: Self-Employed Scheduled Castes in North-West India'. *Economic and Political Weekly* 45, no. 11 (March) 488–500.

Kapur, Devesh Chandra Bhan Prasad, Lant Pritchett, and D. Shyam Babu. 2010. 'Rethinking Inequality: Dalits in Uttar Pradesh in the Market Reform Era'. *Economic and Political Weekly* 45, no. 35 (28 August): 39–49.

Lin, Nan. 1982. 'Social Resource and Instrumental Action'. In *Social Structure and Network Analysis*, edited by Peter Marsden and Nan Lin, 131–45. Beverly Hills, CA: Sage.

———. 1990. 'Social Resources and Occupational Status Attainment'. In *Social Mobility and Social Structure*, edited by R.L. Breiger, 241–71. New York: Cambridge University Press.

Locke, John. 1960. 'An Essay Concerning the True Original, Extent and End of Civil Government'. In *Social Contract: Locke Hume Rousseau*, edited by Earnest Barker, 3–143. London: Oxford University Press.

Marx, Karl. 1844. *On the Jewish Question*. Paris: Deutsch-Französische Jahrbücher. Available at http://www.marxists.org/archive/marx/works/1844/jewish-question. Last accessed on 3 May 2020.

———. 1968. *A Critique of the German Ideology*. Moscow: Progress Publishers. Available at http://www.marxists.org/archive/marx/works/download/Marx_The_German_Ideology.pdf. Lasr accessed on 3 May 2020.

Miliband, Ralph. 1969. *The State in a Capitalist Society*. London: Weidenfeld and Nicolson.

Omvedt, Gail. 2011. *Globalisation & Indian Tradition*. Available at http://www.ambedkar.org/News/Globalisation.htm. Last accessed on 4 February 2015.

Panini, M.K. 1996. 'The Political Economy of Caste'. In *Caste: Its Twentieth Century Avatar*, edited by M.N. Srinivasan, 26–68. New Delhi: Viking.

Porter, M.E. 1980. *Competitive Strategy*. New York: Free Press.

Poulantsaz, N. 1973. *Political Power and Social Classes*. London: New Left Books.

———. 1978. *State, Power, Socialism*. London: Verso.

Prasad, Chandra Bhan. 2008. 'Markets and Manu: Economic Reforms and Its Impact on Caste in India'. CASI Working Paper Series, no. 08-01. Available at https://casi.sas.upenn.edu/sites/casi.sas.upenn.

edu/files/research/Markets%2Band%2BManu%2B-%2BChandra%2BBhan%2BPrasad.pdf. Last accessed on 3 May 2020.

Radcliffe-Brown, A.R. 1940. 'On Social Structure'. *Journal of the Royal Anthropological Institute of Great Britain and Ireland* 70, no. 1: 1–12.

Ramaiah, A. 2004. 'Dalits to Accept Globalization: Lessons from the Past and Present'. Mumbai: Tata Institute of Social Sciences. Available at http://questforequity.org/contents/Papers/Dalits%20to%20Accept%20Globalisation,%20Avatthi%20Ramaiah..pdf. Last accessed on 3 May 2020.

Smith Adam. 2005. *Wealth of Nations*. North Carolina: Hayes Barton Press.

Srinivas, M.N., and André Béteille. 1964. 'Networks in Indian Social Structure'. *Man* 64 (November–December): 165–8.

Thorat, S.K. 2006. 'Caste System and Economic Discrimination: Lessons from Theories'. In *Reservation and Private Sector: Quest for Equal Opportunity and Growth*, edited by S.K. Thorat, Aryama, and Prashant Negi, 73–80. New Delhi: Indian Institute of Dalit Studies and Rawat Publication.

Webster, C.B. 1999. 'Who is a Dalit'. In *Dalits in Modern India: Vision and Values*, edited by S.M. Michael, 76–90. New Delhi: Sage.

10

Ambedkar's Economic Methodology for Social Justice

*The Centrality of Dalits**

PRITAM SINGH

Dr B.R. Ambedkar is popularly known as the principal architect of the Indian Constitution and one of the founding fathers of the Indian republic, and rightly so, but that he was also an original economic thinker is relatively less recognized.[1] The originality of his economic thinking can also be interpreted as eclecticism due to his non-adherence to any one economic ideology, namely Marxism, neo-classical economic thought, support for market economy, or state regulation. However, behind this eclecticism lies a unity and a common running thread in his ideas on different economic issues. This unity was provided by his concern for the Dalit sections of

* I thank R.S. Mann for research assistance while preparing the chapter, and Meena Dhanda and Shree Borkar for discussions on these issues.

[1] Ambedkar's PhD from Columbia University, USA, in 1927 was in economics, and the Doctorate in Science (DSc) which the London School of Economics (LSE) conferred on him in 1923 was also for his contributions to the field of economics. His DSc (1923) thesis at LSE was titled 'Problem of Rupee' and the PhD (1927) thesis at Columbia was on 'The Evolution of Provincial Finance in British India'. Among the political leaders in India, he was the first to receive formal training in economics and to have publications in professional economic journals.

Indian society. In adopting this approach, he can be rightly compared with Karl Marx who, in his own words, was 'ruthless' in his rigorous analysis of capitalism, but that rigour was not merely an academic enterprise but was closely linked with defending the interests of the working class. In both cases—Marx for the working class and Ambedkar for Dalits—there was no compromise in the objective analysis of economic conditions to suit any partisan considerations. On the contrary, both viewed the scientific examination of economic conditions as a necessary measure for advancing the interests of the working class (for Karl Max) and Dalits (for Ambedkar).[2] In the Indian context in particular but the South Asian context in general, the social categories of class and caste overlap with and interpenetrate each other despite their autonomous status. If one were to use Marx's definition of the working class as one dispossessed from the ownership of any means of production and dependent on its sale of labour power to earn enough for survival at the least, this class in the Indian/South Asian context would incorporate the most oppressed castes (Dalits). Similarly, the oppressed castes that Ambedkar identified and came to be known as Dalits constitute the bulk of the Indian/South Asian working class. Undoubtedly, some sections of the Indian/South Asian working class do not come sociologically from Dalit caste backgrounds in a similar manner as some sections of the Indian/South Asian Dalits are not in the working-class category and have moved to the petty bourgeois/middle class or bourgeois class category. In that sense, class and caste do retain autonomy of their own and need

[2] Antonio Gramsci, the Italian Marxist philosopher and revolutionary leader, raised the importance of truth, the aim of scientific enquiry, by saying that 'truth was revolutionary'. The complete sentence is 'Dire la verità, arrivare insieme alla verità, è compiere azione comunista e rivoluzionaria', which translates in English as 'To tell the truth, to attain truth together, is to accomplish a communist and revolutionary action'. It appears in an article Gramsci published in *L'Ordine Nuovo* titled 'Workerist Democracy' (Democrazia Operaia), 21 June 1919. The text in Italian is available at: https://www.marxists.org/italiano/gramsci/19/democraziaoperaia.htm. I am thankful to my friend Stefano Pippa for supplying this information on the original source of Gramsci's words on truth as revolutionary. Stefano adds: 'I am not aware of any other occurrences [of these words], but there may well be something similar in the PN [Prison Notebooks of Gramsci] or in the Letters.'

to be analysed in their own domain. Another strong similarity in Marx's and Ambedkar's methods of analysis is that both picked up a social relation as central to their analysis, and the meaning of other social relations was analytically and politically derived from their relationship to the that central social relation within this framework of analysis. For Marx, the central social relation was between wage labour and capital, and the significance of other intermediate classes was to the extent to which they impacted this relationship. Similarly, for Ambedkar, the central social relationship in the context of Indian society was between Dalits and the upper castes, and the significance of other intermediate castes was to the extent to which they impacted this Dalit–upper caste relationship.[3]

Ambedkar focussed his intellectual energies on three main issues of relevance for Dalits in the economic domain: monetary circulation in the economy, size of land holdings as part of the broader agriculture strategy, and public finance (especially the pattern of federal finance). The subject of federal finance further required that, apart from issues of revenue-expenditure at different levels of governance, the question of centralization versus decentralization of the federal mode of governance was analysed. Ambedkar did take up both these aspects of federal finance.

Monetary Circulation in the Economy

In his writings on money, Ambedkar directly challenged the dominant Keynesian view in the 1930s regarding the delinking of money supply from gold reserves. John Maynard Keynes had argued that due to the development of the monetary exchange mechanism in advanced capitalist economies such as the UK, there was no need to limit the supply of money by linking it with the amount of gold

[3] Mathew (1992, 1283) makes a similar point, though only tangentially, in his reply to Gopal Guru's critical review of his book *Ambedkar: Reform or Revolution*, where he mentions the relationship between the working class and the peasantry in the Marxian framework, and between 'Untouchables' and 'Sudras' in his proposed Ambedkarite framework: 'India's dalit democratic revolution should definitely be the revolution of the ex-untouchables and sudras notwithstanding the contradiction between them ... the leadership would definitely be that of the ex-untouchables, the eternal proletariat of India.'

reserves. Ambedkar opposed this view not because he had any special fascination with gold but because he considered that this delinking of money supply from gold reserves would open up the possibilities of excessive money supply which, in turn, could lead to financial instability and inflation. The system of gold reserves provided a restraint on the expansion of money.[4] From the viewpoint of the poor sections of society, Ambedkar was convinced that both inflation and financial instability would hit them adversely, while the rich might in fact benefit from this by using a range of alternative investment options.[5] The poorer sections of society have zero or a low level of savings, which does not allow them to explore any investment options. This leads to the rich taking advantage of the systemic financial instability to accumulate more, while the poor are thrown into further economic shocks and insecurity. The recent financial crisis of the global capitalist economy since 2007–8 triggered by unregulated financial markets and resulting in huge income and wealth inequalities is a testimony to the prophetic insights of Ambedkar.[6] For him, the seemingly technical question of money supply and gold reserves needed to be assessed from the viewpoint of the impact of the government's stance on this issue on the welfare of Dalits who constituted the bulk of the poorer segment of Indian society. The neo-classical theory or even the Keynesian theory would examine such monetary issues in terms of the overall impact on the economy, while Ambedkar did a partisan analysis of the impact of such monetary phenomena on the Dalit sections of society. By looking at the overall impact, the neo-classical or Keynesian analysis would appear to be neutral in its approach towards different social groups but, by ignoring the differentiated nature of economic phenomena and policies, such 'overall impact' perspective tends to empower the already powerful in the status quo. In contrast, Ambedkar clearly recognized that economic policy changes not only have different levels of impact on different class components of the society but that such impacts

[4] Jadhav (1991) makes a similar point in his reading of Ambedkar's contribution to monetary economics.

[5] Ambedkar has been cited for saying that high internal inflation 'is a gain for one class at the cost of another class in the country' (Rajadhyaksha 2015).

[6] On financial and other dimensions of this crisis, see Singh (2008).

most often are mutually conflicting, that is, benefitting some and harming others. Ambedkar, therefore, examined such phenomena from the position of the economic interests of the Dalits, and, to do this, it was essential that the analysis be truthful and robust.

Federal Finance: Revenue–Expenditure Dimension

The other major issue which attracted Ambedkar's analytical attention was the question of public finance dealing with revenue and expenditure of different layers of governance. His basic premise was that in a federal system of governance, each level of government—centre, province, or the local—needed to have appropriate sources of revenue to meet its expenditure obligations. Ambedkar further argued that along with the quantitative dimensions, it was essential to examine the qualitative dimensions of the revenue–expenditure pattern. A government may be able to generate generous revenue, but it might fritter away that revenue through unproductive expenditure such as luxury spending by the government's ministers and officials. In contrast, even a modest increase in the expenditure of revenue on public goods such as health and education can have a multiplier effect on improving people's quality of life. The provision of such public goods is especially important for Dalits as well as some poorer sections of society. The recent experience of austerity regimes all over the capitalist world shows that in order to decrease the revenue–expenditure gap, public expenditure on public goods such as health and education has been drastically cut (see Singh and Bhushal 2014). Such cuts have disproportionally affected the poorer sections of society in an adverse way. Ambedkar's method or approach holds consistent, for he analysed the revenue–expenditure dimension of federal finance in the context of the impact that changes in this dimension would have on Dalits.

Federalism: Centralization versus Decentralization

In assessing inter-governmental relations in a multi-level governance model of federalism, Ambedkar also examined the impact of centralization versus decentralization on the living conditions of Dalits. From one angle he seemed to be supportive of centralization, but from another, he considered excessive centralization as a threat to the interests of Dalits. In his arguments in support of centralization, he viewed that decentralization could empower the local upper-caste elites over Dalits, whereas centralized institutions could be used to restrain the power of such local elites and thus defend the interests of Dalits. However, Ambedkar also visualized that excessive centralization could lead to creating favourable conditions for the rise of authoritarianism that can weaken democracy. In his view, weakening of democracy was not in the interest of Dalits because strong democratic institutions provided avenues for Dalit mobilization and negotiations. It is precisely for this reason that Ambedkar opposed and defeated a proposal from Jawaharlal Nehru that India's Constitution could be amended by a simple majority in the Parliament. Ambedkar viewed Nehru's proposal as paving the way for increased centralization and, therefore, authoritarianism. Ambedkar defeated the Nehruvian proposal and succeeded in inserting the constitutional provision that a government needed to have at least a two-third majority in the parliament to make a constitutional amendment (see Singh 2005 for a detailed discussion). We see again the applicability of Ambedkar's method in supporting or opposing centralization. His key concern was not with centralization or decentralization per se in an abstract sense but with the implications of centralization and decentralization in defending the political and economic interests of Dalits.

The Question of the Size of Landholdings

Ambedkar discussed the issue of small landholdings in Indian agriculture as part of the general problems surrounding Indian economy at that time.[7] He noted 'two very noteworthy but equally sad facts regarding economic life in India: (1) that it was largely an agricultural country; and (2) that its agricultural productivity is the lowest' (Ambedkar 1979, 458). He looked at the sectoral division of the Indian economy then and argued that, in general, a livelihood could be obtained through the service sector, which in modern economic theory is also referred to as the tertiary sector, and the

[7] The article 'Small Holdings in India and Their Remedies' was originally published in the *Journal of the Indian Economic Society*, Vol. 1, in 1918. It is included in Ambedkar (1979).

industrial sector (Ambedkar 1979, 453). He further divided what he called industry into secondary industry and primary industry,[8] and provided a definition of primary industry thus:

> The primary industries are concerned with extracting useful material from the earth, the soil or water and take the form of hunting, fishing, stockraising, lumbering and mining. These primary or extractive industries are fundamental in two ways: (1) They extract from the physical world useful materials which become the original sources of man's subsistence, (2) They provide raw materials for the secondary or manufacturing industries. (Ambedkar 1979, 453)

In the context of Indian economy, he highlighted the importance of the primary industry, that is, agriculture, and identified the key problems of India's agricultural economy as those related to production: 'what to produce, the proper proportion of the factors of production, the size of holdings, the tenures of land, etc' (Ambedkar 1979, 453). He then focussed his attention on discussing the problem of small landholdings because of its implication on productivity.

Ambedkar noted that due to various historical reasons and laws relating to land inheritance, some countries (such as England) have large landholdings while others (such as France, Denmark, and Holland) have smaller landholdings (Ambedkar 1979, 456). Concerning India, he provided data on the size of landholdings in three tables—the first presented data on four provinces (Assam, Bombay, Central Provinces, and Madras) for 1896–7 and 1900–1, the second on the state of Baroda for 1917, and the third on a village called Pimpala Saudagar, near Poona, for 1927. He concluded on the basis of this comparative data that: '[T]he average size of holdings varies from 25.9 acres in the Bombay Presidency to an acre or two in Pimpala Saudagar' (Ambedkar 1979, 457). Having empirically established the preponderance of small landholdings, he proceeded to dissect other dimensions of this small-scale farming. He highlighted, in particular, the lack of compactness of these

[8] The modern sectoral classification of an economy is: primary (agriculture), secondary (industry), and tertiary (services). Ambedkar used the classification which was, perhaps, prevalent at that time: services (tertiary) and industry—which was further subdivided into primary industry (agriculture) and secondary industry (manufacturing).

small landholdings; that is, spatially speaking, the landholder had small tracts of land in different locations of the village. He rightly characterized this as the problem of fragmentation of landholdings. Such fragmentation, he argued:

> renders farming in India considerably inefficient as it once did in Europe. It involves waste of labour and cattle power, waste in hedges and boundary marks, and waste of manure. It renders impracticable the watching of crops, sinking of wells and the use of labour saving implements. It makes difficult changes in cultivation, the making of roads, water channels, etc, and it increases the cost of production. (Ambedkar 1979, 459)

He concluded: 'These disadvantages of fragmentation are to be recounted only to lend their support to the process of restripping or consolidation' (Ambedkar 1979, 459). After discussing various schemes that involved the legal and social dimensions of consolidation, Ambedkar asserted that the solution to small landholdings caused by fragmentation was not merely to group together scattered plots of land but also to increase the scale of each holding to an economically efficient level. He argued: 'If it is said that Indian agriculture suffers from *small* and *scattered* holdings we must not only consolidate, but also enlarge them. It must be borne in mind that consolidation may obviate the evils of scattered holdings, but it will not obviate the evils of smallholdings unless the consolidated holding is an economic, i.e., an enlarged, holding' (Ambedkar 1979, 464; italics in original). He then examined the various definitions of what could be considered an economic holding. Some definitions suggested arbitrary quantitative sizes that varied between 30 acres to '30 to 50 bighas of fair land' (Ambedkar 1979, 465), where he notes '8 bighas = 5 acres' (Ambedkar 1979, 456), that is, a bigha was about 62 per cent of the size of an acre. He dismissed these quantitative definitions as arbitrary and not worth further consideration. He then examined qualitative definitions that centred on the idea that a desirable size of land should be one which could support a farmer's family. He rejected this approach too because it was based on meeting the consumption needs of the farming family and not on the productive efficiency of the farm. His argument was:

> [C]onsumption is not the correct standard by which to judge the economic character of a holding. It would be perverse accounting

> to condemn a farm as not paying because its total output does not support the family of the farmer though as a *pro-rata* return for each of his investments it is the highest. ... [I]f our social custom compels a farmer to support some of his family members even when he cannot effectively make any use of them on his farm we must be careful not to find fault with the produce of the farm because it does not suffice to provide for the workers as well as the dependants that may happen to compose the family. The adoption of such an accounting system will declare many enterprises as failures when they will be the most successful. (Ambedkar 1979, 466; italics in original)

Recognizing the capitalist nature of the economic system in which the size of holdings was being discussed, without using the word 'capitalist' in this particular instance (though he did it later as mentioned in the next paragraph), he argued:

> It must be premised at the outset that in a competitive society the daily transactions of its members, as consumers or producers, are controlled by a price regime. It is production, then, in a price regime that we have to analyse here for our purpose ... if agriculture is to be treated as an economic enterprise, then, by itself, there could be no such thing as large or a small holding. To a farmer a holding is too small or too large for the other factors of production at his disposal necessary for carrying on the cultivation of his holding as an economic enterprise. Mere size of land is empty of all economic connotation. Consequently, it cannot possibly be the language of economic science to say that a large holding is economic while a small holding is uneconomic. It is the right or wrong proportion of other factors of production to a unit of land that renders the latter economic or uneconomic. Thus a small farm may be economic as well as a large farm; for, economic or uneconomic does not depend upon the size of land but upon the due proportion among all the factors including land. (Ambedkar 1979, 467–8)

To say that the problem of Indian agriculture was one of small holdings, Ambedkar contended, would be a flawed argument. In his view, the problem of small holdings was merely a symptom; the cause of small holdings was that there was a huge amount of surplus labour that was not economically employed in agricultural activities. If the dependence of this surplus labour on land was taken away, there would be basis for what Ambedkar called 'capitalist agriculture' (Ambedkar 1979, 479) which would demand the consolidation and enlargement of holdings.[9] The shifting of this dependence was only possible, Ambedkar argued, by means of industrialization: 'industrialization ... alone can reduce the extreme pressure [of population] which ... causes subdivision of land. Thus, if small and scattered holdings are the ills from which our agriculture is suffering to cure it of them is undeniably to industrialize' (Ambedkar 1979, 479). By looking at data from advanced capitalist economies, Ambedkar placed emphasis on their trend towards a decrease in rural population, while India was experiencing de-urbanization. The data he cited showed that in USA, rural population as a share of the total population had decreased from 87.5 per cent in 1790 to 33.3 per cent in 1911; in the UK, from 49.92 per cent in 1851 to 19.9 per cent in 1911; in France, from 75.6 per cent in 1840 to 57.9 per cent in 1911; but in India, it had increased from 64.4 per cent in 1891 to 71.5 per cent in 1911 (Ambedkar 1979, 479). He used this data to highlight what he called 'too much agriculture in India' (Ambedkar 1979, 479). What Ambedkar did not do was to analyse why this de-urbanization or 'too much agriculture' had taken place. He merely noticed the empirical trend and suggested the remedy of industrialization. Later research on 'deindustrialization' in India has shown that it was the British colonial rule over India that had caused this deindustrialization, de-urbanization, and excessive burden on agriculture (Clingingsmith and Williamson 2004). Similarly, later research has shown that the transfer of rural/traditional-sector population to the urban/modern sector, as suggested by Ambedkar and theorized by Lewes and Schultz, was not an easy and uncomplicated process. The work of Karl Kautsky, a Marxist theoretician and politician, had highlighted how small peasantry, through overwork and under-consumption, struggles to subsist and resist its disintegration caused by competition from large-scale capitalist agriculture (Banaji 1976).[10] The latest data shows that the population dependent on agriculture has declined to about 50 per cent of the total population, and that massive industrialization has led to a decline in the share of agriculture in India's

[9] Students of development economics would immediately recognize this argument as developed by Lewes (1954) and Schulz (1964), for which they were awarded the Nobel Prize in Economics in 1979.

[10] My friend Jairus Banaji informs me that a full English translation of Kautsky has been published by Zwan Publishers in 1988.

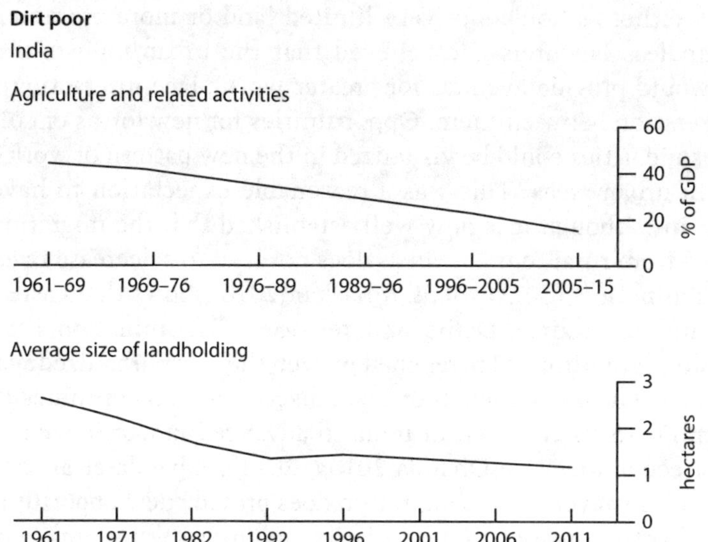

Figure 10.1 Decreasing Share of Agriculture in GDP and the Decreasing Size of Average Landholding in India

Source: Agricultural Census, Ministry of Agriculture (*The Economist*, 2018).

GDP, yet the problem of small landholdings in India not only persists but has, in fact, become even more acute. See Figure 10.1 on the problem of small landholdings in contemporary India.

This data shows that the average landholding has decreased from 2.6 hectares (6.4 acres) to 1.1 hectares since the 1960s.

In my view, Ambedkar's advocacy of industrialization as the solution to small-scale uneconomic landholdings could be attributed partially to the influence of the dominant paradigm in economics at that time, that the problem of 'surplus' rural population can be resolved by its absorption into the expanding industrial sector. Even more importantly, it could be attributed to Ambedkar's view of rural life as the habitat of caste oppression and of the transition to urban life as a means to free oneself from that caste oppression. At one place, he stated this unambiguously: 'The minorities and the Scheduled Castes who are living in the villages are constantly subjected to tyranny, oppression, and even murders by the members of the majority communities. The minorities need an asylum' (Ambedkar 1979, 157–8). Perhaps Ambedkar also identified that Dalits in the rural/agrarian sector were isolated from each other either as holders of very limited land or more prominently as landless labourers. He believed that the urban/industrial sector would provide avenues for greater work-place interaction and cooperation between them. Opportunities for new forms of collective solidarities could be visualized in the new pattern of work and life in urban areas. This was a reasonable expectation to have at that time, though it is now well established that the migration of Dalits from rural to urban areas does not lead to a decrease in caste discrimination against them. Mhaskar (2018) shows that caste discrimination against Dalits and religious discrimination against Muslim minorities is entrenched in even the most urbanized spaces in India. The phenomenon of caste discrimination continues even when Dalits migrate out of India to advanced industrialized capitalist economies (see Dhanda 2013a, 2013b; Dhanda et al. 2014a, 2014b). However, such a migration does provide new opportunities for collective organization, solidarity, and networking.

Ambedkar's work on small landholdings, therefore, demonstrates that despite his minute analysis of the issue as a truth-seeking social scientist, his larger political vision encompassed advancing the cause of Dalit solidarity and liberation from caste oppression. The issue of global climate change and global warming had not entered public consciousness then. With increasing awareness of the threat of global warming to human and non-human life, the discourse on agriculture is now changing in favour of small-scale, local, and of course organic farming.

⋆⋆⋆

For all those who oppose caste and other forms of discrimination, an important lesson to learn from what I have characterized as the Ambedkarite method of analysis is that the concerns of Dalits and other discriminated sections should remain the central determining criterion in assessing different policy options. In the era of global climate change, a creative development of Ambedkar's ideas is necessary to suggest sustainable and egalitarian modes of economic activities. Taking up this challenging task is essential for building an alliance between Dalit and Green perspectives. A Dalit or working-class standpoint is necessary to give the Green perspective an egalitarian orientation, and the Green perspective is necessary to bring the Dalit vision equal to the challenges of the twenty-first century, where global climate change, accompanied by the continuous and massive loss of biodiversity, is the biggest threat facing humanity. Poor Dalit communities would be the worst sufferers if the policy drift on global climate change is not stopped. In the context of the present century, a creative ecological reframing of the Ambedkarite method of defending Dalit interests when faced with alternative policy options is an absolute historical necessity.

References

Ambedkar, B. R. 1979. *Dr Babasaheb Ambedkar: Writings and Speeches*, vol. 1, compiled by Vasant Moon. Bombay: Education Department, Government of Maharashtra.

Banaji, Jairus. 1976. 'Summary of Selected Parts of Kautsky's "*Agrarian Question*"'. *Economy and Society* 5, no. 1: 2–49.

Clingingsmith, David, and Jeffrey G. Williamson. 2004. 'India's De-industrialization Under British Rule: New Ideas, New Evidence'. Working Paper No. 10586, *The National Bureau of Economic Research (USA)*. Available at https://www.nber.org/papers/w10586. Last accessed on 1 June 2020.

Dhanda, M. 2013a. 'Caste and International Migration, India to the UK'. In *The Encyclopedia of Global Human Migration*, edited by I. Ness. New Jersey: Wiley Blackwell.

———. 2013b. 'Certain Allegiances, Uncertain Identities: The Fraught Struggles of Dalits in Britain'. In *The New Indian Diaspora*, edited by O.P. Dwivedi, 99–119. New York: Editions Rodopi.

Dhanda, M., D. Mosse, S. Iafrati, and J.K. Mundy. 2014a. 'Caste in Britain: Experts' Seminar and Stakeholders' Workshop'. Research Report no. 92. Equality and Human Rights Commission, Manchester.

Dhanda, M., A. Waughray, D. Keane, D. Mosse, R. Green, and S. Whittle. 2014b. 'Caste in Britain: Socio-legal Review'. Research Report no. 91. Equality and Human Rights Commission, Manchester.

Jadhav, Narendra. 1991. 'Neglected Economic Thought of Babasaheb Ambedkar'. *Economic and Political Weekly* 26, no. 15 (13 April): 980–2.

Lewes, Arthur. 1954. 'Economic Development with Unlimited Supplies of Labour'. *The Manchester School* 22, no. 2: 139–91.

Mathew, Thomas. 1992. 'Ambedkar and Marxism'. *Economic and Political Weekly* 27, no. 24–5 (13–20 June): 1283.

Mhaskar, Sumeet. 2018. 'Ghettoisation of Economic Choices in a Global City: A Case Study of Mumbai'. *Economic and Political Weekly* 53, no. 29 (21 July): 29–37.

Rajadhyaksha, Niranjan. 2015. 'Ambedkar, Rupee and Our Current Troubles'. *Livemint*, 14 April. Available at https://www.livemint.com/Opinion/rMImvbuYNDk4RvWGfcMtQO/Ambedkar-rupee-and-our-current-troubles.html. Last accessed on 27 July 2019.

Schulz, Theodore. 1964. *Transforming Indian Agriculture*. New Haven, CT: Yale University Press.

Singh, Pritam. 2005. 'Hindu Bias in India's "Secular" Constitution: Probing Flaws in the Instruments of Governance'. *Third World Quarterly* 26, no. 6: 909–26.

———. 2008. 'Contemporary Global Capitalism: Multi-pronged Crises'. *Economic and Political Weekly* 43, no. 41 (11–17 October): 36–40.

Singh, Pritam, and Lok Nath Bhusal. 2014. 'Austerity, Welfare State, and Eco-socialism: With Special Reference to the United Kingdom'. *Economic and Political Weekly* 49, no. 39 (27 September): 111–18.

The Economist. 2018. 'Agriculture in India: Slim Pickings'. 14 July. Available at https://www.economist.com/asia/2018/07/14/indias-government-claims-to-subsidise-farmers-but-actually-hurts-them. Last accessed on 27 July 2019.

11

Economic Justice

Policy and Public Investment for Pasmanda *Muslims*

JAWED ALAM KHAN*

We will have to devise innovative plans to ensure that minorities, particularly the Muslim minority, are empowered to share equitably in the fruits of development. They must have the first claim on resources.

—Prime Minister's address at the 52nd Meeting of National Development Council (2006)[1]

As per the National Commission for Minorities Act, 1992, the term 'religious minorities' includes Muslims, Christians, Sikhs, Buddhists, Parsis, and, of late, Jains. The Indian Constitution guarantees equality of opportunities and freedom of faith and expression to its citizens and prohibits discrimination on the grounds of religion (Articles 14, 15, 14, 29, and 30). Muslims constitute around 15 per cent of India's total population and the largest share—more than 70 per cent—of the total religious minority population (which

* The author is thankful to his PhD supervisor Kaustav Banerjee and colleagues at the Centre for Budget and Governance Accountability (CBGA) for the valuable comments and suggestion made on this chapter's initial draft.

[1] Available at https://archivepmo.nic.in/drmanmohansingh/speech-details.php?nodeid=482. Last accessed on 1 June 2020.

is around 20 per cent of the total population). Further, a large section of the Muslim population constitutes the *Pasmanda*[2] community.

Unfortunately, a large number of Pasmanda Muslims have for long been counted among the most backward sections of the population and have also been under-represented in governance, decision-making institutions, and leadership positions. The issues of identity, security, and stigmatization of Muslims in pre- and post-Independence period have emerged as major hindrances to addressing equity-related matters. Further, there has been continuous neglect on the part of the union and state governments in addressing the development deficit among Muslims.

Additionally, unequal social structures, patriarchy, religious identity, and the discriminatory mindset of the government's administrative apparatus excluded Pasmanda Muslims from the government's development policies. More importantly, due to the presidential ordinance of 1950, Dalit Muslims could not get the Scheduled Caste (SC) status (as did Dalits from the Hindu, Sikh, and Buddhist communities) to avail the benefits of reservation in admission to public educational institutions and government jobs. Moreover, some sections of Muslims were included in the Other Backward Classes (OBC) list, but the Muslim OBCs, who originally were part of the Dalits who converted to Islam, were not able to compete with the Hindu and other non-Hindu OBCs despite the affirmative action policies in north Indian states and at the central level. While discussing the backwardness of Muslims, there has been a tendency to present them as a single, monolithic, homogeneous group not only in the political arena, development and planning, and the policymaking circle but also in social science discourses and media debate, unlike the Hindu community. It was argued on the basis of evidence from decennial censuses that Muslims in India were divided into three broad categories, namely *Ashraf* (noble born), *Ajlaf* (mean and lowly), and *Arzal* (excluded) (Ansari 1960).

An analysis of the Five-Year Programme (FYP) documents since 1951 shows that Pasmanda Muslims were not recognized as a separate category in the public domain until the Fifth FYP. In 1983, the

[2] *Pasmanda*, a Persian term meaning 'those who have fallen behind', refers to Muslims belonging to the Shudra (Other Backward Classes) and Ati-Shudra (Dalit) castes. *Pasmanda* Muslims constitute large sections of (70–80 per cent) the total Muslim population in the country.

Gopal Singh Commission was formed to assess the socio-economic conditions of Muslims. In the same year, the 15 Point Programme for the Welfare of Minorities was announced without a proper implementation strategy.

Prime Minister's High Level Committee under the chairpersonship of Justice Rajindar Sachar assessed the social, economic, and educational status of the Muslim community in 2006. So far, policies and budgetary allocations were largely made for religious minorities by the union and state governments. The NITI Aayog report of 2017 showed that even after 10 years of implementation of the Sachar recommendations, the condition of Muslims in the areas of education and economic development had not changed much. 'Muslims constitute the largest religious minority and lag behind others in terms of economic, health and education parameters. The participation of Muslims in salaried jobs is also low. Muslim workers are largely concentrated in the informal sector which is characterised by low wages, poor working conditions and little or no social security'.[3] The Pasmanda Muslim Community faces exclusion in planning, budgeting, and implementation processes of development programmes at various levels of governance.

Objectives and Research Methodology

The objective of this chapter is to assess the implementation of policies and programmes for minorities in general and Muslims in particular initiated by the union government during the FYPs. The primary research question of the chapter is how development policy initiatives meant for Muslims worked in terms of policy/programme design, availability of financial resources, fund utilization and physical performance, and status of implementation (planning and monitoring) during the Twelfth FYP. In terms of methodology, the chapter heavily relies on secondary-level data sources, scheme design, resource availability, and physical output made under the Prime Minister's New 15 Point Programme (15 PP) for the Welfare of Minorities and Multi-sectoral Development

[3] *Three Year Action Agenda*, NITI Aayog, Government of India, 2017, pp. 152.

Programme (MSDP). MSDP was renamed as Pradhan Mantri Jan Vikas Karyakram (PMJVK) in 2017–18. It has also attempted to analyse the allocation of budget for minorities in some selected states. In terms of data sources, the chapter has used the websites of Ministry of Minority Affairs, Ministry of Finance, Lok Sabha, and State Finance Department. Several reports published by the government, journal publications, and research papers by think tanks and the Central Statistics Office (CSO) have been reviewed to assess the minority-related programme.

Review of Policy Provisions for Minorities in Five-Year Plans

The issues faced by Muslims since Independence are multifaceted and diverse, in having to do with identity, security, and development. Muslims have for long been recognized to be among the backward sections of the society as per government data and reports. Till about the Fifth FYP, minorities had not been addressed in the FYPs at all. It was only in the Sixth FYP that minorities were addressed as a separate socio-economic group and some policy and budgetary provisions were made exclusively for them.

The 15 PP for the Welfare of Minorities was formulated in the Sixth FYP in May 1983. Commonly known as the 'Prime Minister's 15-Point Programme for the Welfare of Minorities', it covered 15 different aspects for action. It was aimed to facilitate the full participation of Muslims and other minority groups in all aspects of national life and, thus, promote the cause of national integration. However, no credible report is available in the public domain on the impact of the 15 PP's implementation.

In 2005, the Sachar Committee carried out a comprehensive study of the condition of Muslims (their demographics, education, employment, and credit availability) and other minority and socio-religious groups (SRCs). The Sachar report notes that the Muslim 'community exhibits deficit and deprivation in practically all dimensions of development' (GoI 2006). The report also found that their situation was especially poor in the states of West Bengal, Uttar Pradesh, Bihar, and Assam. For the implementation of 72 accepted recommendations, the government took 43 decisions by clubbing together recommendations of a similar nature, such as education, skill development, access to credit, special development initiatives, measures for affirmative action, Waqfs and Communal Violence (Prevention) Bill, and the Delimitation Act. However, three recommendations that were not accepted are: enumeration of castes/groups as part of the decennial census exercise; creation of a new all-India cadre of officers for Waqf; having an alternative admission criteria in higher education institutions and absorbing Arzals in the SC list or at least in a separate Most Backward Category (MBC) carved out of the OBCs.

General policy recommendations focus on improving transparency, monitoring and data availability, and setting up a National Data Bank (NDB) to monitor the outcomes. The data has to be digitized so as to be easily accessible to all. The Equal Opportunities Commission (EOC) and Diversity Index provide incentives to various organizations and institutions that promote diversity according to what the diversity index advocates. In this regard, although reports of working groups on setting up an EOC and constructing a diversity index have been submitted, no headway has been made in terms of actual implementation so far.

Specific policy suggestions focus on reviewing the content of government textbooks, increasing schooling facilities, setting up community study-centres, encouraging primary education in Urdu language, and allowing the admission of non-matriculate minority students in Industrial Training Institutes (ITIs). Voluntary reservations should be promoted in institutions of higher studies on the basis of economic, occupational, locational, and caste backwardness of candidates, and madrasa degrees should be accepted for admissions into institutions of higher education. To promote and enhance credit access to Muslims in priority sector advances and to open up more bank branches in the minority concentrated areas, experts should be drawn from minority communities to be a part of relevant interview panels and recruitment boards.

The Sachar Committee advocates the provision of basic infrastructure facilities to all sections of the society, including Muslims. Registration of trusts set up by the community, such as Wakf institutions and mosque committees, should be facilitated. It also talks about the better utilization of Wakf properties for a number of welfare activities.

The Sachar Report came out with data facts on Pasmanda Muslims, but no mention was made in the recommendations of any policy action for them. Further, more than 50 per cent of the total Muslims live in Bihar, Uttar Pradesh, Bengal, and Assam with poor development conditions, but the committee did not make any recommendations for a region-specific policy action. The 15 PP for the Welfare of Minorities and the MSDP have been the only operational policy strategies for the development of minorities since 2006 and 2008 respectively. Moreover, many states are also running their own state-sponsored development programmes for minorities.

Current Policy Provisions and Development Programmes

Prime Minister's New 15 Point Programme for the Welfare of Minorities, 2006

The Eleventh and the Twelfth FYPs, through their core approach of 'faster and inclusive growth',[4] adopted a four-pronged strategy—educational and economic empowerment, access to public services, strengthening of minority institutions, and area development. In 2006, the 15 PP was reformed to focus on issues intimately linked with the social, educational, and economic upliftment of minorities in 15 different aspects and provided for the earmarking of 15 per cent of total outlays/funds in certain schemes.

Nonetheless, in 2006, the Ministry of Minority Affairs (MoMA) was set up as the nodal ministry for the welfare and empowerment of religious minorities. In addition to the 15 PP, a new development strategy (MSDP), which is being implemented since 2008, was designed to address the development shortfalls faced by religious minorities.

With regard to activities, the 15 PP focuses on enhancing opportunities for education, promoting equitable share in economic activities and employment, improving the minorities' living conditions, and the prevention and control of communal riots. Besides MSDP, all the schemes run by the MoMA are also part of the 15 PP, and are entirely meant for the development of minorities.

[4] Twelfth Five Year Plan (2012–2017), vol. 1: *Faster, More Inclusive and Sustainable Growth*, Planning Commission, Government of India, 2013. Available at https://niti.gov.in/planningcommission.gov.in/docs/plans/planrel/fiveyr/welcome.html. Last accessed on 6 May 2020.

Currently, eleven union ministries/departments claim to be involved in implementing the 15 PP, including the Ministries of Rural Development, Water and Sanitation, Urban Development, Housing and Urban Poverty Alleviation, Labour and Employment, Home, Finance, Women and Child Development, School Education and Literacy, Personal and Training, and Minority Affairs. Details of selected schemes from the 11 union ministries/departments are available on MoMA's website. Since 2015, the names of many schemes have gotten changed, and the sharing pattern of funds between the centre and the state has also been revised since NITI Aayog's report on the rationalization of centrally sponsored schemes (CSS). There are other programmes under the 15 PP which are exclusively implemented for minorities, such as the Madrassa Modernization Programme, scholarship schemes, women leadership, skill development, National Minorities Development Finance Corporation (NMDFC), and Maulana Azad Education Foundation (MAEF), all of which aim to address the education deficit in the minority community. The NMDFC focuses on providing microfinance to the poorest of the poor among minorities through NGOs, educational loans to persons belonging to a minority community, facilitating vocational training programmes among the minority community, and financing tailor-made market assistance options for artisans and craftspersons.

Priority Sector Lending to Minorities All commercial banks are advised to ensure a smooth flow of bank credit to minority communities in 121 minority concentration districts having at least 25 per cent of their population constituted by minorities, excluding those states/union territories where minorities are in majority. Access to credit for Muslims is critical as a large proportion of this community is engaged in self-employment activities. While formulating the district plan it has to be ensured that adequate credit is made available to minorities, Muslims in particular, with convenience and ease.

Minorities have shown a steady increase in the volume of credit from 10.6 per cent in 2007–8 to 15.40 per cent in 2017. The community-wise flow under public sector lending (PSL) during 2016–17 is as under: Muslims (45.48 per cent), Sikhs (23.90 per cent), Christians (20.24 per cent), Jains (6.32 per cent), Buddhists (2.39 per cent), and Parsis (1.67 per cent). The data clearly shows that while Muslims constitute 72 per cent of the minority population, they account for 45 per cent of the total credit flow. Besides, several field-based studies have found that in some rural areas their access to credit is even negligible due to many reasons (Khan and Parvati 2012).

Status of Recruitment Giving Muslims a fair share in governance institutions is very critical for their development. Data collated by the MoMA on the status of recruitment of minorities (in central government, public-sector undertakings, banks, and so forth) shows that the percentage of minorities recruited was 6.24, 6.91, 7.89, 8.56, and 7.5 per cent of the total recruitment from 2011–12 to 2015–16. It clearly reflects that minorities have not been given their fair share in recruitment processes. The representation of Muslims is at the lowest level. There is no disaggregated data on religious minorities in terms of recruitment. My own assessment of the representation of Muslim in the central government departments and ministries shows that it does not exceed beyond 2–3 per cent of the total recruitment.

Prevention of Communal Riots In recognition of the fact that security and development initiatives are equally essential for Muslims, there are many clauses under the 15 PP for the prevention and control of communal riots, justice, and rehabilitation of victims. It has been found that the aforesaid commitment has repeatedly been breached by the union and state governments. Incidents of communal violence continue to occur, creating an environment of deep insecurity among minorities, which has a negative impact on equality and inclusive development. Prosecution for communal violence is tardy and victims are not adequately rehabilitated. In this context, it is the responsibility of the present government to act firmly and ensure the prevention of communal tensions and violence, lynching, and illegal detention of Muslims in the name of containing terrorism and cow protection. A time-bound prosecution for offences and a comprehensive rehabilitation based on justiciable and statutory norms are required (Post Sachar Evaluation Committee 2014).

Further, to address all aspects of the issue of communal violence in the country, a bill titled 'The Prevention of Communal Violence (Access to Justice and Reparations) Bill, 2013' was prepared and approved by the cabinet. However, the introduction of the bill was deferred and it has not been taken up since for further discussion.

Multi-Sectoral Development Programme

The MSDP adopted an area development approach with a bouquet of schemes to address deficits related to a number of issues such as male-female literacy and work participation, housing, drinking water, and electricity. It was also seen as a gap-filling measure or a top-up approach to expedite development deficits in 90 minority concentrated districts (MCDs). In the Twelfth FYP, MSDP was extended to 710 minority concentrated blocks (MCBs) of 196 districts and 66 minority concentrated towns (MCTs) having at least 25 per cent minority population. Both 15 PP and MSDP have to be implemented at the state level. Moreover, many states have their own state-sponsored schemes in the areas of education, livelihood, and social security.

Allocation of Financial Resources, Utilization, and Physical Performance

Union Government

It was established in the previous section that many schemes are being implemented by the central and state governments since the Eleventh FYP. It is, therefore, necessary to know the quantum of allocation, extent of fund utilization, and physical target and physical achievement meant for minorities in the MoMA, Department of Education (Ministry of Human Resource Development), Ministry of Civil Aviation, and the 15 PP. Looking at the total budgetary allocation for minorities, it may be noted that only 0.49 per cent of the total union budget of 2016–17 has been earmarked for the development of minorities. The allocated fund for minorities includes 15 PP (100 per cent), MSDP, and 15 PP (15 per cent). The total reported expenditure on minorities by the central government through 15 PP and MSDP has shown a declining trend since 2012–13, although religious minorities constitute 21 per cent of the total population as per the 2011 census (see Table 11.1).

Table 11.1 Budgetary Allocation for Minorities in the Union Budget (in crores)

	2012–13	2013–14	2014–15	2015–16	2016–17
Financial allocation under 15 PP (100 per cent) and MSDP	2,174	3,026	3,089	3,654.86	3,827
Financial allocation under 15 PP (15 per cent)	24,999.1	27,291.86	23,565.33	11,912.28#	6,102.9*
Total allocation/ Expenditure on minorities	27,173	30,318	26,654	15,567.14	9,930
Total Union budget	**1,410,372**	**1,559,447**	**1,663,673**	**1,790,783**	**2,014,407**

Note: #Some schemes do not have full year data.
* Many schemes do not have full year data.
Source: Compiled from Ministry of Minority Affairs, Government of India.

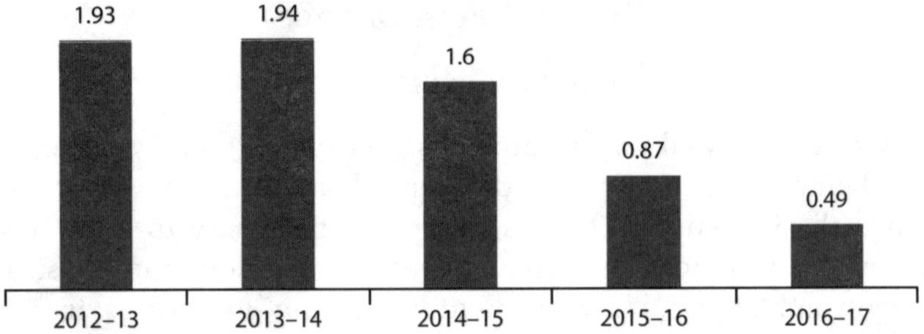

Figure 11.1 Share of Expenditure on Minorities in the Total Union Budget (per cent)

Source: Ministry of Minority Affairs (www.indiabudget.gov.in, last accessed on 16 March 2020).

Ministry of Minority Affairs (MoMA)

The total budget allocation (in absolute number) under MoMA has increased marginally from INR 196 crore in 2014–15 to INR 4,195 crore in 2017–18. The performance of MoMA in terms of fund utilization was unsatisfactory in the Eleventh FYP.

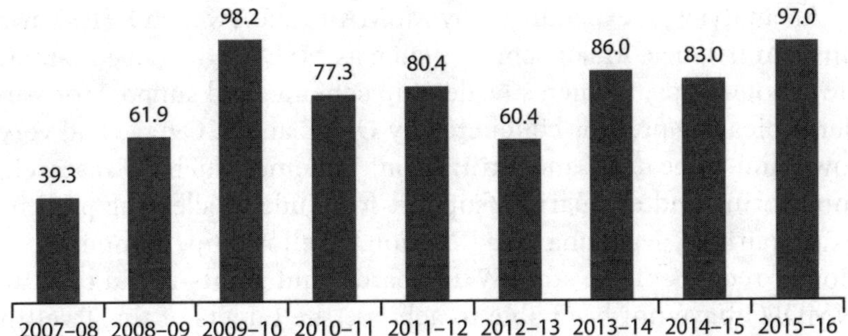

Figure 11.2 Fund Utilization vis-à-vis Fund Allocation (per cent)

Source: Ministry of Minority Affairs (www.indiabudget.gov.in, last accessed on 16 March 2020).

The ministry was able to utilize merely 78 per cent (average) of the total outlay (INR 7,000 crore) earmarked in the Eleventh FYP period. In the Twelfth FYP, the percent of utilization was found to go up to 94 per cent. The MoMA noted that the budget's poor utilization has primarily been due to a delayed start in the implementation of major schemes such as pre-matric scholarship and MSDP for select MCBs and MCTs (Table 11.2).

Table 11.2 Status of Fund Allocation and Utilization under Ministry of Minority Affairs (in crores)

Year	Allocation		Expenditure
	B.E.	R.E.	
2007–8	500	350	196.7
2008–9	1,000	650	619.1
2009–10	1,740	1,740	1,709.4
2010–11	2,600	2,500	2,080.9
2011–12	2,850	2,750	2,292.3
2012–13	3,155	2,218	2,157.9
2013–14	3,531	3,131	3,026
2014–15	3,734	3,165	3,089
2015–16	3,738	3,736	3,654
2016–17	3,827	3,827	
2017–18	4,195		

Note: *Utilization has been reported taking into account B.E. figures; R.E.: Revised Estimate.

Source: Compiled from Ministry of Minority Affairs, Government of India.

An analysis of expenditure by MoMA in the Twelfth FYP shows unspent balance. Major schemes such as MSDP, pre- and post-matric scholarships, women's leadership scheme, and support for students clearing prelims conducted by UPSC and SSC have had very low fund allocation and utilization. Schemes such as research, monitoring and evaluation, support for students clearing prelims examinations, Maulana Azad National Fellowship, computerization of records of the state Wafq boards, and grants-in-aid to state NMDFC have not been able to achieve the targets of the Twelfth FYP, which has been a major cause of concern in terms of effective functioning. Allocation of budget to the Madrasa Modernization Programme (school education) has seen a drastic decline for the last three financial years, from INR 400 crore 2014–15 down to INR 150 crore in 2017–18. In Uttar Pradesh, Bihar, and other northern states, teachers have not received their salary for the last two years.

Multi-sectoral Development Programme

The MSDP has undergone a major revamp in terms of its increase in geographical coverage and changes in its implementation and planning in the Twelfth FYP. However, the expansion of activities and allowing some kind of flexibility in the guideline of CSS for preparing tailor-made projects as per the local needs was not done to the desired level. As per the data reported by MoMA, in the initial 4 years of the Twelfth FYP, the government was able to spend only 41 per cent of total allocation proposed for MSDP (Table 11.3).

Further, it can be seen that there has been very low achievement in physical outcomes across the components of MSDP. Degree colleges, school buildings, lab equipment, teaching aid,

Table 11.3 Financial Achievement under MSDP in the Twelfth FYP as on 31 June 2016

Twelfth FYP proposed allocation (in crores)	5,650
Total cost of project approved in the Twelfth FYP (in crores)	4,478
Fund released for projects approved (in crores)	2,361
Expenditure	1,311
Expenditure over approved fund (in per cent)	29
Fund released over the Twelfth FYP proposed allocation (in per cent)	41

Source: Compiled by CBGA from the Ministry of Minority Affairs.

free cycles, and other such components have a poor completion rate against the unit sanctioned under the MSDP project, while many activities under the MSDP have not yet started. Similar is the case for water supply, housing, and income generating infrastructure (see Table 11.4).

Table 11.4 Physical Achievement under MSDP in the Twelfth FYP as on 31 June 2016

	Unit sanctioned	**Unit completed**	**Work in progress**	**Per cent of completion against sanctioned units**
Activities				
A. Education				
Degree college	15	0	3	0
School building	995	10	126	1
Additional classrooms	12,106	2,664	2,147	22
Hostels	605	77	98	12
Computers	893	381	14	42
Lab equipment	87	0	0	0
Toilet and drinking water in school	1,914	384	373	20
Teaching aid	613	0	4	0
Free cycle	13,960	0	764	0
Cyber gram	371,657	74,293	14,389	19
B. Skill development				
ITI building	96	7	38	7
Polytechnic	16	2	9	12
Skill training	127,605	2,129	750	2
C. Health	1,738	117	242	7
D. AWC	8,357	2,767	2,230	33
E. Drinking water				
Hand pump	13,624	6,825	1,630	50
Drinking facilities	9,853	3,103	4,209	31
F. IAY	44,054	15,782	9,240	35
G. Income generating infrastructure	66	16	35	24
H. Miscellaneous	2,433	0	239	0

Source: Compiled by CBGA from the Ministry of Minority Affairs. Available at www.indiabudget.nic.in, last accessed on 16 March 2020.

Allocation and Utilization in the Prime Minister's New 15-Point Programme

The MoMA collates scheme-wise information on the 15 PP. There are only a few schemes which report financial achievement. Utilization rate for the period between 2006–7 and 2013–14 is found to be low in Indira Awas Yojna (IAY) (70.53 per cent), Swarna Jayanti Shahari Rozgar Yojana (SJRSY) (53.08), and ITI (68.20 per cent) with some degree of variation (Chart 11.1).

For 15 PP's schemes—such as Sarva Shiksha Abhiyan (SSA), Kasturba Gandhi Balika Vidyalaya (KGBV), Integrated Child Development Services (ICDS), and Swarnajayanti Gram Swarozgar Yojana (SGSY) (renamed as Ajeevika)—only the data on their physical achievements is reported without any information on their financial performance. Components related to Jawaharlal Nehru National Urban Renewal Mission (JNNURM) (UIG, Urban Infrastructure and Governance, Urban Infrastructure Development Scheme for Small & Medium Town [UIDSSMT], Integrated Housing and Slum Development Programme [IHSDP], and BSUP) and the Madrassa Modernization Programme did not report the data on fund utilization and physical outcomes regularly (Figure 11.3). Important schemes such as Integrated Child Development Services (ICDS) (59 per cent), Swarnajayanti Gram Swarozgar Yojana (SGSY) (61 per cent), and IAY (82 per cent) have low physical achievements of the target fixed by the government for the schemes, whereas SJRSY has a higher physical achievement. Physical achievement

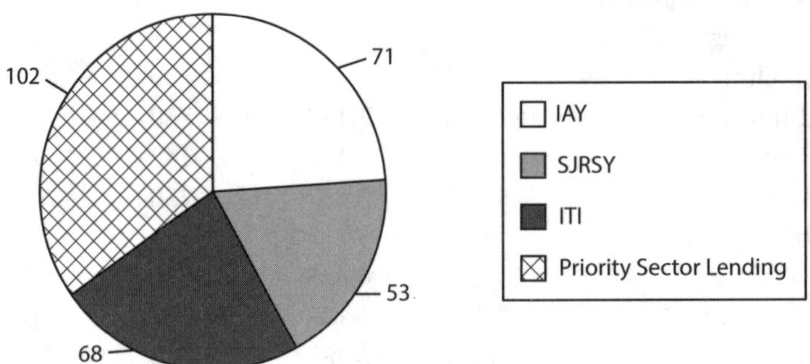

Chart 11.1 Financial Achievement under Various Schemes of the 15 PP (2006–7 to 2013–14) (in per cent)

Source: Ministry of Minority Affairs, Government of India.

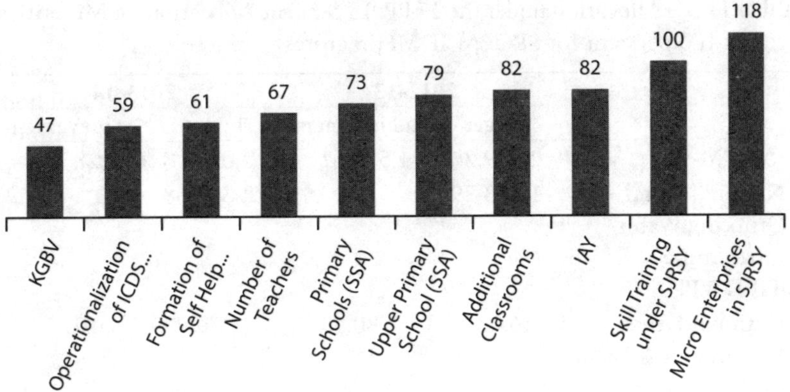

Figure 11.3 Physical Achievement under Various Schemes of the 15 PP (2006–7 to 2013–14) (per cent)

Source: Ministry of Minority Affairs, Government of India.

in SSA is found to be low with some degree of variation across the components (Table 11.5).

Scholarship schemes since their inception have shown over-achievement in terms of physical targets, which are now declining due to low utilization funds. Data on overachievement in scholarship schemes reflects both fresh and renewed scholarships distributed among minority students. Data on physical achievement in scholarship schemes should be reported in two separate columns, under fresh and renewed cases. Here, it is worth noting that scholarship schemes and NMDFC are providing beneficent data on the basis of religious bifurcation.

Budgetary Priorities in State Governments

With regard to dealing with development of religious minorities in states, even before the Sachar recommendations, many states such as Uttar Pradesh, Bihar, West Bengal, Karnataka, and Telangana had their own Department of Minority Welfare at the level of state and district. However, there are states such as Gujarat, Odisha, and Delhi that are dealing with the development work for minorities through an umbrella department called SC, ST, OBC and Minority Welfare Department. State departments for the welfare of minorities do implement many centrally sponsored schemes (15 PP, MSDP)

Table 11.5 Allocation under the 15 PP: 15 per cent Allocation for Minorities Except 100 per cent for SPQEM/IDMI (in crores)

	2012–13		2013–14	
	Target	**Achievement**	**Target**	**Achievement**
IAY/PMAY	2,049.24	1,533.62	2,016.18	1,285.75
National Rural Drinking Water Programme (NRDWP)	1,443.79		2,305.58	
National Urban Livelihoods Mission (NULM)	46.6811	30.38	79.99	101.74
Quality Education in Madarsa (SPQEM)	182.49		182.7338	
Infrastructure Development for Minority Institutions (IDMI)	28.38		24.9899	
DAY-NRLM				
Basic Service to the Urban Poor (BSUP)	7,254.84		6,813.03	
Integrated Housing and Slum Development Programme (IHSDP)	2,235.83		2,237.06	
Urban Infrastructure Development Scheme for Small and Medium Towns (UIDSSMT)	2,642.19		2,821.76	
Urban Infrastructure and Governance (UIG)	9,097.24		10,805.74	
Upgradation of Industrial Training Institutes (ITIs)	18.42	8.82	4.8	23.44
	24,999.1	1572.82	27,291.86	1410.93

Source: Ministry of Minority Affairs, Government of India.

2014–15		2015–16		2016–17	
Target	**Achievement**	**Target**	**Achievement**	**Target**	**Achievement**
2,061.173	1,663.152	2,645.503	1,567.589	5,773.049	
1,830.82		823.02		135.61	
155.7		54.38	51.54		
107.829		294.5074			
11.4471		1.308475		142.02	
29.97	11.9411	27.1407	17.5952	52.2213	2.2035
5,226.47		5,894.89			
1,823.86		2,171.53			
2,048.917					
10,259.78					
9.36	6.126				
23,565.33	1681.219	11,912.28	1,636.724	6,102.9	2.2035

and state-sponsored schemes (pertaining to education, livelihood, social welfare, Urdu education and Hajj, and provision of land for graveyard).

The analysis for 2017–18 shows that Gujarat, Madhya Pradesh, Odisha, Jharkhand, West Bengal, Telangana, Uttar Pradesh, and Karnataka allocated 0.029, 0.039, 0.057, 0.15, 1.9, 0.83, 1, and 1.17 per cent respectively of the total state budget for their minority population. Among these states, only West Bengal, Uttar Pradesh, and Karnataka have crossed the one percentage point (Table 11.6).

The MSDP is one of biggest schemes in the country, jointly implemented by the central and state governments. In Uttar Pradesh, the minority welfare department implemented the Madrasa Modernization Programme and provided grants to recognized madrasas; extended scholarship schemes and provided support for the preparation of civil services examination; and constructed girls' hostels. In West Bengal, the government is running schemes for scholarships, development and welfare of minorities, assistance to government and non-government schools/colleges, housing for women, and setting up of new educational institutions and hostels for minorities. The minority welfare departments of Telangana and Karnataka have run many schemes for the development of

Table 11.6 Priorities in the State Budgets

States	Allocation for minorities	Share of minorities in the state budget (in per cent)	Share of minorities in state population (in per cent)
Gujarat	51	0.029	11.3
Madhya Pradesh	55	0.039	8.15
Odisha	62	0.057	5.04
Jharkhand	117	0.15	18.27
West Bengal	3,471	1.9	28.18
Telangana	1,250	0.83	12.68
Uttar Pradesh	2,457	1	20
Karnataka	2,200	1.17	15.72
Union government	3,827	0.22	19.5

Source: State Finance Department, Government of India.

minorities, among which the establishment of residential schools for boys and girls has been the most effective for the promotion of education among the minority community.

Besides looking at the development policy initiatives (budgetary allocation, fund utilization, and physical achievement) implemented by the union and state governments, it is also necessary to assess the several challenges—such as those relating to the design of schemes, and the planning, implementation, and monitoring of processes and outcomes—encountered while executing these policy initiatives.

Issues in Design of the Schemes and Programmes

The 15 PP was aimed at channelling public resources equitably to minorities, and for 15 per cent of the financial allocation and the physical benefits to be earmarked as the targeted share of the minorities below poverty line (BPL). It is a matter of fact that no list of BPL minorities has been prepared in many states. My own experience in Uttar Pradesh, Bihar, and Haryana is that only a negligible proportion of the Muslim community is included in the BPL list. Also, the phrase 'wherever it is possible' used for financial allocations and deciding the number of beneficiaries lends a lot of ambiguity and confusion to the operationalization of the scheme by departments at the union, state, and district level.

The design of the 15 PP and an assessment of its objectives reveal that the government's intent with the plan was to provide policy-driven benefits to minorities, akin to budgetary strategies such as the Scheduled Caste Sub-Plan (SCSP) and the Tribal Sub-Plan (TSP). The SCSP and TSP promise plan allocations to the SCs and STs in accordance with their proportion within the country's total population through departments at the centre and the state. However, the share of fund flows to minorities through the 15 PP is either not based on the proportion of their population or the needs of their communities.

It has also been found from the author's assessment that minorities have not been included in the budgetary processes of either the union or the state governments. In terms of expenditure reporting and accounting at the union, state, and district levels, the SCSP and the TSP are better placed than the 15 PP. Allocations for SCs and STs are reported under budget (minor) heads 789 and 796 of the Detailed Demand for Grants in the union and state budget documents. Further, the District Annual Plan provides a separate column on resource allocation for the SCs and STs along with general-sector allocation. The Ministry of Finance has to introduce a budget statement in the annual budget for minority-related development schemes to maintain this information on fund allocation, utilization, and beneficiaries.

Moreover, the existing rigid policy guidelines of CSSs covered under the 15 PP do not allow for tailor-made interventions for minorities/Muslims within the general-sector programmes. In the reporting format, there is scant scope to monitor and track the benefits extended to Muslims. The concerned ministries under 15 PP had been urged to report their achievements, both physical and financial, under their respective schemes for the benefit of religious minorities in 2013. The same needs to be reported on a regular basis to the MoMA. The reporting of expenditure under 15 PP by union ministries has been more of the nature of 'retrospective budgeting', where allocations for minorities are earmarked after the budgets for schemes have been finalized without any special measure taken for minorities during the budget preparation phase. The schemes and programmes in 15 PP should prepare exclusive action plans for minority wards and hamlets, considering the specific needs of and challenges faced by Muslims.

Lack of Clarity in Guidelines

Most of the CSSs that are part of the umbrella programme have not been altered in any way (by way of bringing about changes in the scheme guidelines) to cater to the specific disadvantages and needs of the Muslim community. State- and district-level agencies do not have adequate clarity on the share of allocations available towards the programme due to the lack of disaggregated data on BPL minorities for whom the schemes are to be implemented. Besides the weak implementing mechanisms, state-level functionaries and representatives of Panchayati Raj Institutions (PRI) and Urban Local Bodies (ULB) remain unclear about their role in the district-level planning process, which contributes to the concerns about the design of the programme.

Poor Planning in MSDP

With regard to MSDP's development plan for minorities based on their local needs, the Eleventh FYP followed the preparation of two reports, namely a baseline survey of the MCDs and a detailed project report (DPR). Similarly, during the Twelfth FYP, blocks had to prepare a baseline survey of the MCBs, which has not happened in most blocks. Under the 15 PP, the IAY, SJSRY, and SGSY are beneficiary-driven schemes, while other schemes have followed an area-based approach for infrastructure development. Under the area-based approach, districts (and not minority-dominated hamlets or wards) are considered as units for the planning and implementation of infrastructure projects. Hence, in the Eleventh FYP, in many places such as Bihar, Uttar Pradesh, and Haryana, ITIs, Anganwadi centres (AWCs), and school buildings were located in non-minority areas with only a handful of beneficiaries from minority communities. The Twelfth FYP document suggested that the annual targets and outlays for 15 PP/MSDP should be broken down to the level of hamlets/wards. It was expected that in the revised MSDP guidelines the emphasis should be on plans based on local needs to overcome deficits (Khan and Parvati 2012).

Activities related to ensuring girls' education, technical education, and income generation opportunities (as proposed by the district administration in many MCDs) that are essential to advance the educational and economic conditions of the community have been neglected by MoMA in the Eleventh and even the Twelfth FYP. The allocation meant for MSDP was used as a top-up to saturate the targets of the ongoing CSS. For instance, in Darbhanga district in Bihar the proposed scheme of building additional classrooms (ACRs) in recognized madrasas got shot down by MoMA on the ground that the SSA guidelines did not sanction ACRs to madrasas. The baseline survey conducted for MSDP in Mewat district in Haryana suggested that more focus should be given to programmes promoting female literacy in rural areas, but the district administration built additional classrooms, staff quarters, and a hostel in Mewat Model School that already had adequate and quality infrastructure. The vital objective pertains to building neighbourhood schools for Muslims girls with female teachers to improve quality of education. Additionally, promoting gainful employment among the Muslim youth could be furthered by apportioning adequate outlays for the creation of artisan clusters in MCDs across the country. It is needless to add that the success of these interventions would largely depend on the extent and scope of community participation in the planning and implementation of these services.

The new MSDP guidelines for the Twelfth FYP target a large section of the Muslim population through MCB and MCT. However, when it comes to the selection of activities by districts, the bulk of expenditure is directed towards the construction of IAY houses, AWCs, school buildings, and health sub-centres—provisions that cater to the common populace and are not exclusive to the minorities.

The 15 PP should adequately cover schemes and the desired allocations for them, and should have enough scope for tailor-made interventions that suit the specific needs of minority communities. However, very few departments/ministries are allocating the requisite funds to schemes or reporting physical targets in a disaggregated form. A large number of schemes under 15 PP focus on essential services and employment generation, while critical sectors—such as information and technology, commerce and industry, and micro, small, and medium enterprises—that would address the long-term development of minorities remain out of the programme's ambit.

Exclusion and Diversion of Benefits in MSDP and 15 PP

In MSDP, the criteria for identification of MCDs tended to be more exclusionary, which left a significant proportion of minorities out of the Eleventh FYP. The Twelfth FYP recommended the expansion of the scope of 15 PP to include a large number of programmes and the expansion of MSDP to cover more MCDs. The population criterion to identify MCBs and MCTs was suggested to be brought down from 25 per cent to 15 per cent of a block as the unit of planning and implementation (Khan 2018).

There are also instances where funds meant for minorities get diverted to non-minority areas due to lack of clarity in the guidelines of MSDP and 15 PP. With regard to providing housing facilities under the Eleventh FYP, for instance, the district magistrate (DM) of Barabanki in Uttar Pradesh thought that only 15 per cent of the houses were to be allotted to minorities according to the

IAY guidelines for both MSDP and 15 PP. There is no disaggregated data available at national level on the minorities who have benefited from IAY. In Barabanki district, more than half of the total benefits have gone to non-minority communities owing to the non-inclusion of Muslims in the BPL list of the Eleventh FYP. Such a flaw in the programme's design, making the BPL category a prerequisite, leads to the exclusion of the targeted community which is to benefit from the programme. As a result, a majority of BPL Muslims are not considered in the first place. Further, a separate minor head, a budget statement, and physical reporting under minority related programmes are absent, which makes it difficult to track the funds flowing for the welfare of minorities across schemes and programmes in various sectors (Khan and Parvati 2012). In 2013, the Committee of Secretaries' (CoS) minutes of the meeting showed that data reporting on minority related programmes has to be done on a disaggregated level for different groups among minorities, which has not happened so far.

Low Unit Cost in Scholarship Programmes

Currently, a large number of students are deprived of scholarships due to technical glitches at the state level, while many minority-run institutions are not able to register their online scholarship web portal. Many students from rural areas are not able to apply online due to lack of electricity or poor internet connectivity. Therefore, students should be allowed to submit their applications manually, besides the online process, so that they can avail the benefits of such scholarships even if they hail from rural areas.

Besides the absence of clear-cut institutional mechanisms for the submission of application forms, related concerns such as unrealistic unit costs in terms of the amounts provided for admission, tuition, and maintenance, and prevalent eligibility norms of providing the scholarship to not more than two students from a family constrain its effective implementation and a comprehensive coverage of beneficiaries.

Currently under the pre-matric scholarship, each (day-scholar) student of the minority community is allocated INR 1000 per annum, which is insufficient, especially if we take into account the rate of inflation. In 2017–18, INR 950 crore was allocated for pre-matric scholarship. Making some simple calculations for enhanced allocation to pre-matric scholarship, if we exclude the higher-income group (comprising around 20 per cent of the Muslim population) and consider the requirement of the remaining 80 per cent of Muslim children up to class 10 (pre-matric), we find that the total allocation should be around INR 2,493 crore, whereas at present the government is allocating only INR 950 crore. The MoMA itself has acknowledged that this programme needs more resources. In 2016–17, against MoMA's demand for INR 1831.2 crore, the Ministry of Finance allocated the programme only Rs 931 crore (Action Taken Report by the Ministry of Minority Affairs to Standing Committee 2016). Given the deprivation with regard to the educational indicators for Muslims, the government may consider bringing some sort of parity between the per annum unit costs for these minorities and SCs/STs, especially in the educationally backward blocks of the country.

Challenges in Implementation and Monitoring

The MSDP, being the largest area-development programme to address directly the socio-economic deficits among Muslims, was allocated the largest share of MoMA's total budget in the Eleventh and the Twelfth FYPs. However, non-submission of DPR by state governments due to poor capacity at the district level and delays in the submission of Utilization Certificates led to a delay in undertaking and completing projects under the programme. Further, factors such as inadequate institutional arrangements for implementation at the district level, lack of planning capacity, shortage of staff and required infrastructure, and insufficient funds to monitor the programmes have crippled the effective working of these schemes.

Lack of Convergence between Line Departments

The MoMA monitors the implementation of 15 PP, MSDP, and other schemes. Upon scrutiny of available data and perceptions of officials at the state and district levels, it is felt that MoMA has not been consistently proactive in terms of strengthening this implementation. Coordination with other line departments at the central level (such as 15 PP and MSDP) is also found to be weak. At the state level too, minority welfare departments are starved of financial and human resources and implement schemes without a clear policy mandate or an assessment of the community's regular needs. Poor coordination between line departments mars the implementation of schemes even at the sub-state level.

In order to effectively monitor schemes such as 15 PP and MSDP, guidelines[5] are provided for setting up central- (Committee of Secretaries), state-, and district-level committees to report their progress on a quarterly basis. A scrutiny of notifications by the governments of Bihar and Haryana reveals that state-level committees (SLCs) were formed only in 2010, that is after a delay of more than three years.

The implementation of many programmes is poorly monitored despite there being provisions for establishing monitoring mechanisms at the central, state, and district level, along with the mandated involvement of members of Parliament, state legislatures, and NGOs in the monitoring and reviewing processes. As per the MoMA guidelines, CoSs, state-level committees, and district-level committees should convene twice a year, quarterly, and on a regular basis respectively. For monitoring the implementation of MSDP and 15 PP, state- and district-level committees have been constituted in 20 states and union territories, but they have not been functioning properly. Except in Jharkhand, state-level meetings in the other 19 MCD states have not been held as per the programme's guidelines, which stipulate the holding of a meeting at least once every quarter (GoI 2011–12). Further, no CoS meetings have taken place since 2013. Adding to that, either state-level committees have not been constituted or quarterly meetings have not been convened in the states of Madhya Pradesh, Jharkhand, Karnataka, Odisha, Gujrat, and Telangana (Rehnuma 2017).[6]

At the district level too, although district-level committees (DLCs) are constituted, they lack representation from minority communities. Lack of clarity and proper awareness among

[5] Guidelines for the implementation of the Prime Minister's New 15 Point Programme are accessible at: http://www.*minorityaffairs*.gov.in/sites/upload_files/moma/files/pdfs/pm15points_eguide.pdf, last accessed on 16 March 2020.

[6] Two meetings of the SLCs have been held in Assam, two in Bihar, three in Haryana, six in West Bengal, and nine in Uttar Pradesh since early 2007.

government officials is also believed to inhibit the effective implementation of schemes exclusively for the welfare of minorities. Further, the prevailing perception among government functionaries that interventions focusing only on Muslims might lead to social disruption also compounds the problem.

In this regard, the onus lies with MoMA to actively engage with other departments and push for greater attention towards the concerns of Muslims in schemes falling within the 15 Point Programme. Lack of availability of social group–wise disaggregated data at the state level also affects monitoring the coverage of Muslims in government jobs, credit facilities, and prevention of communal riots—another commitment of the 15 PP.

Besides the several problems encountered in the implementation of development programmes, there are two important factors due to which marginalized communities such as Muslims have suffered the most. First is the overall weak administrative apparatus (inadequate or less-capable staff, lack of need-based planning, and poor monitoring and accountability) and indifferent and callous governance with regard to all social-welfare programmes. Second, there are certain communities, such as Dalits and Muslims, that experience discrimination as well as humiliation. Due to educational and economic deprivation, Muslims not only face discrimination but are also at times stigmatized. In this regard, Pasmanda Muslims have suffered most: on the one hand they are discriminated as Muslims by the majority community, and on the other hand they are treated as lowly by Muslims from the upper strata. They are further discriminated against and marginalized when they are classified as part of the OBCs (as is done by many state governments) but are not able to avail the benefits extended to OBCs due to their Muslim identity. They face many difficulties in getting the OBC certificate from government offices (Centre for Peace Studies 2014).

***

Assessment of the implementation of 15 PP and MSDP from 2007 to 2017 shows that the government's policy initiatives towards the development of minorities in general and Muslims in particular leave a lot to be desired. The commitments made in the Eleventh and Twelfth FYPs in terms of policy priorities and budgetary allocations have not been fulfilled yet. Pasmanda Muslims have largely not benefitted from the schemes and programmes meant for them, and the community faces exclusion in the planning, budgeting, and implementation processes of development programmes at various levels of governance.

Certain corrective measures pertaining to budgetary allocations, fund utilization, design problems, and the implementation of 15 PP and MSDP have to be taken. Adequate focus has to be given to the development of Muslims through special provisions for the inclusion of the Pasmanda community in public policies and programmes. The need of the hour is to put in place targeted strategies, well-designed interventions, and needs-based allocations for the overall development of Pasmanda Muslims. First, in order to ensure adequate funds, the existing guidelines of earmarking 15 per cent (wherever possible) should be revised to make it proportionate to the size of the minority population or even above it.

Second, it is suggested that MSDP and 15 PP should work in synergy rather than the former duplicating the latter. Also, 15 PP should take care of sectoral investments/ongoing CSSs, while MSDP should fill the gaps for those particular communities or settlements which have not been covered under the existing CSSs.

Third, a regular revision of the unit cost of scholarship schemes should factor in the effects of inflation. Moreover, the government should do away with the two-children norm in scholarship schemes and all eligible minority students should be covered following a demand-driven approach. While assessing the implementation of provisions under the Twelfth FYP, not much headway has been made except regarding the expansion of MSDP's coverage from 90 to 196 MCDs and its planning and implementation at the block and town level.

Fourth, the design of MSDP and 15 PP does not leave much scope for creating tailor-made projects that suit the needs of the Muslim community. Both these programmes adopt the norms and guidelines of the existing CSSs, which are not flexible for addressing these needs. The government has to improve the governance and service-delivery performance of 15 PP and MSDP through better transparency and effective implementation mechanisms (preparation of disaggregated data, employing adequate human resource, decentralized needs-based planning, and strong monitoring and evaluation).

Fifth, MSDP guidelines should be revised to focus on undertaking initiatives that are needs-based, instead of topping up approaches adopted in existing CSSs and covered under 15 PP. The MSDP should push towards plans that overcome the local development deficit instead of aiming to saturate the coverage of already existing national programmes. Secondary and senior secondary schools constructed under MSDP in many MCDs or MCBs need to be made functional at the earliest. The MSDP should consider opening schools for minorities in each of the 710 blocks and 66 towns, following after the Department of Minorities Welfare, Government of Telangana, which opened and now oversees the running of senior secondary schools for minorities in the state. Further, there is a need to establish degree colleges and construct women's hostels in MCDs for the promotion of higher education among minority communities.

Sixth, considering the problems in the schemes' guidelines and designs, 15 PP could be implemented along the lines of the SCSP and TSP. It would also help to consider minorities in budgetary processes through the introduction of separate minor heads for minorities and a separate budget statement on minority-related programmes in the union and state budgets, as is already being done for the SCs and STs (for expenditure reporting). Plan funds for minorities should be allocated in proportion to their population. Out of these fund allocations, a larger share should be utilized for needs-based projects exclusively aimed at the development of Muslims.

Finally, district and state-level agencies should be granted more clarity on scheme guidelines and mechanisms of resource allocation under 15 PP. Social auditors should get access to data on physical targets and outlays from wards and hamlets for providing actionable feedback. The process of setting up a National Data Bank on the outcome development of minorities has to be given top priority. The implementation of the recommendations of the Equal Opportunity Commission (EOC) needs to be expedited and those on the study of the diversity index need to be applied in private- and government-run institutions for providing jobs and education to Muslims.

References

Centre for Peace Studies. 2014. *Broken Promises, A Study on the Socio-economic Status of Indian Muslims: Seven Years Post Sachar*. Centre for Peace Studies. Delhi: Danish Books, supported by Action Aid.

Government of India (GoI). 2006. 'Social, Economic and Educational Status of the Muslim Community of India'. Delhi: Prime Minister's High Level Committee.

———. 2011–12. *Report of the Steering Committee on Empowerment of Minorities*. Delhi: Planning Commission.

Khan, Jawed A. 2018. 'Policy Challenges: Have Development Schemes Meant for Muslims Worked Effectively?' In *Vision 2025: Towards an Inclusive India*, edited by Amir Ullah Khan and Abdul Azim Akhtar, 37–52. New Delhi: Institute of Objective Studies.

Khan, Jawed A., and Pooja Parvati. 2012. 'Government's Commitment towards Development of Muslims: A Post-Sachar Assessment of Uttar Pradesh and Haryana'. In *India Social Development Report 2012*, 250–62. New Delhi: Oxford and Council for Social Development.

Rehnuma. 2017. *Minority Appeasement Myth or Reality: A Ground Report on Minority Welfare*. Supported by UN Women and European Union. Ahmadabad: Centre for Social Justice.

Index

Editor and Contributors

Editor

Aakash Singh Rathore is the author of *Ambedkar's Preamble: A Secret History of the Constitution of India* (2020) and a regular contributor to the *Indian Express* and *Outlook* magazine. Rathore has taught at Jawaharlal Nehru University (JNU), University of Delhi, and Jindal Global University, India; Rutgers University and University of Pennsylvania, USA; University of Toronto, Canada; Humboldt University of Berlin, Germany; and Libera Università Internazionale degli Studi Sociali (LUISS) Guido Carli, Italy.

His twenty previous books range in theme from political philosophy, law, and religion to literature, sports, and wine. These include *Hegel's India: A Reinterpretation, with Texts* (2017) and *B.R. Ambedkar's The Buddha and His Dhamma: A Critical Edition* (2011). He is also the author of the forthcoming book, *B.R. Ambedkar: A Biography.*

Contributors

Upendra Baxi is an honorary professor at the National Law School of India University, Bangalore, India. He has co-edited many volumes and is a contributor to the *The Oxford Encyclopaedia of Human Rights* (2009); *The Oxford Handbook of Legal Studies* (2003); *The Blackwell Companion to Postcolonial Studies* (2005); *The Routledge Handbook of International Human Rights Law* (2016); *The Oxford Handbook of Indian Constitutional Law* (2015), and so on.

Some of his leading publications include: *The Indian Supreme Court and Politics* (1980); *The Crisis of Indian Legal System* (1982); *Inhuman Wrongs and Human Rights* (1994); *The Future of Human Rights* (2008); and *Human Rights in Posthuman World: Critical Essays* (2007).

Vijay Gudavarthy is assistant professor at the School of Economics, University of Hyderabad, India. He is also the secretary of the Centre for Social Concerns, an activist academic society, and a member of Workers Solidarity Network (WSN). He has previously taught Economics of Business Organization at the Institute of Public Enterprise (IPE) an ICSSR institute, and Law and Economics at the National Academy for Legal Studies and Research University (NALSAR), which operates under the auspices of the High Court of Telangana and Andhra Pradesh, India. He has also worked as a research fellow at the Institute of Human Development (IHD), New Delhi.

Jawed Alam Khan is a doctoral candidate at Jawaharlal Nehru University, New Delhi, India. He works with the Centre for Budget and Governance Accountability. His work focuses on fiscal decentralization, issues in fund utilization in social sector programmes, implementation of SDGs and responsiveness of budgets to disadvantaged groups such as minorities, Dalits, and Adivasis. He has more than thirteen years of experience in research and has authored several research reports and papers in his areas of interest. He has an MPhil in economics.

Antje Linkenbach is a long-term fellow at the Max Weber Centre for Advanced Cultural and Social Studies, Erfurt, Germany. Her publications include: *Forest Futures: Global Representations and Ground Realities in the Himalayas* (2007); 'Sustainable Development in a Dharmic land? Environmental and Political Protest in Uttarakhand', *Unfolding Central Himalaya: The Cradle of Culture* (2017); 'Environmental Justice in India? Examining the Compatibility between Sustainability, Social Justice and the Gandhian Legacy', *Journal of Social and Economic Studies* (2017); 'Gender Dynamics and Equality in India: A Plea for an Integrative Approach to Social Justice', *RDWU Journal of Social Sciences and Humanities*, vol. 2.

Arvind Narrain is the co-founder of the Alternative Law Forum, a human rights advocacy and research organization based in Bangalore, India. He is also the co-author of *Breathing Life into the Constitution: Human Rights Lawyering in India* (2017) and co-editor of *Law Like Love: Queer Perspectives on Law* (2011).

Aseem Prakash is professor and chairperson, School of Public Policy and Governance, Tata Institute of Social Sciences, Hyderabad, Telangana, India. His most recent books are titled *Dalit Capital: State, Markets and Civil Society in Urban India* (2015) and *The Indian Middle Class* (co-authored with Surinder Jodhka, 2016).

Anupama Rao is TOW associate professor of history and associate professor, Middle Eastern, South Asian, and African Studies (MESAAS), Columbia University, USA. She is a senior editor for *Comparative Studies in South Asia, Africa, and the Middle East*. Rao has research interests in gender and sexuality studies; caste and race; historical anthropology; social theory; comparative urbanism; and colonial genealogies of human rights and humanitarianism. She is the author of *The Caste Question* (2009) and the edited volume *Gender, Caste, and the Imagination of Equality* (2017). She is currently working on a book on the political thought of B. R. Ambedkar, and a project titled *Dalit Bombay*.

Pritam Singh is professor of economics at Oxford Brookes University, UK. His works *Federalism, Nationalism and Development: India and the Punjab Economy* (2008), *Economy, Culture and Human Rights: Turbulence in Punjab, India and Beyond* (2010), and *Hindu Bias in Indian Constitution* (2017) have received critical acclaim as path-breaking works of scholarship. His co-edited books, *Punjabi Identity in a Global Context* (1999, reprint 2015) and *Equal Opportunities in the Curriculum* (1999), have been pioneering works in their respective fields.

R. Sudarshan was a Rhodes scholar at Balliol College, Oxford University, and a research scholar at St. John's College, Cambridge University, UK. He is an alumnus of Delhi School of Economics, India. He has worked in the Ford Foundation for over seven years and with UNDP in New Delhi, Jakarta, Oslo, and Bangkok for

22 years. He joined the Jindal School of Government and Public Policy as the founding dean in July 2012.

Joseph Tharamangalam is emeritus professor of sociology and anthropology at Mount Saint Vincent University in Halifax, Canada. His research focuses on agrarian class conflicts and peasant movements, secularism and communalism, and more recently on comparisons of 'models' of human development with particular reference to Kerala and Cuba as well as India and China. He is the author of two books and numerous research papers which have appeared in journals such as the *Journal of Peasant Studies*, *Economic and Political Weekly*, *Critical Asian Studies*, and *Canadian Journal of Development Studies.*

Umakant is an independent scholar based in New Delhi, India. In 1998, he got associated with the National Campaign on Dalit Human Rights (NCDHR). Later on he worked for the Indian Institute of Dalit Studies in New Delhi from its inception in 2003 and continued till October 2004. He has been writing on issues related to Dalit politics, Dalit leadership, Dalit human rights issues, and has worked on several reports for different UN bodies. His work is focussed on gender, development, rule of law, governance, public policy, and civil society. He co-edited a book with Sukhadeo Thorat, *Caste, Race and Discrimination: Discourses in International Context* (2004).